Park Campus
Library

Superbrands®

Annual 2018

superbrands.uk.com

STEPHEN CHELIOTIS

Chief Executive, TCBA

& Chairman, Superbrands / CoolBrands UK

BRAND LIAISON DIRECTORS

Anna Hyde

Liz Silvester

Daren Thomas

BRAND LIAISON MANAGERS

Jumoke Moiett

Javier Mulvoy-Ten

EDITOR

Angela Cooper

CREATIVE

Verity Burgess

Also available from TCBA in the UK:
CoolBrands® 2016/17 ISBN: 978-0-9932998-2-7

To order further books, email brands@superbrands.uk.com
or call 020 7079 3310.

Published by
The Centre for Brand Analysis (TCBA) Ltd
5th Floor
Holden House
57 Rathbone Place
London
W1T 1JU

© 2018 Superbrands Ltd

MIX
Paper from
responsible sources
FSC® C015829
www.fsc.org

Contents

CONTENTS

THOUGHT PIECES

APPENDIX

Key

B - Business Superbrands Qualifier

C - Consumer Superbrands Qualifier

Endorsements

REBECCA CROOK

Managing Director
Marketing Agencies Association

2018 will be a challenging year for brands globally. Consumers are more savvy and sceptical of brands than ever before with new entrants to the market making traditional brands raise their game so much more than ever before. That is why to be defined as a Superbrand means you've got it right or almost right (there is always room for improvement)!

A Superbrand needs to be way more than a brand you just recognise. They need to lead their category, have the ability to change and adapt to external market conditions, delighting their customers 24/7. We live in an 'always on' society where consumers are looking for experiences and genuine meaning from brands they interact with. Digital, data and personalisation can help with this but the challenge will be how brands integrate humanity in this digital era to connect with customers.

CATHERINE MASKELL

Managing Director
Content Marketing Association

The success of these Superbrands comes at a time when the marketplace is beset with more challenges than ever before. All brands have to work hard to maintain their positions, but the brands featured here have to work harder than anyone else, building and reinforcing consumer trust, confidence and loyalty to always be one step ahead in an unforgiving arena with constantly changing rules and systems.

Brand success depends on forging a deep and meaningful bond with your customers, giving them a relationship that goes way beyond the physical product. Whether that relationship is forged with fantastic customer service, inspirational marketing or products that enrich their owners' lives, the bestowing of Superbrand status is a genuine honour and something to cherish.

The Content Marketing Association is pleased and proud to be associated with Superbrands and the brands that have reached Superbrand status, many of which use content as a central pillar in their marketing strategies. We also congratulate the CMA members that have created that content and helped shape the future success of these iconic brands.

JOHN NOBLE

Director
British Brands Group

Which of the Superbrands depicted in this book do you find evocative, compelling, nostalgic, heart-warming? Which ones leave you cool, or even cold?

As you look through the pages, it may be worth taking a moment to consider what you feel about what you see. We may like to think we are wholly rational beings, making our choices on factual assessments of performance, quality and price, but is that how we really behave and act? Superbrands engage the emotion as well as the brain, and the emotional triggers within us help us make a faster decision than we could ever achieve through rational analysis. In this way brands ease our lives and in turn allow us to navigate confidently complex markets with myriads of choice. It is heart-warming to see them celebrated here.

CAREY TREVILL

Managing Director
The Institute
of Promotional Marketing

Brands are not what they say we are, they are what we say they are. To feature in these hallowed pages means you've made it as a brand and the public out there have understood not only what these brands do, how they do it and importantly why they do it.

We could talk about how competitive and tricky life is, cutting through the noise and the tough environment brands exist in. The reality is the brands featured in this year's Superbrands bible are the brands that have risen to great heights because they got it right. At every step, purpose and values shone through connecting with what we as consumers understand unequivocally and instantly – this is a brand we want to buy.

At the heart of what we strive for as marketers is brand success. The work supporting the brands here delivers it's 'why' above and beyond just promoting the brand. Superbrands can help the audience understand more about the brands commitment to the environment, sustainability and delivering a message of trust to the market – something we know is lacking in our field. So, here we celebrate the Superbrands and we'd like to congratulate every brand featured.

About Superbrands

Superbrands is the definitive benchmark for brands who've set the agenda, outwitted the competition and built enviable reputations.

The UK's Superbrands are identified annually through an **extensive and robust research process** that measures the equity of thousands of brands, in both direct-to-consumer and business-to-business markets.

Only the most highly-regarded achieve the status of Superbrand. The Superbrands Annual, first published in 1995 and now in its **19th volume**, tells the story of many of these successful brands, **exploring their history, development and achievements**, showcasing why they are much-loved. These case studies provide **valuable insights into the strategies and propositions of the brands** that consumers and business professionals trust and admire.

The Superbrands organisation identifies and pays tribute to exceptional brands throughout the world. The UK programme is run under license by The Centre for Brand Analysis (TCBA).

arco®

Experts in Safety

Arco is the **UK's leading safety company,** distributing quality products and delivering training and expert advice to help keep people safe at work. **Founded in 1884, with a heritage spanning four generations,** Arco integrates **traditional family values with pioneering innovation** to offer a world-class range of **more than 170,000 quality assured products.**

more than 170,000 branded and own-brand products, for head-to-toe protection across all industries. The range of products includes personal protective equipment, clothing, footwear, gloves, workplace safety and hygiene products with specific solutions to meet most requirements and a price range to suit every budget.

Arco works with strategic suppliers to offer premium industry brands; it also invests its own expertise in the design and development of innovative new products, working with customers to understand their needs. This provides solutions that have been designed by experts, tested to the right standards and are fit for the job.

Arco is the only safety distributor to have its own in-house, Product Assurance Laboratory. This is accredited by United Kingdom Accreditation Service and SATRA, recognised authorities in the industry. The laboratory gives the ability to test products to the limits and beyond, complementing routine certification and due diligence testing regimes, offering unrivalled quality assurance.

Market

Since the company was first formed, Arco has continued to evolve, and today plays a leading role in shaping the UK safety agenda. Arco is the leading brand in the safety business, putting people and their wellbeing at the centre of everything it does. Arco offers training and consultancy services, managing customers' risks and provides personal protective equipment and workplace solutions to ensure safety in the workplace.

Arco understands that each industry has its own hazards and specific needs when it comes to safety clothing and equipment. It provides solutions across all sectors including manufacturing, food, utilities, transport, oil and gas, as well as construction. Arco also has many customers across the public sector and supplies numerous central and local government organisations.

Product

Arco offers the most extensive range of workwear and safety equipment in the UK and is able to supply

DID YOU KNOW?

Arco keeps over two million UK workers safe.

Achievements

Arco prides itself on achieving a positive, healthy and happy working environment for all employees throughout the company and was recently awarded 'One to Watch' status, in The Sunday Times Best Companies Survey, recognising very high colleague engagement levels.

Arco's continued growth and commercial success enables it to put more back into the communities in which it operates.

Arco is dedicated to its Corporate Social Responsibility programme supporting local charities by donating in excess of 1% of pre-tax profits annually.

As for sponsorships, the company's most recent partnership is with iconic London attraction, The O2. Its safety equipment ensures the 100,000 people who climb over the dome every year are kept safe and comfortable with bespoke designed climb suits and shoes, as well as safety harnesses to ensure the best possible experience.

Arco is a proud supporter of the Yorkshire Air Ambulances, which provide a rapid response emergency service to five million people across Yorkshire. Arco provide hazardwear, including flight suits, for the paramedics.

Arco has also partnered with the Bloodhound SSC project as it planned, designed and built a supersonic car to raise the world land speed record to 1,000mph. Arco is providing expert advice and protective equipment to keep

Brand History

1884 The company is founded as Arthur Stanley Morrison & Co. in Duke Street, London.

1903 The Martin Family, now in its fourth generation, join the company.

1941 The King Edward Street shop in Hull is destroyed during the Blitz.

1967 The acquisition of Budgen & Hare heralds the development of the Arco branch network.

1980 The company officially changes its name to Arco Ltd.

2000 The National Distribution Centre opens, launching the first publication of a single integrated catalogue: The Big Red Book.

2003 Arco Clothing Centre opens in Preston. Arco Charity Committee was set up by Jo Martin (who died in 2008).

2014 Arco opens independently accredited Product Assurance Laboratory ensuring unrivalled quality across product portfolio.

---

engineers and designers safe during the build and testing process.

Arco was the first distributor in the safety industry to become a member of the Ethical Trading Initiative, a groundbreaking alliance of companies, trades unions and voluntary organisations who work in partnership to improve the lives of workers across the globe.

Recent Developments
Following Arco's focus on safety from the 1960s, it has continued to build the strongest team of safety experts in the industry. To ensure customers' hazards and risks are managed in the best way possible, Arco has a dedicated Training and Consultancy Division. This was recently expanded with the acquisition of two leading companies in its field. Total Access is the UK's leading supplier of Height Safety Training and Services. Confined Space Training Services Ltd is a specialist confined space, health and safety education provider. These acquisitions further expand

DID YOU KNOW?

Every year, Arco supplies over 200 million quality safety items.

Arco's services proposition into hire and rescue services, firmly establishing it as a market leader in the provision of working at height and confined space safety training and consultancy services.

Promotion
The Arco brand is displayed across retail outlets nationwide and has grown through the commitment of the 1,500 colleagues who each uphold its brand values and deliver expert advice to customers. Arco is proud to promote its mission to keep people safe at work through its award-winning communication platform 'It's not just safety gear',

recently awarded Best Brand Campaign in the B2B Marketing Awards. Arco's partnership with The O2 allows it to communicate directly with millions of people who experience their entertainment at London's premier venue, knowing they are kept safe through Arco's products and services. Arco prides itself on the best quality, service and value, and ensures that customers can access these in the most convenient way possible.

Brand Values
Arco believes that everyone who goes to work each day has a basic human right to return home safely to their loved ones. Arco aims to help customers do just that by offering expert advice and safety products to prevent accidents in the workplace and save lives. The company's core values are: Respect for people, Excellence in reputation, Hard work and Enterprise.

'Vorsprung durch Technik,' three words that define Audi. They mean the restless pursuit of advancement. **For 35 years, the strategy has reflected the brand's technical credentials,** design prowess, performance power and distinctive tone of voice. Always ahead, always exciting and always with a twinkle in the eye.

DID YOU KNOW?

Every Audi is **dusted with emu feathers** before painting.

Market

While the total automotive market contracted in 2016, the premium sector has continued to grow, and Audi remains a major contributor to that growth. The brand has a 6.9% share of the total market and outperforms its key competitors in the retail (consumer) market, with a 7.6% share.

The automotive industry is set to change more over the next 10 years than it has during the last 50, with drivetrain electrification and

unprecedented automation of the driving experience being among the key disruptors. In its capacity as innovator and challenger to the status quo, Audi is in the vanguard of development in both fields, with the world's first system to enable conditional automated driving (SAE level three) due for integration into its A8 luxury saloon during 2018 and an all-new fully electric SUV – the e-tron – also waiting in the wings.

Product

Audi offers an extensive range of models across a series of premium segments – from the A1, which was described by What Car? magazine as "one of the best small cars on the market", to the luxury class A8. Audi also offers a wide range of SUVs, from the compact, city-friendly Q2 through to the spacious seven-seater Q7. In addition, its portfolio of high-performance Audi Sport models, including the RS range and iconic R8 supercar, have attracted a sizeable following.

DID YOU KNOW?

The side of every Audi is **two-thirds metal and one-third glass.**

In 2017, Audi's numerous product launches included the new A5 and S5, RS 3, RS 4 Avant and SQ5 as well as the A8 luxury saloon. Looking to the future, these segments will expand to embrace the increasing move towards electrification.

Achievements

Audi sold 177,304 cars in 2016, a 6.4% increase on 2015. The UK remains the largest export market for Audi in Europe, and the fourth largest market globally. According to third

Butter wouldn't melt.

The new Audi RS 4 Avant.

Brand History

1909 August Horch Automobilwerke GmbH is created in Germany. The eponymous founder uses the name 'Audi', Latin for listen and meaning 'hark' in German.

1932 Audi merges with Horch, DKW and Wanderer, to form Auto Union AG. The four rings of the Audi badge symbolise the four brands coming together.

1964 Volkswagenwerk AG acquired the majority of shares in Auto Union GmbH with Audi becoming a fully-owned VW subsidiary from the end of 1966.

1982 Audi employs BBH as its advertising agency. 'Vorsprung durch Technik' is born.

1990s Audi dominates British Touring Cars with its A4.

2000 Audi wins the Le Mans 24-hour race for three consecutive years and the brand becomes renowned as a premium brand with sporting and performance credentials.

2017 Audi's safety technology campaign 'Clowns' wins Campaign magazine's Film of The Year Award.

party brand tracking from Millward Brown, Audi leads the total automotive market for Brand Desirability.

Audi won a raft of awards in 2017, including Best Executive Car for the A4, Best Luxury SUV for the Q7, Best Family Car for the A3 Sportback as well as Best Coupé for the TT in the What Car? Awards and was also awarded in the What Car? Used Car Awards (for 2018). In addition, the brand was also recognised by Honest John, Auto Express, Fleet News, International Engine of the Year, BusinessCar as well as Carbuyer, Best Cars (for 2018).

Furthermore, Audi's 2017 safety technology campaign 'Clowns' won Campaign Magazine's Film of The Year Award as well as the overall Creative Grand Prix Award across all industries.

Recent Developments

Being 'Vorsprung' and embracing innovation is at the heart of everything Audi does. The recently launched A8, for example, is the first production vehicle in the world with level three autonomous driving. Audi has also revealed a series of concept electric vehicles to embrace the march towards electrification. This spirit of innovation is not confined to its products but also infuses Audi business strategies and communications.

Promotion

First used by the ad agency BBH for the brand in 1982, the line 'Vorsprung durch Technik', loosely translated as 'Advancement through Technology', is continuously being reinvented.

In 2017, work focused on the intelligent technologies that have become increasingly prevalent across the Audi model portfolio. While consumers have always appreciated the beauty of the Audi range, they haven't necessarily been aware of the sophistication of the electronic 'brains' behind it. Films such as 'React' and the award-winning 'Clowns,' aim to bring the benefits of these technologies to life in dramatic and charming ways.

Brand Values

'Vorsprung durch Technik' drives everything Audi does. The brand aims to deliver unforgettable experiences for its customers, not only through exciting, desirable cars that push aesthetic and technological boundaries but also at every physical and digital touchpoint on the purchase journey to those cars and beyond.

AUTOGLASS®

Autoglass® is a **leading consumer and business automotive brand**, providing vehicle **glass repairs and replacements to over one million motorists** every year. With the widest reaching auto glazing network in the UK, Autoglass® **employs more than 1,200 mobile technicians. It operates 24 hours a day**, 365 days a year.

Market

Autoglass® is the nation's favourite vehicle glass repair and replacement specialist and the UK market leader. Autoglass® is part of Belron®, which operates in 34 countries and serves over 11 million motorists worldwide.

Windscreens play an integral role in modern automotive design and today's cars typically use 15% more glass than 10 years ago. The windscreen is important for vehicle safety – its correct fitting and bonding can save lives. Windscreens can also incorporate complex technologies, such as cameras to enable Advanced Driver Assistance Systems (ADAS) that form part of the journey to autonomous driving, such as Autonomous Emergency Braking, and heads-up display components.

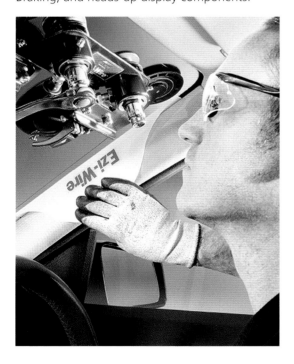

Autoglass® is exceptional in its market by having its own dedicated research and development centre, Belron® Technical. This is a team of innovators and thinkers – all focused on driving technical standards and developing innovations that break new ground to better the service it provides to its customers.

Autoglass® works with insurance, fleet and lease companies – large and small – across the full spectrum of each industry. Autoglass® handles the vehicle glass claims for many of the top UK motor insurance companies, providing a world-class service to motorists.

The company also has a dedicated specialist glazing division, Autoglass® Specials, repairing and replacing vehicle glass on everything from trains to trucks and combine harvesters to coaches.

Product

Autoglass® exists to solve people's problems with real care. By providing exceptional customer service at every touch point and being an ambassador for road safety through its marketing communications, Autoglass® has become one of the UK's most trusted service brands.

Autoglass® fixes damaged glass on any make, model or age of vehicle. The company operates a 'Repair First' philosophy, ensuring that, wherever possible, it will repair a chipped windscreen rather than replace it; a safe solution that saves time and money, and is better for the environment. If the damage is beyond repair, Autoglass® will replace the glass. It only uses Original Equipment Manufacturer (OEM) standard glass, ensuring that each replacement windscreen is as good as the original.

Achievements

Autoglass® has more than 70,000 customer reviews online with an average score of 4.4 out of five, the highest number of reviews from any UK-based vehicle glass repair and replacement specialist.

Autoglass® is proud of being a trusted and respected company in the eyes of its people, customers and partners. Corporate Social Responsibility is in its DNA. Its work for charity is extensive and in 2017, Autoglass® helped to raise a record £1.1m for the charity Afrika Tikkun through its Spirit of Belron® Challenge athletics event. Autoglass® is also committed to achieving continual improvement in Environmental

as well as Health and Safety management. It is certified to ISO 14001, ISO 9001 and OHSAS 18001 standards and constantly strives to reduce its relative use of non-renewable fuel and CO_2.

Recent Developments

Autoglass® prides itself in being at the forefront of innovation in the automotive after-market. In 2016 it was the first to offer a nationwide Advanced Driver Assistance System (ADAS) calibration service.

DID YOU KNOW?

The **glass recycled by** Autoglass® **each year weighs more than the Eiffel Tower.**

ADAS collectively describes the advanced features in newer vehicles, including systems that warn the driver of hazards (for example, Lane Departure Warning) and more advanced systems that take some level of control of the vehicle, such as Autonomous Emergency Braking. Typically, these safety technologies are controlled by cameras located on the windscreen, and require calibration if the windscreen is replaced, to ensure the system operates correctly. Autoglass® has heavily invested in understanding the implications of these technologies and is committed to making calibration as easy as possible for its customers. Throughout 2017 Autoglass® continued to expand its ADAS offering including growing its network of calibration centres. Together with its parent company, Autoglass® has quickly become established as the global market leader in this burgeoning new field.

In 2017, AutoRestore®, the mobile body shop network that is part of Belron® in the UK rebranded to Autoglass® BodyRepair. The two companies have always shared the same values and purpose,

AUTOGLASS®   0800 222 777   autoglass.co.uk

so it was a natural step to align the brands. A new brand identity was launched to support the national service which repairs cosmetic damage to vehicles.

In 2017 Autoglass® also unveiled a series of new technologies designed to support technicians and further improve its vehicle glass repair and replacement service for drivers, fleets and insurers. These included Advanced Repair Technology (ART), and a new Facebook chatbot.

Promotion
Autoglass® became a household name in the 1990s after becoming the main sponsor of Chelsea Football Club. Since then, it has invested in a number of high profile brand campaigns to ensure it remains at the forefront of motorists' minds, cementing its position as a great British brand. In 2005, its 'Heroes' advertising campaign was launched, featuring real technicians. Autoglass® firmly believes its people are 'everyday heroes' that

deliver its brand promise consistently to customers. This format has been extended throughout the company's brand communications, with employees appearing on vans, lorries and online. Sonic branding, in the form of the famous 'Autoglass® Repair, Autoglass® Replace' jingle, is one of the most recognisable assets of the brand.

In 2017, Autoglass® hosted its ninth biennial Best of Belron® UK competition, to find the UK's best vehicle glass technician. The final was hosted in the Milton Keynes Arena and was won by Ryan Millar from Nairn in Scotland. He will travel to the international Best of Belron® competition in Frankfurt during 2018 to represent the UK globally, with the opportunity to win a year's salary if he brings home the title.

Brand Values
Autoglass® makes a difference by solving people's problems with real care.

Brand History

1972 Autoglass Supplies Ltd is launched, providing mobile vehicle glass replacement across northern England.

1982 Autoglass Ltd becomes part of Belron®, the world's largest vehicle glass repair and replacement company.

1983 Autoglass Ltd merges with Windshields Ltd and becomes Autoglass Windshields, rebranding to Autoglass® in 1987.

1990 The windscreen repair service is launched.

1994 Autoglass® becomes a registered trademark.

2005 Autoglass® launches the 'Heroes' advertising campaign.

2007 Autoglass® becomes the first vehicle glass repair and replacement company to offer online booking.

2009 The Autoglass® Specials brand is launched.

2009 Autoglass® introduces its unique repair resin and wins the prestigious Best of Belron® competition to crown the world's best technician.

2013 The Vanbrella®, a proprietary wet weather solution, is rolled out across the fleet.

2015 Autoglass® leads the industry with its Advanced Driver Assistance Systems (ADAS) calibration investment.

2016 The new ADAS calibration service is rolled out nationally, the first service of its kind in the UK.

2017 AutoRestore® rebrands to become Autoglass® BodyRepair.

BARCLAYS

With over **325 years of history and expertise**, Barclays is a transatlantic consumer and wholesale bank with global reach. **Operating in over 40 countries**, offering products and services across personal, corporate and investment banking, credit cards and wealth management, **it has a strong presence in the UK and US**, its two home markets.

Market

Barclays has two clearly defined divisions, Barclays UK and Barclays International, which provide diversification by business line, geography and customer, enhancing financial resilience and contributing to the delivery of consistent returns through the business cycle. Its strong core business is well positioned to deliver long-term value for Barclays shareholders.

Product

Barclays operates in over 40 countries and employs approximately 85,000 people. It moves, lends, invests and protects money for customers and clients worldwide, utilising the latest technology in unison with its wealth of banking expertise.

Achievements

Barclays is a long-standing industry leader in championing diversity and inclusion both within the workplace and in delivering services. It was the first bank to have a female branch manager back in 1958 and in 2017, for a 10th consecutive year, was named a Top 50 Employer for Women by The Times in the UK.

It was also the first bank to roll out 'Talking' ATMs and high visibility debit cards in the UK. With 98%, Barclays was the highest-scoring organisation listed in the Business Disability Forum benchmark in 2017.

Always, aiming to understand its colleagues' needs, Barclays was the first company in the UK to make 'Dynamic Working' an option, even for new employees. It was also named in the Stonewall Top Global Employer list for 2017, the leading charity for the rights of Lesbian, Gay, Bisexual and Transgender people. Furthermore, Barclays was awarded the 2017 Global Ally Programme of the Year award.

Recent Developments

Barclays has continually played a part in driving economic growth and social progress, supporting access into employment by helping people develop the vital skills they require.

In 2016, Barclays entered an innovative multi-year partnership with Unreasonable Group to launch Unreasonable Impact, focused on scaling up entrepreneurial solutions that will help employ thousands worldwide while solving some of the most pressing societal challenges by supporting high-growth entrepreneurs. The project provides advice and guidance thorough a global community of world-class mentors and industry specialists, including experts from Barclays.

Barclays LifeSkills programme has one single-minded ambition – to inspire young people to get the skills they need for a better future. The focus is on inspiring young people primarily aged 11-19 to get job ready. Not just online, but in class and through valuable real-world experiences.

Barclays Connect with Work is another innovative employability programme that up-skills individuals to be ready for entry-level jobs, while supporting companies, including Barclays' clients and suppliers. Since its launch in the UK, more than 650 people have successfully secured employment through the scheme.

Barclays Social Innovation Facility (SIF) supports innovative financial products, which have a social impact, such as The Impact Series Research Reports and the Women In Leadership Index. SIF also launched a multi-asset impact investing fund with seed funding from Big Society Capital – the social investment institution established by the UK Government. SIF worked with more than 500 entrepreneurs in 2017 supporting one-on-one mentoring and a day-long hackathon. SIF has developed a powerful network across the bank, bringing together different cultures, ages, and corporate grades around purpose driven work.

Also in 2017, Barclays launched a banking service for armed forces customers, with a range of products to specifically suit the needs of military personnel. Products include bank accounts, mortgages and credit cards, enabling customers to use garrison addresses when applying for new accounts. This builds on Barclays long standing support for Armed Forces Personnel including programmes which help them transition back into civilian life after service and improve employment outcomes. Over the past year, the Barclays customer base in this segment has grown by 29%.

Promotion

In 2017, Barclays UK continued to promote Fraud Awareness in above-the-line campaigns and continued to promote the role of the Barclays Digital Eagles – employees helping people become more confident with technology.

Barclays Eagle Labs are in 13 locations nationwide to help communities and businesses Create, Innovate and Grow. Advice and digital skills have been provided to 100,000 individuals to date.

Brand History

1690	John Freame and Thomas Gould start trading as goldsmith bankers in London.
1728	Freame and Gould move to 54 Lombard Street, beneath the sign of the Black Spread Eagle.
1920	William Morris is invested in, helping him become the biggest car manufacturer in the UK.
1958	Barclays appoints the UK's first ever female branch manager, Hilda Harding.
1966	Barclaycard, the UK's first credit card, is launched.
1967	The world's first ATM is unveiled by Barclays.
1975	The British-led expedition to conquer the South West face of Everest is sponsored by Barclays.
1987	Barclays launches the UK's first debit card.
2007	Barclays launches the UK's first contactless payment card.
2012	Pingit launches, the first payment service allowing customers to transfer money via their mobile phones.
2014	bPay wearable payment devices are launched.
2015	Barclays launches Rise, a community for Fintech startups to connect, co-create and scale innovative ideas.
2016	Voice Security is launched to UK retail customers.
2017	The first solution for corporate clients that combines biometric technology with advanced digital signing, biometrically tying a transaction to an individual, is launched.

Barclays UK was the headline sponsor in 2017 for Pride in London for the fourth year, taking part in the parade and handing out flowers as part of its 'Share the love' campaign. This campaign also ran internally as well as in London branches and across social media channels.

Another innovation is Bank in a Box, a mobile facility that helps university students open a bank account on campus at times such as Fresher's Week. During trials in 2016, 500 accounts were opened in nine days across eight campuses. Plans are in place to roll out the concept to 50 universities in 2018.

Meanwhile, Barclays International's Ideas Ignite Growth content marketing platform, focuses on the concept that the best financial ideas help growth and innovation flourish.

Barclay's C-suite and institutional investor audiences are highly competitive and zealous because their time is at such a premium, but they are naturally curious and hungry for information. Barclays engages this group in long-term strategic dialogue, through ideas and video-based storytelling. With the aim of delivering the Investment Bank's deep understanding across sectors, asset classes and economies, thought-leading insights provide a transparent view into the way Barclays works with clients and the real impact its services can have on their businesses.

In 2016, the Corporate Bank facilitated the first global trade transaction executed using blockchain technology, alongside Wave, a graduate of Barclays Accelerator. This is a 13-week programme designed to accelerate Fintech start-up businesses.

In 2017, to help customers feel more confident online and to prevent malware and remote access trojan fraud, the first solution for corporate clients that combines biometric technology with advanced digital signing was launched. This solution biometrically ties a transaction to an individual as well as introducing Behavioural Biometrics across digital channels.

Brand Values

The delivery of Barclays strategy is underpinned by the energy, commitment and passion of its people, clear on the common Purpose: to help people achieve their ambitions, in the right way. Barclays' Shared Values transcend the way employees work and how they act, guiding the choices made every day. Everything that the bank does is underpinned by five Values: Respect, Integrity, Service, Excellence and Stewardship.

Biffa provides **collection, recycling, treatment, disposal and energy generation** services to households, businesses and the public sector across the UK. Its scale and breadth of operations places it at the **centre of a dynamic and growing sector,** providing indispensable services to local communities.

Market

Biffa is a leading integrated waste management business operating across the UK since 1912 – handling the collection, treatment, processing and disposal of waste and recyclable materials. The brand is highly recognisable, with its distinct red trucks and containers that now cover 95% of UK postcodes. With an unbeatable service offering, the company boasts a critical mass of 197 operating locations, including depots, waste transfer stations as well as processing and energy generation facilities.

The business employs 7,800 members of staff providing for 72,000 industrial and commercial customers and 2.4m domestic waste customers nationwide.

Product

In addition to providing waste management for commercial and domestic customers, the team also works with the production and sale of energy derived from waste and the sale of recovered commodities such as paper, glass, metals and plastic. Biffa's customer base for these services includes local authorities (which includes the collection of waste from households), large corporate businesses and SMEs, and purchasers of end-product commodities and energy – covering a vast range of UK business sectors, including manufacturing, retail, and hospitality.

DID YOU KNOW?

Richard Biffa is actually Italian. He changed his name from Ponte to Biffa when he moved to London.

Biffa offers recycling services for dry mixed recycling including plastic, paper, tin, cardboard, card and glass; as well as organic recycling for food and garden waste. The company's waste management services also covers general waste – anything that is non-recyclable, green waste, and street cleaning.

Achievements

Health and safety standards have always been a priority for Biffa, and in 2017 the company became the first waste management company to receive prestigious health and safety award, the Sword of Honour, presented by the British Safety Council.

Biffa is one of just 56 organisations worldwide that have achieved this accolade in health and safety. As the waste industry is often reported as one of the most dangerous industries to work in, this is an incredible achievement.

In 2017, Biffa also achieved its highest ever health and safety ranking and score of over 97%, securing the British Safety Council Five Star Award in a combined review of H&S and Environmental management systems.

Recent Developments

Biffa has made 21 company acquisitions in the last three years and in 2016, Biffa became a listed company on the London Stock Exchange, driving an increase in net revenue by 8%.

Biffa has also recently extended its OneCall service offering to include the new 3-2-1 Gone service, responding to customer feedback asking the firm to deal with smaller quantities of unplanned waste quickly and

Brand History

1912 Biffa is launched in Wembley by Richard Henry Biffa.

1930s Biffa introduces the first fleet of motorised lorries.

1959 Biffa wins several bulk refuse contacts with London Borough Council.

1989 The company introduces integrated waste management.

1996 Biffa becomes the first operator with a European landfill site achieving Environmental Management and Audit Scheme (EMAs).

2011 Poplars AD starts generating electricity from food waste.

2014 Aerobic digestion plant works with Sainsbury's to power the local store with its own food waste.

2016 Biffa is listed on the London Stock Exchange.

2017 Biffa becomes the first waste management company to receive the prestigious award of Sword of Honour for health and safety excellence, presented by the British Safety Council.

responsibly. This allows small waste items to be collected, separated, and disposed of, with all recyclable items being put to better use – a reassurance to businesses that they are doing their part to positively impact the environment.

This development follows last year's successful launch of Biffa OneCall – a rapid emergency waste removal service for businesses across the UK, operating 24 hours a day, seven days a week, with a dedicated fleet of purpose built collection vehicles.

Promotion

Biffa has a passionate communications team who create strategies across all creative channels to highlight important waste management and public safety issues to businesses and the general public.

In 2016, Biffa teamed up with Recycle Now to launch the Wasteaters campaign; which saw 15 Biffa trucks with their own individual monster paint job hit the streets, ready to 'guzzle' the waste loaded into their 'giant bodies'.

The trucks visited primary schools across the UK to help educate children about the waste journey and the importance of recycling. The public were encouraged to look out for the trucks, take a photo if they spotted them, and tweet it to @biffa using #wasteater. Biffa also launched a dedicated website containing profiles of all of the Wasteaters, as well as clues of where they can be spotted.

As well as educating the next generation on waste management, Biffa also campaigned for the safety of the community with the launch of DRoPs: Driving Recklessly on Pavements. Every month it is estimated that more than 30,000 incidents of reckless driving on pavements take place across the UK, often as impatient drivers try to get around waste collecting vehicles, resulting in collisions that can be fatal.

Biffa worked with police services and local author ties to raise awareness of the issue, receiving national coverage and great results for local councils across the UK – including Cannock District Council who reported their incidents had been more than halved thanks to the campaign.

Another campaign close to Biffa's heart is the People Sheltering in Bins campaign. In recent years there has been a surge in the number of homeless people using waste containers as a place of refuge – despite this being highly dangerous. A number of initiatives have been enlisted by Biffa to help tackle this issue, including a robust partnership with charity Streetlink and vans being fitted with CCTV cameras to identify people before the bins are emptied.

Brand Values

Biffa takes its responsibilities to customers and their communities very seriously, operating by five key values; be safe, be innovative, be customer focused, be a team player, be accountable. The company strives to deliver an excellent customer experience, as well as serving to protect the environment, employees, and the public.

The team develops and grows its innovative range of services to ensure it is providing for all waste-related needs across the UK, while encouraging businesses and households to dispose of waste in a way that's beneficial to the environment and local communities.

British Gypsum, part of the Saint-Gobain group, is a **100-year old UK manufacturer of interior lining systems**. Its vision is to **create spaces for better living in every kind** of building – **from homes to offices, from hotels to hospitals** – British Gypsum helps to create spaces which keep people warm, comfortable and safe.

Market

British Gypsum is the UK's leading manufacturer of interior lining systems for the residential and commercial construction sectors. Operating from five UK manufacturing sites in Barrow upon Soar and East Leake in Leicestershire; Kirkby Thore, Cumbria; Robertsbridge, East Sussex and Sherburn-in-Elmet, North Yorkshire. All sites provide nationwide next-day distribution capability, keeping the nation's construction sites operational and meeting the needs of a diverse customer base, from specifiers to installers.

Product

The British Gypsum product range includes well-known brands such as Thistle plasters, Gyproc plasterboard, Gypframe metal framing systems as well as a range of ceiling products, accompanied by a wide range of accessories and ancillary products. However, the real value British

Gypsum delivers to its customers is its system based approach – internal partitions, wall linings as well as floors and ceilings are designed to deliver the performance that is required for the particular building type, whether thermal, acoustic, fire or robustness. Moreover, all of the different systems are tested and substantiated to provide evidence that they meet, if not exceed, the claimed performance levels as well as all relevant regulations. All of this information is found in the iconic White Book, the industry's leading publication on drylining, which was first published over 40 years ago.

Achievements

British Gypsum goes beyond building regulations, setting the bar and raising standards in everything it does. For 100 years it has been helping people build better, delivering confidence and certainty, by offering access to the strongest base of expertise in the industry. This commitment to high standards helps build trust amongst British Gypsum's

DID YOU KNOW?

British Gypsum is one of the **UK's largest mine operators**, with five locations throughout the UK.

customers who also benefit from a complete package of support. This includes on-site technical advice and supervision as well as access to the company's Technical Advice Centre, one of the largest in the industry providing over 20,000 hours of technical advice each year.

British Gypsum's SpecSure® lifetime system warranty, guarantees that systems are built from the highest quality components and rigorously tested to meet even the most demanding building requirements. British Gypsum holds over 13,000

actual test and substantiation reports from The Building Test Centre, which is a UKAS-approved testing laboratory, first established by British Gypsum in 1967.

British Gypsum opened its first Training Academy in Kent over 50 years ago. Since then, more than 500,000 days of training have been delivered through the network of Academies for Installers, Clients, Architects and Main Contractors. Recognising the need to support its current and future plasterers and dryliners in the construction industry, the Thistle Partnership supports over

75 colleges nationally including supporting students through the national SkillBuild and WorldSkills competitions.

British Gypsum is also driving innovation through the construction industry by recognising the importance of independently verified Responsible

Brand History

1917	The British Plaster Board company is founded.
1964	Gypsum interests are amalgamated to form British Gypsum.
1967	British Gypsum opens its first dedicated training facility.
1972	The White Book is first published.
1975	British Gypsum launches the first performance plasterboard.
1978	British Gypsum introduces metal framing into drylining systems.
1989	Next day delivery is introduced – an industry first.
1991	The UK's largest plaster mining and manufacturing facility is built at Barrow upon Soar, Leicestershire.
2001	British Gypsum introduces a Plasterboard Recycling Service for it customers.
2003	SpecSure® lifetime system warranty is introduced.
2008	British Gypsum gains full ISO 14001:2004 certification for environmental management systems across its mine and manufacturing sites in the UK.
2012	British Gypsum becomes the first UK gypsum manufacturer to achieve BES 6001 'very good' rating.
2014	New Gyproc Habito® super strong plasterboard launches.
2018	New and improved Gypframe metal frame system is launched.

Sourcing Certification. This aims to provide assurance to customers that it is sourcing materials responsibly and sustainably. The company was the first manufacturer of interior lining systems to achieve a BES 6001 'Excellent' rating for its plaster, plasterboard and metal partition systems.

With a commitment to give back to the community, British Gypsum supports CRASH, the construction industry's charity for the Homeless as well as contributing to many local charities and initiatives close to its sites.

Recent Developments
Over the past three years, significant investment has been made in people as well as capital investment in manufacturing facilities. Production capability in terms of people and processing equipment has been added at all plants in order to respond to the demands of the market as well as maintaining modern and efficient facilities.

Promotion
British Gypsum believes that value lies in ident fying opportunities in conjunction with its customers; for example working with clients and architects to challenge the way schools, offices or healthcare facilities are designed with more focus on end user comfort. Over the last two years the British Gypsum Certified Plasterer scheme has worked with Plasterers to promote new innovative plasters and reinforce the skill and craft of plastering.

The company is also working with housebuilders to futureproof the design, comfort and flexibility of homes for generations to come. This includes the introduction of three thought provoking concepts: Thistle Magnetic Plaster which provides a wall surface that will attract magnets; the creation of super strong walls using Gyproc Habito®, a radically different plasterboard, which is extremely durable

BRITISH GYPSUM ARE PART OF €39 BILLION SAINT-GOBAIN, ONE OF THE TOP 100 INDUSTRIAL GROUPS IN THE WORLD

and damage resistant compared to standard walls and much easier to fix to; and finally, solutions that deliver substantially enhanced levels of sound insulation.

Brand Values
British Gypsum has three key principles at the heart of its business, which it defines as 'Build better. Build with confidence. Build with technical expertise'.

british-gypsum.com

Carlsberg was **founded in Copenhagen in 1847** by J.C. Jacobsen; a visionary who actively brought science into brewing. **Jacobsen dedicated his life's work to the consistent pursuit of better beer,** always sharing new findings freely with other brewers and the wider world. His pioneering **spirit and open-minded philosophy still fuels the brand's progress today**.

Market

Carlsberg Group is one of the biggest brewers in the world, operating in more than 140 markets. One of the top five beer brands in the UK's highly competitive alcoholic drinks sector, more than 400m pints of Carlsberg are enjoyed by consumers every year. With wide-ranging distribution across the UK, from national supermarkets and pub chains to independent bars, restaurants, and convenience stores, wherever you are, there's probably a Carlsberg nearby.

Product

As well as the iconic Carlsberg Pilsner, the Carlsberg portfolio also includes Carlsberg Expørt, a premium-strength lager, alcohol-free Carlsberg 0.0%, and Carlsberg Special Brew, a super-strength lager that was originally brewed to mark Sir Winston Churchill's first visit to Copenhagen, in 1950.

All Carlsberg brews include a specific strain of purified yeast; Saccharomyces Carlsbergensis, which was first discovered by Prof. Emil Christian Hansen, at the Carlsberg Laboratory, in 1883. This was a truly ground-breaking discovery,

DID YOU KNOW?

30% of Carlsberg's global profits are invested in the Carlsberg Foundation, which **funds scientific research projects** worldwide.

which meant that beer could be consistently produced to a high quality. True to his ethos, J.C. Jacobsen shared this discovery with other brewers and today, almost all modern-day lagers are derived from the original yeast.

Achievements

In 2017, Carlsberg Pilsner was one of the top five beer brands, by volume and value, in the UK (Source: Nielsen ScanTrack, CGA OPMS).

Carlsberg's latest campaign, 'The Danish Way', was shortlisted for Campaign of the Year,

and Carlsberg for Creative Marketer of the Year, at the Campaign Big Awards. In addition, the launch TV film, starring Danish actor Mads Mikkelsen, was ranked in the Top 10 for Campaign Magazine's Ads of the Year. Carlsberg Expørt's new packaging, fount, and glass were named best in the category by consumers. Furthermore, the design has won numerous awards including Gold at the FAB awards, Silver at the Drum Roses awards, Silver at the Food and Beverage awards, and bronze at the Penta awards.

In addition to the success of the new Carlsberg Expørt relaunch, The København collection – a limited-edition design for Carlsberg Pilsner – has won multiple awards including the D&AD Wooden Pencil; double Gold at the Brand Impact Awards as well as silver at the Brand Impact and Penta Awards.

Recent Developments

Friday, 10th November, 2017, marked the 170 anniversary of the very first beer brewed at the Carlsberg brewery in Valby, Copenhagen. Today, 51% of Carlsberg is owned by the Carlsberg

The Elephant Gates, at Ny Carlsberg brewery, Copenhagen

Award-winning København Collection

Brand History

1847 J.C. Jacobsen founds the Carlsberg brewery in Copenhagen.

1875 J.C. Jacobsen founds the Carlsberg Laboratory with the vision to share its knowledge.

1876 The Carlsberg Foundation is born, as one of the world's first industrial foundations.

1883 The Carlsberg Laboratory revolutionises the brewing industry by creating the world's first pure yeast.

1909 Danish chemist Dr. Søren P L Sørensen, develops the pH scale at the Carlsberg Laboratory.

1913 J.C.'s son, Carl, donates the now-iconic Little Mermaid statue to the city of Copenhagen.

1950 Carlsberg creates Special Brew to commemorate Winston Churchill's visit to Copenhagen.

1957 Queen Elizabeth II visits the Carlsberg brewery in Copenhagen.

1975 Orson Welles is the first actor to read the 'Probably the best beer in the world...' strapline.

1994 Global sales reach one million barrels.

2015 Globally, 60m consumers see Carlsberg's 'Best poster in the world'.

2017 Mads Mikkelsen becomes the latest actor to read 'Probably...' for the Danish Way.

Mads Mikkelsen stars in latest campaign, The Danish Way

Foundation; one of the world's oldest industrial foundations and each year, 30% of Global profits are invested into the foundation, funding outstanding scientific research to address global challenges, producing universal benefit.

2017 saw Carlsberg launch a new sustainability initiative, Together Towards Zero, which outlined four key ambitions: Zero Carbon Footprint, Zero Water Waste, Zero Irresponsible Drinking, and Zero Accident Culture. As part of this, Carlsberg has committed to eliminating carbon emissions from all breweries, achieving a 30% reduction in the carbon footprint by 2030.

In 2018, Carlsberg will continue its pursuit of better in all areas, from launching revolutionary innovations in packaging to creating exciting new brews.

Promotion

Carlsberg has always been synonymous with strong advertising. From the iconic brand mark, created over 100 years ago by legendary

440M PINTS OF CARLSBERG WERE SOLD IN THE UK DURING 2017

THAT'S 14 PINTS EVERY SECOND

Danish designer, Thorvald Bindesbøll, to the famous "Probably the best beer in the World" slogan, which is one of the most well-loved straplines of all time. The classic "If Carlsberg did…" strapline has also been adopted and re-worked by consumers over a number of years, to become a figure of speech in its own right.

April 2017 saw the launch of The Danish Way, a £15m, integrated marketing campaign to breathe new life into its Carlsberg and Carlsberg Expørt brands in the UK with a progressive positioning, reflective of its

rich history and Danish provenance. In 2018, Carlsberg will continue to bring a little bit of Danishness to the UK, motivating consumers to take action and adopt a 'Probably…' mindset into their everyday lives. A new partnership with Live Nation's UK festivals and venues will connect Carlsberg with a new generation of music lovers, whilst long-standing sponsorships, such as the 25-year old partnership with Liverpool FC, will continue to connect Carlsberg to sports fans across the world.

Brand Values

Carlsberg's relentless pursuit of better beer is best summed up by the Latin motto, Semper Ardens, or 'Always Burning', which is inscribed above the famous Elephant Gates (pictured left) that greet all arrivals to the Ny Carlsberg brewery in Copenhagen.

A City & Guilds Group Business

City & Guilds believes in a world where people and organisations have the capabilities to prosper, today and in the future. As workplaces evolve, so does City & Guilds. That is why it has been setting the standard for skills that transform lives, industries and economies since 1878.

Market

City & Guilds is a household brand and a global leader in skills development. Over one million people earn a City & Guilds qualification every year, providing them with the skills they need to thrive in the workplace.

In the global economy, the ability to compete depends on building a skilled, competent and confident workforce. City & Guilds understands the value of portable skills and globally recognised standards that enable people and organisations to succeed. It partners with

Skills that transform careers, businesses and economies

governments, employers and educators in over 50 countries, across five continents, to advise them on developing high-quality skills training that meets the needs of the global workforce, without compromising local demands.

Product

City & Guilds' focus today is the same as it has always been: to help people into a job, develop on the job and move on to the next job. It works closely with employers across the world to make sure that its products and services are industry relevant, and the people who study with City & Guilds have the skills that meet the needs of business, today and in the future.

City & Guilds offers qualifications across 26 industries from construction to customer service, plumbing to playwork, animal care to automotive and hairdressing to health and social care. As part of the City & Guilds Group, the brand is able to meet evolving employer demands from management skills to innovative new ways of recognising skills in the workforce.

Achievements

City & Guilds is a trusted advisor to employers and governments across the world. In the UK, it has been integral in implementing the new apprenticeship system and was invited to advise on the majority of the recent Government appointed apprenticeship trailblazers. Its experts also sat on the panel of Britain's leading cross-party think-tank, DEMOS, on apprenticeships.

City & Guilds worked with Barclays to accredit its Digital Wings programme, which rolled out to thousands of staff across the globe, resulting in a significant uplift in customers using its Digital Products.

City & Guilds helped Dubai World Central, Dubai's second airport, train and upskill its staff following a radical expansion. Offering passengers the quickest and smoothest process to get to a million destinations meant that the customer had to be the number one

DID YOU KNOW?

For over 100 years, City & Guilds has run its annual Medals for Excellence and Lion Awards to recognise excellence in vocational education globally.

priority. To date over 1,000 staff have been trained in customer service, leadership and management.

In September 2017, Qualifications Wales awarded and appointed City & Guilds and WJEC to be the sole providers to deliver qualifications for health, social care and childcare in Wales.

Also in 2017, City & Guilds was recognised for the Best B2B Marketing Campaign for its apprenticeships campaign at the annual Dotmailer awards.

Recent Developments

City & Guilds is part of the City & Guilds Group. In recent years the business has diversified to meet changing market needs making a number of acquisitions which includes Kineo, ILM, The Oxford Group, Digitalme and Gen2.

Together, the businesses set the standards for corporate learning, on-the-job development, and skills recognition around the world – making skills and careers portable. In the coming years the Group will continue to expand its portfolio.

Through the wider Group offer, City & Guilds is able to provide its customers with products and services that accredit and recognise the skills of the global workforce at every stage of their careers.

Brand History

1878 The City and Guilds of London Institute is founded by the City of London and the Guilds (16 livery companies).

1879 City & Guilds awards its first certificates in cotton manufacture.

1881 HRH The Prince of Wales becomes the first President of the City and Guilds of London Institute.

1951 HRH The Duke of Edinburgh becomes President of the Institute.

1990 City & Guilds International is established.

1998 City & Guilds awards its one millionth NVQ certificate.

2011 HRH The Duke of Edinburgh steps down as President of the Institute and HRH The Princess Royal takes over.

2011 City & Guilds acquires Learning Assistant, an online portfolio allowing learners and tutors to share, track and moderate coursework and projects.

2011 City & Guilds is the premier sponsor of WorldSkills London.

2012 City & Guilds is the premier sponsor of the Skills Show.

2014 The City & Guilds Group acquires Mindset Software Technologies, which develops tools and services to support the delivery and administration of learning and funding for colleges, training providers and employers.

2017 City & Guilds and WJEC are appointed to be the sole providers to deliver particular qualifications by Qualifications Wales.

Over the last few years, it has also carried out a rebrand of the 140 year-old brand that has shaped the vocational educational sector since 1878. To align to the changing environment, City & Guilds, 'unleashing tomorrow's talent' is the essence of the brand today.

Promotion

City & Guilds traditional market has changed dramatically over the past five years. This is due to significant policy changes that affect the delivery of its core products, such as the introduction of the apprenticeship levy and the forthcoming T-level qualifications. City & Guilds has moved from being largely a provider of products and services to colleges and training providers to being a business that also works directly

DID YOU KNOW?

City & Guilds is 140 years old this year.

A City & Guilds Group Business

Unleashing tomorrow's talent

A global leader in skills development

- Recognised and developed by industry
- Develop your career faster
- Get your global passport

with employers to meet their skills needs. This has changed the audiences that it communicates with and the way in which the brand communicates.

City & Guilds' marketing activity with its customers in further education focuses on keeping them abreast of changes in the sector and what it means to them as well as innovations in the products and services in its offer. City & Guilds engages customers using a range of channels such as email and social media, customer events and webinars, sponsorship of trade shows as well as customer-focused publications and public relations activity with further education publications.

To build its employer engagement, City & Guilds works in partnership with employer organisations to deliver thought leadership on the skills issues

that affect them most. This includes a collaboration with Changeboard, a global community of HR and business leaders, where City & Guilds will be headline sponsor of their prestigious annual conference. It has also developed a multi-media marketing campaign focusing on employer issues, launching in early 2018.

Brand Values

City & Guilds brand values are leadership, imagination and integrity. These values run through everything from recruitment to project evaluation. City & Guilds believes in a world where people and organisations have the confidence and capabilities to prosper, today and in the future. Its ambition is to make a difference by helping people into a job, develop on the job and move on to the next job.

Clarks

Innovation and craftsmanship were at the heart of Clarks when it was founded in Somerset, almost **200 years ago** by Cyrus and James Clark. Craft and creativity live on in the brand today, but are **evolved in response to the modern world,** driven by a desire to keep moving forward.

Market

Clarks operates on a global scale, with more than 1,650 stores and 20,000 wholesale selling points throughout Europe, Asia and the Americas, supported by eight e-commerce sites. It is one of the world's leading casual footwear brands, employing around 16,000 people worldwide. In the UK, it is the number one casual footwear brand (Source: Kantar Market Data, 2017).

Product

There are approximately 16 different methods of footwear construction and Clarks can lay claim to commercialising more than half of them. Shoemaking is both an art and a science and every one of Clarks' shoes starts with a handmade last, a skilfully crafted form that has a shape similar to that of a human foot and fundamentally dictates the shape of a shoe. The initial designs are brought to life through razor-sharp, cutting-edge technology. Clarks has a longstanding reputation for quality and its commitment to creating without compromise, combining advanced construction techniques and contemporary materials with the specialist skills that can only be acquired over time helps to maintain this esteemed position. Innovation is important to Clarks with rapid prototyping and 3D printing all being utilised to keep Clarks at the forefront of product development.

The Clarks product range combines the practical and the emotional; beautifully designed products that capture the spirit of the brand and reflect the priorities of consumers. The unique Clarks design code is applied to Men's, Women's and Children's footwear and has created some of the most iconic products in the casual category.

Achievements

The iconic Clarks Desert Boot is a distinctive ankle height boot with a crepe rubber sole. It was designed in 1950 by Nathan Clark, the great-grandson of company founder, James Clark, and is still a popular product today, transcending classification to resonate with both streetwear influencers and more classic mainstream consumers. In addition, the much loved Wallabee, first launched

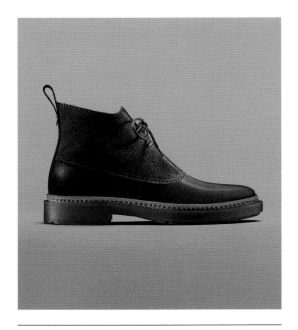

50m **CLARKS SOLD PAIRS OF SHOES IN 2017**

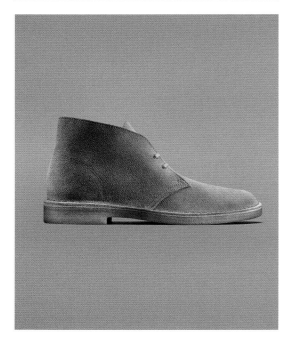

in 1967, has developed a cult following and counts singer Drake and NBA star, Lebron James, among its fans. The Wallabee has a moccasin construction making it simple, beautiful and versatile and has been translated into endless colour and material combinations.

These products redefined the footwear market when they were first introduced, ostensibly creating the 'casual dress' category and driving the creation of the Clarks design code – craft, comfort and creativity.

Clarks is again focused on creating icons. The launch of Nature IV in Spring/Summer 2017 saw a modern, elevated interpretation of Clarks' iconic Nature product, first introduced in 1982. Another new addition is Trigenic that represents a unique Clarks take on the athleisure category. Available to men, women and children, the collection uses natural, foot-shaped designs and three-part flex soles to create an athleisure inspired silhouettes, which resonates with the modern consumer.

Clarks also places importance on creating a strong retail environment to showcase its products. The windows of its Regent Street store were recognised when it received the Retail Focus Reader's Choice Award 2017. In addition, the shop fit of its Manchester Store, by Pure, was highlighted by Retail Week as one of the Top UK Store Designs of 2017. Clarks has also received the accolade of Best Children's Shoe Brand from Little London Magazine Awards 2017.

Recent Developments

Clarks store design was in the spotlight again when the flagship Market Street, Manchester store was praised by Retail Week for creating an environment that customers feel at ease in. With modern, modular, simplicity in mind, the shoes take centre stage. This innovative design concept has also been rolled out in Buchanan Street, Glasgow. Retail Week also highlighted the "mid-shop internally lit display boxes, screens with promotional videos around the perimeter and dramatically lit cash desk",

Brand History

1825 Cyrus Clark, a fellmonger, woolstapler and tanner begins producing whole sheepskin rugs.

1828 Cyrus hires his brother James as an apprentice and the innovative production of slippers, made from sheepskin off-cuts, begins.

1833 The production of slippers is successful and the business begins trading as C. & J. Clark.

1880s William Clark, James' son, creates the first mechanised shoemaking process in the country.

1904 John Walter Bostock comes from the US to teach advanced manufacturing techniques to employees and becomes a company director in 1928.

1937 The company officially becomes a retailer after acquiring all of the Abbotts chain of shops in London.

1950 The iconic Clarks Desert Boot is designed by Nathan Clark, great grandson of James Clark.

1967 The Wallabee design is created.

1980s The Nature, sports casual hybrid, makes its debut.

1997 The iconic 'Act Your Shoe Size Not Your Age' campaign launches.

2010 CEO, Melissa Potter, restructures the business globally, overseeing the creation of an online store.

2017 Nature IV is launched and the award winning flagship Manchester store design heralds a new era for Clarks.

describing the retail environment as "a highly contemporary store".

With future facing strategic thinking, Clarks has recently reoriented the business around its portfolio of brands. Creating new distinct opportunities to interact with differentiated consumer demographics and putting the Clarks brand is at the heart of the business has been key.

Promotion

Clarks' brand campaigns aim to convey the essence of the brand – liberal, free-spirited, optimistic – to emotionally engage consumers. The brand has worked with Cass Bird, the acclaimed world-class photographer, to create atmospheric, visually stunning work.

January 2017 saw the coordinated global launch of Nature IV. In the UK, this included an Oxford Circus takeover.

Clarks also creates world-class brand partnerships to work with specialists and innovators from other fields. For example, it has a long-standing relationship with iconic streetwear brand Supreme. In addition, its collaboration with Drake's OVO brand, titled OVO x Clarks, saw the much discussed first drop of Desert Boots in black, beige and purple, sell out in just 12 minutes.

December 2017, saw the launch of a further collaboration with Star Wars, to co-inside with the release of Star Wars: The Last Jedi. Taking inspiration from the strong female lead, Rey, the range

of women's and girl's boots were designed with both style and durability in mind.

This strategic approach enables Clarks to tell authentic stories, create new opportunities to talk to new consumers, access new distribution channels as well as support the brand positioning.

Brand Values

The founders of Clarks were pioneers with a transformative mind-set. This remains at the heart of the brand today. The brand purpose is defined as 'comfort in movement through innovation', inspiring the creation of market leading products that feel unique and relevant to their consumer target.

Continental

As an **international tyre manufacturer and leading automotive supplier**,
Continental **develops technologies for transporting people safely, whatever the wheel**.
The corporation sets the future in motion with five strong divisions –
Chassis & Safety, Interior, Powertrain, Tyre and ContiTech.

Market

Generating sales of €40.5bn in 2016 and currently employing over 233,000 people in 56 countries, Continental's market position as a leading premium tyre manufacturer is underlined by winning four out of five independent tyre tests in Europe. With best in braking across all weather conditions, Continental tyres are fitted to one in three new cars across Europe. The German manufacturer shapes the automotive landscape for a safer future. As one of the world's leading automotive suppliers, it strives towards a world of zero accidents.

Product

With a rich heritage of developing groundbreaking technologies and mobility solutions over the last 145 years, Continental offers a range of tyre fitments for all applications. Continental works with manufacturers to develop groundbreaking solutions such as ContiSeal, a tyre that features a sticky viscous layer in the tread that seals punctures up to 5mm. It invests heavily across its ranges, with its latest PremiumContact 6 offering 'perfect grip and comfort' in all situations.

DID YOU KNOW?

Continental has now become an **official partner of the Tour de France**, supplying tyres for all official support cars and motorcycles on the Tour.

At the forefront of tyre development, Continental innovates for the future with revolutionary products such as ContiSense and ContiAdapt. ContiSense is based on the development of electrically conductive rubber-based sensors that continuously monitor both tread depth and temperature. ContiAdapt combines micro-compressors integrated into the wheel, meaning the system can modify the size of the tyres contact patch to the road: a decisive factor for both safety and comfort.

Achievements

The market-leading approach of Continental has been frequently recognised with a range of UK tyre test wins and international awards. In 2017 it took the top spot in both summer and winter tyre tests. Continental's commitment to technical excellence and innovation ensures its tyres deliver superb braking, handling and performance. It is the only tyre manufacturer to have an automated braking test centre, enabling year-round testing. Continental completes more than 700m test miles annually and more than 200 rubber compounds daily. Continental is the leading tyre choice for the world's top car manufacturers, with over 500 current model approvals. If the manufacturer trusts the tyre brands products, drivers can too.

Recent Developments

Over recent years Continental has developed a range of partnerships to maximise its brand awareness across audiences, reiterating its safety-first approach for all road users.

Brand History

1871 Continental-Caoutchouc- und Gutta-Percha Compagnie is founded in Hanover.

1882 The rampant horse is adopted as a trademark.

1904 Continental presents the world's first automobile tyre with a patterned tread.

1914 There is a triple victory for Daimlers fitted with Continental tyres at the French Grand Prix.

1979 The takeover of the European tyre operations of Uniroyal, Inc., USA, gives Continental a wider base in Europe.

1993 Continental has approximately 2,000 tyre retailers and franchises across 15 European countries.

1998 Continental adds sites in Argentina, Mexico, South Africa and Slovakia.

2001 Majority holdings are purchased in two Japanese companies.

2003 The world's first road tire approved for speeds up to 360km/h – the ContiSportContact 2 Vmax – is unveiled.

2006 The automotive electronics business of Motorola, Inc. is acquired by Continental.

2016 Continental's SportContact 6 makes its UK tyre test debut, taking first places in the evo tyre test.

2017 Recognition in UK tyre tests continues by winning the Auto Express summer and winter tests. The ContiPremiumContact 5 and TS 860 both topped their test groups to round off a successful tyre test year.

Working closely with adidas, Continental brings advanced tyre technology to the soles of trainers, creating rubber compounds with exceptional grip in wet and dry conditions. Continental proudly activates its partnership with adidas to the running community through Conti Thunder Run, an endurance race to test the ultimate traction off road.

The brand's commitment to safety extends to its sponsorship as Safety Partner at Prudential RideLondon, widely known as one of the greatest cycling festivals in the world. Continental is a leading producer of bicycle tyres, and the top eight riders in the 2016 Tour de France rode on Continental rubber. The event is a natural choice, showcasing to over 100,000 riders that Continental offers the 'perfect choice for grip – whatever the wheel'.

Continental also continues as a Partner in Excellence at Mercedes-Benz World, the pioneering brand experience centre located at Brooklands motor racing circuit. In 2017 over 500 people experienced the benefits of free driving demonstrations held over the year. Guests got to experience the importance of premium tyres through a range of driving demonstrations, along with latest safety systems such as Autonomous Emergency Braking.

Promotion

Over recent years, its five-strong divisions have helped establish Continental as one of the top automotive suppliers globally, with such technologies contributing to zero accidents and fatalities in the future, known as Vision Zero. A partnership with the New Car Assessment Programme through its Stop the Crash campaign has further enhanced Continental as a leader in automotive technology and safety. As a proud corporate supporter of TyreSafe, Continental brought safety to the streets, educating motorists about the simple tyre safety checks all drivers should undertake.

Brand Values

With its tyre technologies, and automotive knowhow, Continental works towards its vision zero initiative of zero road accidents. Its contributions make not only for an exciting driving experience, but a safe one. Continental's pioneering safety technologies, paired with educating road users globally, show a company that is truly committed to road safety.

Deutsche Bank is one of the **best-known financial services brands in the world.**
The iconic **Deutsche Bank logo is the basis of a versatile brand identity system**
that provides **consistency in execution and attitude in print and online**
across the bank's many client groups, businesses and markets.

© Anit Lennon

Market

Deutsche Bank operates in a highly competitive global banking industry alongside other leading names such as Barclays, Citigroup, Goldman Sachs, HSBC, JPMorgan Chase, Morgan Stanley and UBS. It is one of the few European banks with a genuine global presence. At home, Deutsche Bank is Germany's leading bank with a long history of connecting German business to the rest of the world.

Product

The Corporate & Investment Bank division provides corporate finance, equities, fixed income and currencies, and global transaction banking services for companies, governments and institutional investors globally.

The Private & Commercial Bank supplies retail banking and commercial banking services to more than 20m companies, small and medium-sized businesses and private individuals

in Germany under the Deutsche Bank and Postbank brands. It will launch a new digital bank for younger clients in 2018. It also provides global wealth management services for high net worth individuals and families.

Asset Management operates under the DWS brand. Providing traditional and alternative investments across all major asset classes for individuals and institutions, it is one of the world's leading investment managers.

Achievements

Recent awards include Best Global Trade Finance Provider for the third year in a row in the annual Euromoney Trade Finance Survey, and best for fixed income research from Institutional Investor for the seventh consecutive year. The bank recently won International Financing Review's Europe High-Yield Bond House award for the third consecutive year. In its Fixed Income and Currencies business, it also won three awards from Risk Magazine: Currency Derivatives House, Quant Research House and Institutional Investment Product of the year.

Deutsche Bank was recognised as Best Fintech Partnership in the Financial Innovation Awards and Best Treasury and Capital Markets Project at the Banking Technology Awards. It received two awards from the German Brand Institute in 2017 for the strategy, creative execution and promotion of its global social enterprise

programme, Made for Good. For the 15th year running, the bank has also been recognised among the best places to work for members of the LGBTQ community.

Recent Developments

Recognising the new expectations of banks following the global financial crisis, in 2017 Deutsche Bank redefined the purpose of its business. A new brand position of #PositiveImpact expresses Deutsche Bank's commitment to enabling economic growth and societal progress through the financial, commercial and human outcomes that result from its work for clients. It's a message that confirms Deutsche Bank's belief in long-term partnerships and sustainable business practices. It also demonstrates a wider and longer-term view of value beyond the narrow pursuit of profit that has undermined public trust in the banking industry. As it approaches 150 years in business, Deutsche Bank is moving forward with a renewed sense of its founding purpose as a partner that can help clients achieve their plans, ambitions and dreams.

Promotion

The use of a hashtag in the tagline #PositiveImpact is another indication of the repositioning – and modernisation – of the Deutsche Bank brand. The bank says the hashtag reflects its commitment to engagement and dialogue about its role in business and in life.

Brand History

1870 Deutsche Bank is founded in Berlin. Its mission is to promote trade between Germany, Europe and overseas markets.

1873 Deutsche Bank opens its first London branch.

1926 The Bank makes its name in the UK with deals for BP and London Underground.

1974 Graphic design pioneer Anton Stankowski creates the famous 'slash in the square' logo to represent the modern Deutsche Bank.

1989 The takeover of Morgan Grenfell gives Deutsche Bank a new presence in the City of London and begins an expansion that will see it become one of the world's leading investment banks.

2008 Deutsche Bank emerges from the global financial crisis with its reputation enhanced, having stood strong and supported clients through the upheaval.

2010 Deutsche Bank adopts a more confident and minimal approach to branding with the iconic logo appearing without words alongside it.

2011 The BrandSpace opens in Frankfurt, inviting visitors to experience the Deutsche Bank brand in new ways.

2017 Deutsche Bank launches its #PositiveImpact positioning.

Before going public with #PositiveImpact in 2018, the bank began a global internal communications campaign to embed this new purpose inside the bank and rally employees around it. The launch in May 2017 was led by a message to all employees from CEO John Cryan. A film showing real-life examples of positive impact for clients was shown on hashtag installations in major regional offices in London, Frankfurt and New York, on screens in public areas and on the bank's intranet. Offices worldwide were dressed with posters and vinyls to encourage employee participation.

We're not just advising SMEs on financial matters.

We're helping Steiff make friends for life.

#PositiveImpact

Watch the film
positiveimpact.db.com

25% OF DEUTSCHE BANK EMPLOYEES VOLUNTEER IN LOCAL COMMUNITIES ACROSS THE UK

Employee brand champions from all regions helped create a series of themed videos providing personal perspectives on positive impact. These were posted on a dedicated digital hub that provided the central focus of internal activity, where employees could see and share personal examples of positive impact. To date, almost 75,000 employees have visited the hub and posted 3,000 #PositiveImpact statements of their own.

Deutsche Bank's longstanding corporate social responsibility programme provides another avenue for employee involvement. The bank invests millions of euros annually in the support of education, enterprise and community projects worldwide, which are complemented by volunteering and giving by employees through the bank's 'Plus You' programme. It uses a large format newspaper called 3D to report on its global CSR activities, with regional inserts that contain a snapshot of local projects.

Projects in the UK include 'Playing Shakespeare with Deutsche Bank', which uses cultural learning to support the academic achievement and social mobility of young people. The Deutsche Bank Awards for Creative Enterprise has launched the careers of hundreds of third year and post grad students studying creative subjects.

The bank's UK Charities of the Year programme is a two-year partnership with two charities chosen by UK employees. It has raised more than £17.5m since it began in 1999 through employee fundraising activities.

Brand Values

Deutsche Bank's brand characteristics are dependable, high performing and human, which together illustrate the attitude and behaviours required to fulfil its promise of positive impact. It has chosen dependability because partnership demands integrity and truth. High performance shows the bank's commitment to doing the best for its clients. Humanity provides the warmth, humility and emotional intelligence required to deliver all of the dimensions of positive impact.

Dreams

As the **UK's leading bed specialist**, Dreams is passionate about providing the perfect night's sleep. Committed to providing the **highest standard of expert customer service** and advice, Dreams offers an **extensive selection of high quality products including mattresses, bed frames, divans, bedroom furniture and soft furnishings**, primarily hand-crafted in the UK.

DID YOU KNOW?

Dreams' Headquarters, based in High Wycombe, is called Bedquarters.

Market

As the population continues to recognise the importance of sleep to their wellbeing, the bed and mattress market is subsequently growing. Dreams' current market share is circa 17% based on sales vs. total market. The retailer, with over 190 stores nationwide, and a delivery fleet of nearly 120, is continuing to grow, having recently opened its second Bed Factory in the Midlands. Dreams is also a valued member of the National Bed Federation, the trade association representing UK manufacturers of beds and mattresses.

Product

Dreams' commitment to delivering a perfect night's sleep is accomplished by providing comfortable, quality beds and mattresses with outstanding customer service.

Mattresses continue to be at the forefront of Dreams' product offering and in 2017 Dreams added multiple new brands to its range including Tempur Cooltouch, Sleepeeze, a new Flaxby range, Doze and Sleep Essentials. Dreams continues to sell its own brand mattresses, the Dreams Workshop range, all of which are manufactured at the Dreams Bed Factory in Oldbury, UK.

Dreams has also invested heavily in its bedframe offering over recent years and the latest launch in April 2017 saw bedframes rise to 25% of the sales mix.

As well as high quality product, Dreams understands that listening to customers is the key to its success. Pillow Talk, a customer feedback tool, was introduced

DREAMS DELIVERS OVER 300,000 MATTRESSES EVERY YEAR THAT'S ENOUGH TO FILL 50 OLYMPIC SIZED SWIMMING POOLS

in 2014 to gather customers' comments on their purchase experience. This year, responses reached over 225,000 and boasts a customer satisfaction rate of 94%.

Achievements

2017 was an exceptional year for Dreams having won a number of industry accolades including Retail Week's Speciality Retailer of the Year Award which recognises Dreams' strong growth over the past three years. Dreams also won Retail Week's Supply Chain Award for its recycling and had two employees shortlisted in the coveted Retail Week Rising Star awards.

The Dreams factory celebrated winning a Silver award from The Royal Society for the Prevention of Accidents and winning an award for safety from the British Safety Council for the third year running. Dreams' bed in a box brand, Hyde and Sleep won a Which? Best Buy Award and an Express Home & Living Awards for it's Next-Gen memory foam mattress.

Dreams prides itself on achieving its brand purpose of being the UK's most recommended bed company and in 2017 it reached its highest Trustpilot score of 9.5 with over 13,000 five star reviews.

Throughout 2017, Dreams continued to raise money for its chosen charity, The Fostering Network with many employees embarking on fundraising activities including running the Paris Half Marathon and delivering a bed to the

DID YOU KNOW?

None of Dreams' customer collected waste ends up in landfill and instead, is made into insulation, refuse derived fuel and even pet cushions.

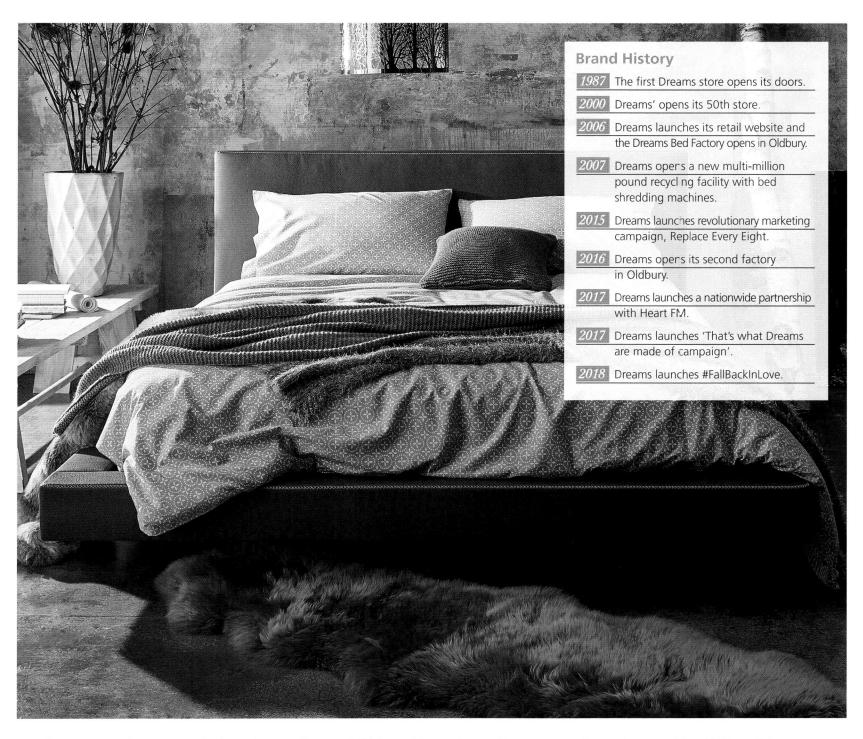

Brand History

1987	The first Dreams store opens its doors.
2000	Dreams' opens its 50th store.
2006	Dreams launches its retail website and the Dreams Bed Factory opens in Oldbury.
2007	Dreams opens a new multi-million pound recycling facility with bed shredding machines.
2015	Dreams launches revolutionary marketing campaign, Replace Every Eight.
2016	Dreams opens its second factory in Oldbury.
2017	Dreams launches a nationwide partnership with Heart FM.
2017	Dreams launches 'That's what Dreams are made of campaign'.
2018	Dreams launches #FallBackInLove.

top of Mount Snowdon. Dreams also hosted an inaugural Charity Golf Day and has raised over £100K for the charity over the past 18 months.

Recent Developments

Dreams' biggest investment in the last 12 months was announced this summer when it opened a state-of-the-art extension to its factory, increasing production capacity by nearly a third and creating 60 new jobs.

2017 saw Dreams focus on the additional services it offers to customers and made the decision to launch Free Delivery on all orders over £100. This was a first for the industry and successfully positioned Dreams ahead of its competitors. Dreams also invested in additional training for its delivery drivers to ensure customers receive the same quality of care throughout the entire purchasing journey.

To further enhance its customer service, Dreams has been developing a re-platforming project over the last 12 months. Branded 'Dreams 360', it combines online and in-store propositions to create a joined-up shopping experience. The platform is set to be launched in multiple stages throughout 2018, and will streamline the journey between shopping online and in store for all its customers.

Promotion

Dreams' most successful campaign to date is 'Replace Every Eight' which advises consumers to replace their mattresses every eight years. 2017 saw Dreams launch its third iteration of this campaign titled Fall Back in Love, demonstrating how a new mattress and better sleep is beneficial to your relationship. For the past 12 months, Dreams has also been promoting the campaign, 'That's what Dreams are made of' which brought to life its end-to-end quality and care, as well as its UK manufacturing credentials.

2017 also marked the beginning of Dreams' partnership with Heart FM. The collaboration allows Dreams to provide its unparalleled sleep advice to over 9.6m listeners every week.

Dreams' partnership with Heart FM gave it the opportunity to sponsor one of Global Radio's festivals, Rewind. This type of activity was a first for Dreams and enabled the company to reach a completely different audience in an engaging way.

Brand Values

For over 30 years Dreams has been passionate about providing everyone with the perfect night's sleep. The brand is committed to continually offering a wide range of quality products and the very highest standard of expert customer service.

Dreams truly understands the importance of sleep and making the right choice of mattress; therefore, the retailer offers a 40 Night Comfort Guarantee to give peace of mind to all its customers who are free to change their mattress should they not be entirely satisfied.

Dulux
let's colour

Manufactured for more than 80 years, Dulux™ paint has an established reputation for **quality, whilst offering the tools and services** that make it easy for consumers and professionals to decorate. The brand is instantly recognisable thanks to its iconic Dulux mascot, the **Old English Sheepdog, that made his debut in a 1961 TV advert.**

Market
With approximately 328m litres of paint sold in the UK last year, the DIY and Professional market is highly competitive. However, Dulux remains a strong market leader in the category, and continues to drive innovation throughout its products, services and guidance to inspire beautiful living spaces.

Product
With a comprehensive portfolio of decorating products, Dulux has always led the market in terms of innovation such as its unique product, Dulux Easycare™, with its stain repellent technology. DIYers can feel free from the worry that everyday living will damage the look of their beautiful home as spills simply bead off and stains are even easier to wash away.

Professional decorators are under increasing time pressure, resulting in demand for a paint that will perform straight from the tin without the need to thin. The new Dulux Trade Vinyl Matt™ has an improved in-can consistency that can be applied with or without thinning for optimum results. The new formulation has a smooth flow for easy application

and the benefit of reduced fly-off for a more enjoyable and efficient decorating process. The improved consistency also supports the delivery of a high quality uniform finish, whilst continuing to deliver outstanding opacity and coverage.

DID YOU KNOW?

In 2017, Brandz accredited Dulux as the 'healthiest UK brand overall.'

Achievements
In January 2017, Dulux unveiled pop-star-turned-presenter Rochelle Humes as the ambassador for 2017 Colour of the Year, Denim Drift™.

Carefully curated by an elite group of global colour experts, Denim Drift also became the UK's second most bought online tester in 2017 and one of the top five colours bought in the Easycare range.

In July 2017, Dulux hosted its first Facebook Live event with a Puppy Playdate, where delegates could virtually interact with nine adorable Dulux puppies. The online event reached almost one million people and raised awareness of the 'Fun Living with Dulux' campaign; which encouraged families to turn any room in the house into a playroom, and play together without worrying about the walls with Easycare.

In September 2017, a new centre of production for Dulux UK formally opened as the world's most advanced and sustainable paint factory. Based in Ashington, the state-of-the-art factory is capable of doubling current UK production levels whilst reducing the carbon footprint of a litre of paint by 50%.

Recent Developments
In the Trade side of the business, Dulux recently launched a new colour tool set to inspire and assist building owners and managers in the specification process. The Dulux Colour Schemer™ is easy to use and provides professionals with unprecedented access to an extensive range of colour schemes, tailored to meet the needs of a variety of market sectors such as Healthcare,

Brand History

1919 Naylor Brothers, long-established varnish makers, set up a factory in Slough.

1926 Dulux paint is sold to the building trade for the first time.

1953 The Dulux brand is introduced to the consumer market for the first time.

2006 The Light + Space™ range launches, introducing a paint that reflects up to twice as much light as existing paints.

2007 Dulux unveils its new campaign – 'We Know the Colours that Go' – sparking a new wave of personalisation and colour.

2008 Dulux launches PaintPod™ – the biggest innovation in painting since the roller and tray.

2011 The Dulux dog celebrates his 50th anniversary as company mascot and the Ecosense™ paint range launches.

2014 The 10-year anniversary of ColourFutures™ and the launch of the Dulux Visualizer app take place.

2016 The Dulux Academy opens its doors to industry professionals.

2017 The Ashington paint production site, the world's most sustainable paint factory, opens and Dulux Easycare™, with stain repellent technology, is launched.

Education and Housing. In just three simple steps, users of the Colour Schemer can select the relevant sector and desirable outcome, choose colour schemes and create specific designs that most suit the brief. A key feature of the new tool is the ability to coordinate design specifications with the core colours of a project. By choosing a core colour, users can be assured that their chosen schemes will coordinate and complement existing fabrics, flooring or furniture.

In 2016, Dulux updated its augmented reality app the Dulux Visualizer to include features such as e-commerce, social sharing and live visualization. The Dulux Visualizer app enables people to see what different colours look like on their walls in real time. The helpful colour tool can be used to identify the nearest Dulux shade to a favourite colour chosen from the real world and apply this colour live to a room, helping consumers decide on a colour with confidence. Since the updated version was launched in the UK in April 2017 there have been over 19.5m visualizations.

Promotion

Through all communications in 2017, Dulux focused on giving DIYers the confidence to decorate. The TV campaign starred the Dulux dog and featured, Easycare, a durable product where spills bead off the walls, making them easy to clean. In March 2017, the UK's first state-of-the-art training academy for the painting and decorating industry celebrated its first birthday. The Dulux Academy provides Continuous Professional Development (CPD) for professional decorators with courses that teach new techniques and ways of working. Hundreds of experienced tradesmen and apprentices have received expert advice in applying paints and coverings as well as gaining an advanced understanding of developments within areas essential to their careers including colour, design, sustainability and business skills. Since its launch, the Academy has also won 'Excellence in Training' at the British Coatings Federation (BCF). Dulux Academy's ambition by 2020 is to have trained 10,000 decorators.

Brand Values

Through Adding Colour To People's Lives™, Dulux aims to transform people's surroundings, their moods, their views and attitude to life. Dulux hopes to inspire consumers to decorate by celebrating the power of colour and the ongoing positive change that comes from creating a beautiful living space.

The **original disruptor of the e-commerce** world, eBay has come of age –
but it's still **shaking up traditional retail with a global marketplace** that
welcomes big brands, **empowers entrepreneurs** and serves
23.5 million customers a month in the UK alone.

Market

eBay was the first online marketplace.
Today, it's a household name. A regular feature
in lists of best loved brands, it connects millions
of buyers and sellers, helping customers to find
the item they're looking for from its 1.1bn listings.

With buyers in 190 markets, trade is fast. The UK
website sells a car part every second, and searches
for must-have items, like 2017's fidget spinner,
regularly top 50 searches a second.

This incredible interest directly benefits the small
businesses who trade on eBay, giving them access
to an audience once unthinkable for a small shop
on the high street.

Product

Whether an item is new or nearly new, luxurious
or rare, fashionable or one-of-a-kind, it is probably

DID YOU KNOW?

eBay has **168 million active
buyers** around the world.

for sale on eBay.co.uk. The brand's mission
is to be the place where the world shops first,
and a continued focus on its powerful search –
including image recognition and voice control through
Google Home – gives power to that promise.

While eBay remains true to its marketplace roots,
88% of the items for sale on eBay are now offered
at a fixed price and 81% are brand new. The UK's
big retail brands also continue to gravitate towards
the marketplace, setting up their own eBay stores
to be where British consumers are shopping.

All sellers on eBay benefit from one of the
most popular mobile apps in the market –
downloaded more than 380m times
and counting – along with a ready-made
web presence that is fast, mobile and secure.

Achievements

Throughout its history, eBay has helped many
thousands of small businesses to succeed.
Small British firms regularly rank in the top five
grossing sellers on eBay.co.uk's biggest trading
days like Black Friday, and over a thousand
British sellers who started with a shop on eBay
are now running million pound businesses,
providing jobs to people in their communities.

By partnering with sellers in this way,
eBay.co.uk has helped hundreds of thousands
of British entrepreneurs over its 22-year history.
As a hub of retail in the UK, the marketplace
also continues to welcome top brands to the
site – including Currys, Halfords, GoPro, Canon,
BooHoo and more.

eBay also makes it easy for customers to give
to charitable organisations. Using eBay for Charity,
sellers can donate a portion of their sales and
buyers can shop while supporting their favourite
causes – adding to the £100m that eBay.co.uk
has raised for UK charities to date.

Recent Developments

With a wealth of 'firsts' to its name, eBay remains
at the forefront of online retail.

The marketplace created one of the first-ever
mobile apps, and today over 60% of international
buyers shop on eBay through their mobile device,
putting the products of small businesses directly
into the hands of consumers whenever they
want to shop.

Fast forward to 2017 and eBay is still driving new
developments: artificial intelligence, the ability
to search from a photograph and the world's
first virtual reality department store experience,
to name a few.

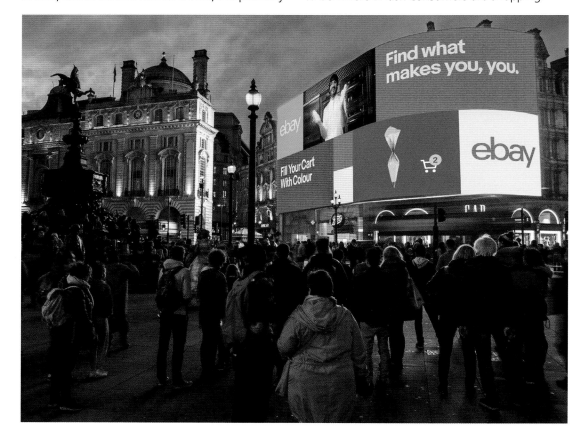

Brand History

1995 eBay founder, Pierre Omidyar, launches AuctionWeb. By the following year, $7.2m worth of merchandise is sold.

1997 Feedback is introduced, allowing members to rate their transactions – a first for the web that's now an industry staple.

2000 Buy It Now, allowing users to buy an item instantly at a set price, is introduced.

2002 eBay purchases PayPal, followed by Gumtree three years later.

2008 eBay is one of the first companies to launch on an iPhone, featuring during the Apple app store launch.

2009 eBay receives a 100% rating from the Human Rights Campaign, which it has continued to receive every subsequent year.

2016 In partnership with Myer, eBay launches the first-ever virtual reality department store as well as a smart, personal shopping assistant, powered by AI.

2017 eBay's 22nd year in the UK sees Image Search and Find It On eBay launching, allowing shoppers to search using a picture.

Innovating in mobile has also meant an expansion into social media, a natural partner to the marketplace. eBay.co.uk's Mother's Day Snapchat lens was one of the most popular filters of 2017 and a new generation of customers are finding deals through this medium.

Promotion

In Autumn 2017, eBay's Fill Your Cart With Colour campaign launched in the UK and around the world. Advertising ran across all channels, mirroring the offering of the eBay marketplace; encouraging shoppers to celebrate their individual passions and shopping 'like nobody else' –

23M BRITS A MONTH ARE SERVED BY EBAY IN THE UK

But did you check eBay?

Fill Your Cart With Colour

ebay

something the brand says is possible only on eBay thanks to its unrivalled choice.

For Christmas 2017 eBay brought the campaign to central London, with a range of UK influencers, to bring the brand to life. eBay was also the first to invest in mood advertising – ads with the ability to react instantly to the mood of consumers – on the iconic screens of Piccadilly Circus.

eBay regularly partners with other high profile brands who understand the power of the marketplace in bringing products to life. In late 2017, eBay once again joined forces with Disney ahead of the much-anticipated release of Star Wars: The Last Jedi. The brand's dedicated Star Wars Hub (ebay.co.uk/starwars) featured more than 12,000 pieces of official merchandise and

sold a lightsaber every 15 minutes. It is one of a range of product hubs built for brands including Dyson, Canon and GoPro, and sits alongside specialist categories including physical media, Curve clothing and newly added wine and beer categories.

Brand Values

eBay's vision for commerce is one that is enabled by people, powered by technology and open to everyone. eBay focuses on providing opportunity for all, allowing charities, businesses and individuals to participate in – and benefit from – global commerce. This is bolstered by eBay for Charity, allowing people to easily support their favourite charities when buying and selling.

ECHO FALLS

The essence of Echo Falls is to **celebrate and be a part of spontaneous,** fun filled social occasions – whether that is an evening in, summer picnics or unplanned evenings out. The brand is all about providing an unpretentious introduction into **enjoying wine in a relaxed way.**

Market

Echo Falls, owned by Accolade Wines, is currently the second largest wine brand in the UK behind Hardys, which is also owned by Accolade Wines. As one of the largest wine companies in the world and the largest producer of wine in the UK, Accolade Wines is in the enviable position of holding an 11% share of the UK wine market.

In 2015 Echo Falls released its innovative Fruit Fusion sub-brand, which blends wine with appealing combinations of fruit flavours, successfully carving out a new mainstream market within the UK. Furthermore, within two years it has grown the market from being worth £20,000 per annum to more than £70m, of which Echo Falls currently occupies 84% of the entire market.

In total, the Echo Falls brand is worth in excess of £170m annually, selling a staggering 26m litres of wine a year.

Product

Echo Falls specialises in approachable, easy drinking red, white and rosé wines that are ideally suited for those starting their journey into wine with a range of blends and varietal wines from around the world. Its sweeter styled Fruit Fusion sub-brand, which combines wine with other fruit flavours, encompasses combinations such as strawberry and lime, raspberry and cassis and the UK's favourite Fruit Fusion, Summer Berries.

Central to the Echo Falls brand is to create a feeling of being approachable in the way in which it talks to the consumer who is often put off wine by the formalities surrounding it. Echo Falls also has the vision of being an accompaniment to a wide variety of relaxed social situations.

Keeping up with the ethos of 'there's an Echo Falls for everyone', there is also an alcohol free sparkling offering, which is a market leader, with a 33% share of the No Alcohol Sparkling category.

@georginahartofficial and photography by @jadegreenbrooke

@alan_stokes and @phillylewis

The recent redesign of Echo Falls saw the brand connecting with its Facebook audience to influence the way the bottles looked. Using a survey on the social media platform its 127,000 followers chose which words they would use to describe each of the wines in the portfolio. This gave each wine a 'personality' that is now featured heavily in the approachable back label copy and on all social platforms. Most recently, Echo Falls worked with hand picked social influencers that best matched the personality of the wine, which was seen by over 200,000 people online.

Achievements

The brand took a bold move with the introduction of its Fruit Fusion range, which has proved to be a very successful addition and has won several awards including the Federation of Wholesaler Distributors, Drinks Brand of the Year 2015; the Retail Industry Awards 2015, Product Launch of the Year in the Alcohol category; and was also a Grocer Gold Award Finalist in 2016.

DID YOU KNOW?

Echo Falls **sold nearly 47 million bottles in 2017.**

The owners of the brand, Accolade Wines, wants to lead in its corporate responsibility and sustainability strategy through working in the areas encompassing water and the environment, alcohol and responsibility, and offering support for communities where its production facilities are located.

Accolade Wines has been supporting the disadvantaged community of Kayamandi Township in South Africa since 2003 through various school projects, actively helping the community and investing over R6m in the local pre-primary school to date. Contributions have included the construction and furnishing of new school buildings as well as financial assistance enabling additional teachers and cleaners to be hired.

Recent Developments

Building on the success of Fruit Fusion, development is underway to take this range to the next level with some fresh flavour innovations, aiming to redefine what it means

54%

OF ECHO FALLS
SALES WERE INCREMENTAL
TO THE TOTAL
UK WINE MARKET

to be a wine brand. This will focus on consumer trends to develop products that fit in with the lifestyle of the target audience.

The brand's focus on product development has also seen the release of Summer Berries Vodka in November 2017, drawing on the trust amongst consumers of the Echo Falls brand, this moves into an entirely new category, which opens up huge potential for further development in the future.

During 2018 a focus is also being placed on large-scale above-the-line exposure, with a media value of £5m. This will give an ideal opportunity to showcase the way in which the brand is expanding the product range in an exciting way.

Promotion

Echo Falls' first TV advert was launched in 2007, which helped make it a household name. Since then, it has aligned itself with the fun and exciting side of wine. For example, in 2012 it began sponsoring Channel 4's Come Dine With Me, in which dinner party guests make the most of an evening with the fellow diners that they have just met, the perfect spontaneous evening for the brand to link up with.

Echo Falls has also held sampling opportunities at UK festivals, using a brightly coloured branded double decker bus to promote its range of Spritz cans. Echo Falls also sponsored Ladies Day at Chester Races in 2015 and 2016. Using a branded VW Camper Van to sample the Fruit Fusion range, Echo Falls surprised 10 hen parties each year with race-day hampers and also ran competitions throughout the day.

Further to this, the brand has also teamed up with designer Holly Fulton, to create striking limited edition fashion-inspired labels for its bottles.

Brand Values

Echo Falls has three key points that are central to its DNA, firstly Vision – to be an approachable and friendly first step in to wine; Values – vivacious, friendly, unpretentious and optimistic; and finally Personality – joyfully sassy and spontaneously sociable.

Brand History

2003	The Echo Falls brand is launched.
2007	The brand's first TV advert is aired.
2008	Echo Falls becomes the eighth largest wine brand in the UK, worth over £100m.
2012	Echo Falls sponsors Come Dine With Me on Channel 4.
2013	Labels have a make-over by designer Holly Fulton.
2015	Echo Falls becomes the third largest wine brand in the UK.
2015	The Fruit Fusion sub-brand of Echo Falls is launched.
2016	Fruit Fusion grows to become worth over than £50m annually.
2017	Echo Falls becomes the second largest wine brand in the UK.
2017	Echo Falls launches its first fruit flavoured vodka.

EDWARDIAN HOTELS
LONDON

Offering a collection of individual hotels, inspired by London and rooted in the neighbourhoods the hotels inhabit, from stylish boutiques through to **luxury on the grandest scale,** each hotel boasts stunning interiors and exceptional comfort. With complimentary wifi throughout, chic bars and concept restaurants, **Edwardian Hotels London's service ethos delivers unforgettable experiences.**

Market

Founded by Jasminder Singh, OBE in 1977, Edwardian Hotels London is intrinsically linked to the capital, with 11 of its 12 properties being in London and one in the heart of Manchester. Edwardian Hotels London has been committed to establishing upscale hotels in the city for decades and is inimitably embedded within the London landscape. The luxury London hotel market is a highly competitive environment and Edwardian Hotels London is able to stand out from the crowd with stunning four and five-star properties in key London locations. What helps to distinguish the brand from other key players is its individuality. As a family business, Edwardian Hotels London offers top quality and unique design combined with a style of service that is genuine.

Product

Known for its presence in London's most sought after locations; Edwardian Hotels London has eight hotels in Zone One alone. With strong and sustained investment across the portfolio and a contemporary environment in each hotel, the hotels are designed for comfort and convenience. Adorned with tactile furnishings and original art throughout, each hotel is distinct in its look and feel.

DID YOU KNOW?

The **Radisson Blu Edwardian, Vanderbilt** takes its name from the influential American family, **the Vanderbilts,** who converted the building from **ten 19th century town houses into a single hotel** in the 1920s.

Staying in an Edwardian Hotels London property is an experience. From Kensington to Covent Garden or Bloomsbury to Mercer Street, each has a unique personality. The group's 'Yes I Can!' service philosophy means nothing is ever too much trouble.

Achievements

Edwardian Hotels London has been ranked as one of the best hotel groups in the UK in Which? Travel consumer magazine.

Focused on creating bespoke experiences, each hotel is a one off, and strives to achieve the best in hospitality by creating exceptional memories. This ethos is further evident at its Manchester property, winner of The Beautiful South Gold award, as well as Manchester Tourism's Hotel of the Year over consecutive years. Sustainability is also high on the agenda, with numerous awards cementing the brand's reputation as one of the UK's greenest hotel groups, including a Green Tourism Business Scheme Gold Award, Best Carbon Reduction in a Hotel Chain, and a Sustainable Restaurant Association Two Star badge. Edwardian Hotels London is the official corporate fundraising partner to Cancer Research UK, with funds raised by the wider company going to the Francis Crick Institute in London, a world-leading centre of biomedical research and innovation.

Digital innovation is also at the forefront of Edwardian Hotels London's mind with a number of new enterprises, ensuring a seamless guest experience. Shortlisted for a Catey award and Best Multi-Channel Customer Service 2016, its virtual host 'EDWARD' has been a huge success. An automated, intelligent text-based interaction service, EDWARD responds to and executes guests' requests, enquiries and bookings via mobile phone. Online check-in and check-out has also become a popular feature, with guests given the freedom to choose their room prior to arrival and check-out quickly and easily.

Recent Developments

Edwardian Hotels London remains part of one of the world's fastest growing upscale hotel

groups, while retaining its individuality as a privately owned hotel collection. 2017 saw the company expand its restaurant and bar offerings, with the Hampshire hotel launching Leicester Square Kitchen and collaborative pop-up, At The Hampshire Lounge Bar. The former embraces the art of shared dining in the heart of Leicester Square, showcasing a contemporary selection of Mexican and

Peruvian small plates, complemented with the finest wines and signature cocktails. The latter offers a range of inspirational food and drink, changing throughout the year to reflect the partner brand or theme during its residency.

DID YOU KNOW?

The May Fair Hotel was launched in 1927, with **King George V** presiding over the official opening.

The latest exciting development in Leicester Square comes in the form of a new hotel, opening its doors to the public in 2019. The 350-room property will comprise a number of bars, restaurants, two Odeon cinemas, a banqueting suite as well as leisure facilities.

Promotion

The group's brand communications remain distinctive. Through cherry-picked partnerships and a cross-channel brand activation calendar, every hotel continues to weave itself into the fabric of the community in which it resides. In the capital, Radisson Blu Edwardian, London properties demonstrate their affinity with the arts through longstanding partnerships with the National Theatre, Royal Shakespeare Company, and The Donmar Warehouse, to name three of its extensive partnership portfolio. The May Fair Hotel continues its status as the official hotel partner to London Fashion Week and the London Film Festival. While in the north, Radisson Blu Edwardian, Manchester continues to cement its place in the heart of Manchester through its title as the Official Hotel of Manchester Pride. In 2017, celebrities and customers were invited to join the brand's social media campaign, which called for people to show their support by Tweeting or Instagramming their 'pride moments' using #BeeProud. The Manchester Bee, has been a symbol of the city since the industrial revolution and represents the city's energy and sense of community.

Brand Values

The essence of the Edwardian Hotels London brand is its core 'Yes I Can!' philosophy – an approach not only to service, but also to the way it does business. This positive attitude enables the delivery of a customer promise that makes people feel special with individual service aiming to build mutually beneficial relationships with a commitment to create business. With authenticity at its core, the environment and experience guests enjoy at Edwardian Hotels London is uniquely cosmopolitan.

Brand History

1977 Edwardian Hotels is established by Jasminder Singh, OBE.

1992 A marketing agreement with Carlson is signed to increase global reach and the brand becomes Radisson Edwardian Hotels.

2004 The first hotel outside London opens in Manchester, a five-star hotel at the city's iconic Free Trade Hall.

2007 The company opens a brand new hotel opposite The O2 at New Providence Wharf.

2012 An agreement is signed with Carlson Rezidor Hotel Group to become part of the global Radisson Blu brand portfolio and the brand becomes Radisson Blu Edwardian, London.

2013 Radisson Blu Edwardian, London launches Steak & Lobster as well as Scoff & Banter.

2016 May Fair Kitchen opens at The May Fair Hotel, Monmouth Kitchen opens at the Radisson Blu Edwardian Mercer St. Hotel and Leicester Square Kitchen opens at the Radisson Blu Edwardian, Hampshire hotel.

2017 Plans are underway for Edwardian Hotels London's new hotel development in Leicester Square.

Since 1969, **Embraer has been delivering aircraft that air forces, pilots, passengers** and operators worldwide love to fly. From **Commercial Aviation to Executive Jets to Defense & Security,** the brand **challenges convention to create fresh and exciting solutions** that enable partners and customers to outperform their goals and ambitions.

Market

Embraer is a global company with headquarters in Brazil. Its businesses span Commercial and Executive aviation, Defense & Security and Services & Support. It designs, develops, manufactures and markets aircraft and systems and is recognised worldwide as the leading manufacturer of commercial jets up to 150 seats.

Product

Embraer have a portfolio of aircraft products that span the range of sectors and partner needs. These include the E2, E-Jet and ERJ families of commercial aircraft. Soon to enter service, the E2, the most efficient single aisle aircraft, is setting a new benchmark in sustainability and performance in the segment.

In Defense & Security, Embraer leads the sector in Latin America. From the A-29 Super Tucano light attack and advanced trainer to the multi-mission transporter, the KC-390, Embraer provides a full line of integrated solutions and applications. Embraer products are present in more than 60 countries.

Embraer Executive Aviation offers a home away from home concept combined with performance

DID YOU KNOW?

Every **10 seconds** an **Embraer aircraft takes off** somewhere in the world.

in the form of the Phenom, Legacy and Lineage Business Jets. Showcasing the latest innovation and technologies, they are supported by the world's number one ranked product support team.

Achievements

In 2017, Embraer was awarded the title of Most Innovative Company in Brazil for the second year running.

The E2 Family has been awarded the Crystal Cabin Award, the only international award for aircraft interiors, for its innovative design.

Embraer Executive Jets are consistently ranked number one for customer support.

Recent Developments

In March 2017, Embraer opened its first Silicon Valley and Boston based innovation offices. These new Embraer facilities will explore and develop the ways that flight contributes to the future of society by seeking out partnerships with new business models and technologies.

April 2017 brought a partnership with Uber – named Uber Elevate – to explore the potential deployment and development of small electric vertical take-off and landing (eVtol) vehicles for short urban commutes.

At the end of 2017 Embraer delivered the 1400th E-Jet, an E175 to Envoy Air who will operate it for American Eagle.

In 2017 the brand established Services & Support, which furthers a commitment to create and supply custom made solutions to operators enabling maximum efficiency, availability and profitability.

Entering service in early 2018, the E2 'Profit Hunter' aircraft has been launched to help operators sustain profitability in an increasingly tough environment.

Brand History

1969 Embraer is formed by the Government with a view to producing two Bandeirante aircraft per month.

1974 The EMB 200 Ipanema, an agricultural airplane, is released. One of the first successes for Embraer, the aircraft is still manufactured today.

1983 The EMB 312 Tucano, an acrobatic turboprop plane for advanced military training, leaves the hangar.

2001 Embraer goes public on both the Sao Paulo and New York stock exchanges. The Legacy program is launched and starts Embraer's entry in executive aviation.

2002 The E-Jets family is announced, a milestone achievement for Embraer Commercial Aviation.

2005 Embraer expands its Executive Jets footprint by launching a dedicated Business Unit and enhancing its portfolio with the Lineage and Phenom product lines.

2009 Embraer signs a contract to produce the largest military transport jet ever produced in Brazil, the KC-390.

2013 Embraer announce the launch of the E2 Jet Family, the second generation of the popular E-Jet family.

2017 The KC-390 military transport and aerial refueling jet completes a relevant milestone: the achievement of the Initial Operational Capability (IOC).

2018 On April 24th, the E2 enters service, on budget and ahead of schedule.

Promotion

At the Paris Air Show in 2017 Embraer unveiled a new brand proposition that shows what the company has done best over the past 47 years: overcome challenges by creating great products that enable customers to outperform. The brand brought several aircraft to the show from a number of business units including: the E195-E2 commercial jet, the KC-390 military transporter, the Legacy 450 business jet, and the ERJ 145 regional jet.

At the event Embraer unveiled the new 'Profit Hunter' advertising campaign, painting the face of a golden eagle onto the nose of the aircraft. The name and eagle were chosen as they perfectly represent the aircraft's personality and features – with an eye for an opportunity, excellence in tough environments and with outstanding efficiency in the air. This activity

SINCE 1969 EMBRAER HAVE DELIVERED OVER 8,000 AIRCRAFT

brought widespread attention being featured on BBC News, the Daily Telegraph and other global communication channels.

The brand has introduced innovative technology across its marketing, utilising Virtual Reality to create immersive, memorable experiences at international exhibitions.

It has also started running an international advertising campaign to consolidate the KC-390 as a major player in the airlift market.

Embraer continues to be an active presence at major aerospace exhibitions, and in the industry press, attending more than 60 events in a calendar year.

Brand Values

The brand's DNA can be summed up in three words: Challenge. Create. Outperform.

By constantly challenging the boundaries of what is possible, and the expectations of convention, creating solutions that enable customers to outperform again and again. It's more than a way of working, it's an approach to life that comes from inside. It's what makes the brand unique and defines the competitive point of difference.

FedEx Express provides rapid, time-sensitive delivery to more than 220 countries and territories, linking more than 99% of the world's GDP. Unmatched air route authorities and transportation infrastructure, combined with leading-edge information technologies, make it the world's largest express transportation company, providing fast and reliable services for more than 5.5m shipments each business day.

DID YOU KNOW?

FedEx Express has set goals to **reduce aircraft emissions 30% by 2020.**

Market

FedEx Corporation provides customers and businesses worldwide with a broad portfolio of transportation, e-commerce, and business services. With annual revenues of $61bn, the company offers integrated business applications through operating companies competing collectively and managed collaboratively, under the respected FedEx brand. Consistently ranked among the world's most admired and trusted employers, FedEx inspires its team of more than 400,000, to remain 'absolutely, positively' focused on safety, the highest ethical and professional standards, and the needs of its customers and communities.

Product

FedEx Express offers time-definite, door-to-door, customs-cleared international delivery solutions, using a global air-and-ground network to speed delivery. It can deliver a wide range of time-sensitive shipments, from urgent medical supplies, last-minute gifts and fragile scientific equipment, to bulky freight and dangerous goods. Each shipment sent with FedEx Express is scanned 17 times on average, to ensure that customers can track its location online 24 hours a day.

In addition to the international product range offered by FedEx Express, FedEx UK provides

DID YOU KNOW?

FedEx Express has **transported rare cargo** such as **polar bears** and elephants.

customers with a wide range of options for domestic shipping. Within the UK this includes time-definite, next-day and Saturday delivery services. All services are supported by free and easy-to-use automation tools, allowing customers to schedule pick-ups and track their packages online.

Achievements

FedEx Express, which started life in 1973 as the brainchild of its founder Frederick W. Smith, CEO of FedEx Corp., has amassed a long list of 'firsts' over the years. FedEx Express originated the overnight letter, was the first express

Brand History

1973 Federal Express establishes operations.

1983 Federal Express reaches $1bn in revenue – the first US business to achieve this status.

1994 FedEx launches fedex.com the first transportation website to offer online package status.

2000 FedEx announces an expansion of its global network connecting Europe to Asia.

2009 FedEx Express introduces FedEx International Economy® service for less time sensitive shipments from more than 90 countries and territories around the globe.

2013 FedEx Express surpasses its self-imposed vehicle fuel efficiency improvement target ahead of schedule with more than 22% cumulative improvement in fuel economy for its vehicles.

2017 FedEx Express agrees to purchase 50 clean-sheet design Cessna SkyCourier 408 aircraft.

---

transportation company dedicated to overnight package delivery, and the first to offer next day delivery by 10.30am. It was also the first express company to offer a time-definite service for freight and the first in the industry to offer money-back guarantees and free proof of delivery. In 1983 Federal Express (as it was then known) made business history as the first US company to reach the $1bn revenue landmark inside 10 years of start-up, unaided by mergers or acquisitions.

This history has resulted in multiple awards and honours. In 1994 FedEx Express received ISO 9001 certification for all its worldwide operations, making it the first global express transportation company to receive simultaneous system-wide certification. In 2008 FedEx Express and FedEx UK were granted the highly regarded, internationally accepted ISO 14001:2004 certification for environmental management systems.

Recent Developments

FedEx Express has agreed to purchase 50 clean-sheet design Cessna SkyCourier 408 aircraft, with options to purchase up to 50 additional aircraft. Delivery of the first aircraft is expected in mid-2020, with subsequent deliveries on a schedule of one aircraft per month over a four-

DID YOU KNOW?

FedEx Express has **three core focus areas of investment**, Emergency and Disaster Relief, Child Pedestrian Safety and Environmental Sustainability.

---

year period. This continues the successful fleet modernisation strategy, which will improve fuel efficiency, reliability and operating costs and will grow business in small and medium-sized markets.

Promotion

It is FedEx's third year as Main Sponsor in the UEFA Europa League. The sponsorship commenced with the start of the 2015/16 season and will extend through to 2018. A major European football cup competition, The UEFA Europa League is the largest club competition in the World, bringing together 190 teams from across Europe, which aligns with the FedEx presence and network in the region. The sponsorship also extends into UEFA's digital

channels including the FedEx Performance Zone which tracks, analyses and ranks the performance of the heroes in the UEFA Europa League. The sponsorship builds on FedEx's history of sports partnerships, including sponsorship of the ATP World Tour and Ryder Cup.

Brand Values

The FedEx corporate strategy, known to FedEx employees as the 'Purple Promise', is to 'make every FedEx experience outstanding'. The Purple Promise is the long-term strategy for FedEx to further develop loyal relationships with its customers. The FedEx corporate values are: to value its people and promote diversity; to provide a service that puts customers at the heart of everything it does; to invent the services and technologies that improve the way people work and live; to manage operations, finances and services with honesty, efficiency and reliability; to champion safe and healthy environments; and to earn the respect and confidence of FedEx people, customers and investors every day.

FINASTRA

Misys and D+H joined forces in June 2017 to create Finastra – the third largest Fintech company in the world. The same brand attributes that awarded Misys Superbrand status for the past two consecutive years are now deeply embedded in Finastra – an even stronger company with a large global footprint and deep domain expertise.

Market

In an era of increasing choice and regulation, all customers – corporate, institutional and retail – are demanding greater value from financial services. They expect greater agility, innovation, integration and security than ever before. Finastra helps its customers to break the shackles of closed, legacy systems that limit transparency, block innovation and ignore vast amounts of data. Its scale and geographic reach means that Finastra is able to serve customers better, regardless of their size or geographic location – from global banks, to community banks and credit unions. Unlocking this potential today means that financial institutions can embrace the future with confidence and assure their position in the banking world of tomorrow.

Product

Utilising the latest technology and standards, Finastra is committed to delivering FusionFabric.cloud – a platform as a service solution built on open architecture and technology that embraces a wide ecosystem of customers, partners, system integrators and co-innovators.

This unique strategy will see the company open its technology platform and core systems to third parties, who can leverage the platform to build, sell and consume their own apps.

DID YOU KNOW?

Finastra has
9,000+ customers
in 130 countries.

FusionFabric.cloud helps financial institutions to become more customer focused by:

Accelerating growth – An open ecosystem delivers competitive advantage through better business insights, rapid innovation cycles and faster time to market for new products and services.

Improving experience – Next-generation capabilities enable both its clients, and their

customers, to save time and adopt self-service models with ease.

Optimising cost – Finastra helps financial institutions modernise and rationalise their application infrastructure to enable true digital transformation of financial processes.

Mitigating risk – Customers gain a complete view of their risk exposures to improve decision-making and out-of-the-box reporting to meet regulatory requirements.

Achievements

Drawing on achievements of the past and as a testament to the strength of the two legacy brands – Finastra has already earned several awards in 2017.

Finastra was the winner of Best Lead Generation for Enterprise LinkedIn Marketing. The company leveraged LinkedIn's targeting capabilities to reach C-suites through Sponsored Content and Sponsored InMail. This account-based-marketing approach led to a 30% increase in registrations for all events,

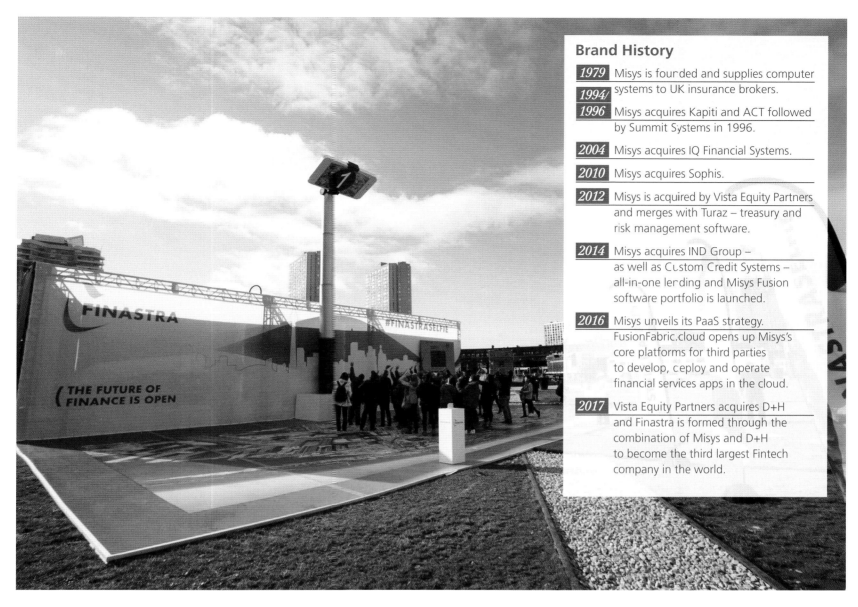

Brand History

1979 Misys is founded and supplies computer systems to UK insurance brokers.

1994/ 1996 Misys acquires Kapiti and ACT followed by Summit Systems in 1996.

2004 Misys acquires IQ Financial Systems.

2010 Misys acquires Sophis.

2012 Misys is acquired by Vista Equity Partners and merges with Turaz – treasury and risk management software.

2014 Misys acquires IND Group – as well as Custom Credit Systems – all-in-one lending and Misys Fusion software portfolio is launched.

2016 Misys unveils its PaaS strategy. FusionFabric.cloud opens up Misys's core platforms for third parties to develop, deploy and operate financial services apps in the cloud.

2017 Vista Equity Partners acquires D+H and Finastra is formed through the combination of Misys and D+H to become the third largest Fintech company in the world.

with 15% of these attendees becoming sales qualified opportunities.

Customer-centricity is a core belief held by Finastra and this commitment helped Finastra top the UK Customer Experience Awards 2017 in the Technology and Telco category.

DID YOU KNOW?

48 of the top 50 banks globally are Finastra customers.

Recent Developments
In anticipation of the combination of Misys and D+H, the two firms engaged a world-leading brand agency to help create the new brand in under six weeks. Finastra launched on day one of the new organisation with, The Future of Finance is Open, strapline and the vision statement –'Finastra unlocks the potential of people and businesses by creating a platform for open innovation in the world of financial services.' For Finastra, these principles are the driving forces behind its strategy, and encapsulate its vision to transform the global financial services industry.

To represent Finastra's commitment to open architecture and stand out in a crowded Fintech market, a logo design was developed that represents openness, agility, energy and innovation. A vibrant fusion of colour in the 'ribbon' asset brings energy and differentiation into marketing materials.

Promotion
To spread the word and amplify the new brand on launch day, Finastra leveraged social media, employee advocacy and traditional marketing and communication channels – everything from a coordinated organic outreach with employees posting 'The Future of Finance is Open' to a new finastra.com website promoting a film and message from the CEO.

Finastra unveiled the newly combined company at Sibos – a large financial technology conference in October 2017, attended by customers and partners from all over the world. Delegates were welcomed at Toronto airport with luggage carousel screens, branded eco-caps and out-of-home advertising. In addition to over 300 meetings at its stand, Finastra had a little fun by inviting Sibos delegates to Strike a Pose and take their very own selfie at the world's largest selfie stick. Photos were downloaded from finastraselfie.com and shared all across social media.

Brand Values
The name – derived from FIN for Finance and ASTRA meaning star in Latin – embodies the expertise and strength through which Finastra will unlock the potential in finance. It represents a new star, born in the wide universe of financial software. The following unique attributes enable Finastra to lead customers into the open future of finance.

Comprehensive – With a large global footprint and deep domain expertise, Finastra serves clients of all sizes spanning retail and corporate banking, lending, treasury, capital markets, investment management and enterprise risk.

Innovative – Finastra is leading the way in which financial software is written, deployed and consumed in the world of financial services. As a pioneer in SaaS and cloud, Finastra delivers next-generation financial software – open, reliable, secure, agile – either on premises or on the cloud.

Collaborative – The Fusion architecture and open platform approach stimulate co-operation and co-innovation. Finastra delivers fully integrated solutions by working together with clients and their existing software.

Note: Misys was the brand voted on in the 2018 Superbrands voting process but has subsequently rebranded to Finastra.

GREEN &BLACK'S

Green & Black's was founded on Portobello Road, London in 1991 by **Craig Sams and Jo Fairley** – sustainability pioneers. Since then, Green & Black's has **brought many firsts to the market** and continues to achieve its ambition for even more people to discover and enjoy the brand.

Market

The UK chocolate market is currently worth £2.9 bn per year. Premium Chocolate contributes towards £0.3bn of this and in 2017 grew by 5.4% versus 2016. This is largely driven by the growth in UK shopper's confidence, meaning that quality has become increasingly important with key purchase drivers shown to be 'a taste I love' and 'intense pleasure'. Green & Black's appeals to this need through offering a unique taste profile, finest ingredients and high quality products. As a result, Green & Black's is growing slightly ahead of the market at 7.3%, in 2017, driven by its Tablets and Gifting formats.

Product

To achieve its ambition for more people to discover and enjoy the Green & Black's brand, the 2017 Green & Black's range has expanded across new occasions such as 'indulgent moments for me' and 'be the thoughtful gift of choice'.

DID YOU KNOW?

Green & Black's **Maya Gold** was the **first product** in the UK with the **Fair Trade mark**.

Within its tablets and gifting formats, Green & Black's has recently launched its new Velvet Edition range – a super smooth dark chocolate; providing consumers with self-treat, informal sharing, token gifts and small gesture formats.

Of the total Green & Black's range though, Green & Black's classic Dark 70% continues to be the most popular product in the range, contributing towards 19% of Green & Black's Tablets total value sales.

Achievements

Green & Black's starts and ends everything it does with taste and quality. Therefore, the brand always works with chefs and taste specialists when creating new bars. This has been recognised by the brand receiving stars at the Great Taste Awards 2016 and Silver and Bronze awards at The Academy of Chocolate 2015/16 for the Green & Black's Classic and Thins ranges.

Green & Black's is also proud to have been voted as a CoolBrand for the past 11 consecutive years.

Recent Developments

Green & Black's know people who choose the brand do so because it combines a passion for high quality, delicious chocolate with a commitment to sustainability, and will never compromise on this.

However, it also knows that there are chocolate lovers in the UK who haven't tried Green & Black's yet, who are attracted by Green & Black's philosophy, but may associate the taste with more complex, strong flavours.

Due to this, the Green & Black's team of chocolate experts have created Green & Black's Velvet Edition – a smooth textured chocolate with nutty, vanilla notes made with high quality, ethically sourced cocoa beans to provide the perfect entry point for people to discover the Green & Black's family. The beans used have been deliberately chosen for their distinctive taste. They are sourced from Ghana in West Africa, and are not available to order in organic bulk, but are sustainably sourced, independently verified beans from the Cocoa Life programme.

This is about providing consumers with more choice through expanding the Green & Black's offering, in addition to its classic organic range, which remains a key part of the brand's portfolio and will see continued investment during 2018.

Brand History

1991 Green & Black's is founded on Portobello Road by Craig Sams and Jo Fairley and the UK's first ever 70% Cocoa Bar is launched.

1994 Maya Gold becomes the first product in the UK to carry the Fair Trade Mark.

2006 Green & Black's achieves Coolbrand status.

2011 The complete Green & Black's range becames Fair Trade marked across more than 30 countries.

2016/ 2017 The brand achieves Great Taste and The Academy of Chocolate awards.

2017 The brand achieves Superbrand status, launches Green & Black's Velvet Edition and releases its first ever TV advert.

Promotion

Experiences form a part of what Green & Black's like to do as it is an award winning, delicious tasting chocolate, consumers are invited to discover the brand through taste trials in order to experience it for themselves.

October 2017 marked Green & Black's first ever TV advert going live as well as its Dark Tales Retold PR event. Both celebrated the recent launch of Green & Black's Velvet Edition – a new, sumptuously smooth dark chocolate. The event was hosted in Soho, London and invited press, bloggers and influencers to enjoy an immersive chocolate experience and create new and fun content. Green & Black's has always worked closely with influencers. Historically, due to the fact that the classic range over indexed in this preference, these bloggers tended to be of a foodie nature. However, since the launch of Green & Black's Velvet Edition, which is targeted at a younger, female audience, the strategy has changed slightly across each of the social media

GREEN & BLACK'S
LAUNCHED THE UK'S
FIRST 70% COCOA BAR

platforms to increase the relevance to these new consumers and appeal to those with an interest in travel, lifestyle and fashion as well as food.

Brand Values

Contrary to popular belief, there is no Mrs Green or Mr Black. Green symbolises the commitment to 100% ethically sourced cocoa, a simple ingredient line and no artificial colours and preservatives. Black stands for the high quality, delicious tasting chocolate and sourcing the finest ingredients.

Green & Black's was one of the first brands to work directly with the the cocoa bean farmers in order to support local communities and give them a fair price for their beans. By 2022, the Cocoa Life Programme will invest $400m to empower 200,000 cocoa farmers and reach one million community members across six countries.

One of the **world's first super-premium ice creams**, Häagen-Dazs was introduced in 1961 by Reuben Mattus, whose vision was to make the best ice cream in the world using only the finest ingredients. In doing so, he **pioneered a new luxury category in the ice cream sector.** The company has remained true to its founder's principles and is so proud of its **original Vanilla ice cream that the recipe has not changed in over 50 years.**

Market
Häagen-Dazs is one of the most successful and indulgent brands in the world, sold in more than 80 global markets. It is a leading player in the UK's luxury ice cream sector – currently the number one brand for absolute growth in 2017, number two in luxury pints and number one in minicups (Source: Nielsen Scantrack data, w/e 31 December 2017).

Product
All that Häagen-Dazs ice cream is made of the four kitchen friendly ingredients (real cream, milk, egg yolks and sugar) to which only the best ingredients are added. It took six years, for example, to find the perfect strawberries for its Strawberries & Cream flavour. Its flavours, dense, creamy texture and innovative products all reflect Häagen-Dazs' deep commitment to quality.

Achievements
Häagen-Dazs is currently valued at £67m in a largely luxury ice cream category worth £360m. Häagen-Dazs value sales growth continues to out-perform the category, with a 42% growth (Source: Nielsen Scantrack data, w/e 31 December 2017).

DID YOU KNOW?

Häagen-Dazs has a **very low overrun** (the amount of air incorporated into the product during freezing) **which is why it takes longer to be able to scoop once it comes out the freezer,** providing the **creamy, thick, indulgent texture.**

Recent Development
2017 heralded a bold new brand reinvention for Häagen-Dazs as it once again redefined the rules of ice cream for a new, trend-setting millennial consumer, seeking unique and authentic experiences they can participate in as well as share online.

In spring 2017, Häagen-Dazs launched its new brand positioning 'Everyday Made Extraordinary' accompanied by a pack transformation and engaging local marketing activations in its determination to become iconic again. Häagen-Dazs commissioned more than a dozen globally renowned artists that brought the deliciously creamy texture and engaging flavours to the pack. Each artist was asked to illustrate different Häagen-Dazs flavours using their own styles. The result was a stunning collection of highly photographable packs inviting consumers to discover the 'luxurious creamy taste of Häagen-Dazs'.

The new brand image was brought to life through a experiential campaign in collaboration with the renowned culinary architects Bompass & Parr. The immersive multi-sensory Häagen-Dazs experience called 'My Extraordinary Life' invited people to discover a series of interactive rooms designed to help consumers take the best ice cream photographs ever.

Thanks to consumer demand for more ice cream variety and new experiences Häagen-Dazs has launched two new innovations. These include expanding into 'on-the-go' with a range of bars designed to fit in with people's busy lifestyles and minicup collections providing an easy option for ice cream lovers wanting to discover new flavours.

The stick bar range is three-strong and answers growing consumer demand for convenient take-home, handheld snacks. The ice cream stick bars benefit from an emphasis on quality within both the rich Belgian chocolate coating as well as the ice cream inside. Tapping into current trends for sweet and salty flavour combinations, as well as increased consumer interest in nut-containing products, the bars include the following flavours; Salted Caramel, Vanilla Caramel Almond and Mango & Raspberry.

The minicups collections included Vanilla, Caramel and Fruit, together with a new Sorbets Collection to offer a refreshing option. The format

Promotion

In summer 2017 as part of its Wimbledon partnership, Häagen-Dazs turned the classic Wimbledon strawberries and cream signature flavour pairing of on its head, aiming to elevate it into a new tradition for everyone: Strawberries & Cream ice cream. Making Strawberries & Cream extraordinary and celebrating the traditional serve by adding a playful twist.

Häagen-Dazs delivered a major TV burst with a bespoke tennis-themed spot as well as a high-reach social media push on Facebook and Instagram, featuring a large-scale micro influencer outreach.

Adding another twist to the iconic summer pairing, Häagen-Dazs brought back its Limited Edition Strawberries & Cream ice cream bar. Building on its Scandinavian inspired heritage, Häagen-Dazs has partnered with the Swedish sports fashion brand Björn Borg, renowned for its iconic tennis heritage, to create a limited edition design in a true celebration of the summer of tennis.

Häagen-Dazs chose the glamorous annual WTA Pre-Wimbledon Party at The Roof Gardens, Kensington to debut and serve up its Limited Edition bar to some of the biggest names in women's tennis, fashion and entertainment. Keeping in theme, it installed a Strawberries & Cream Swing where a leading British tennis player unveiled the Wimbledon Limited edition bar. It was a big draw with all attendees given the opportunity to create their perfectly photographable 'Strawberries and Cream' moment.

Brand Values

Today Häagen-Dazs is more committed to its founding values of quality and craftsmanship than ever before, using only the finest quality ingredients possible to create a super-premium ice cream that helps consumers create those extraordinary every day moments.

taps into consumer demand for packs that offer variety around one flavour as well as providing an easy option for consumers wanting to discover new flavours. Additionally, the mini-cup format is an ideal and convenient option for those in single-person households or those with less freezer storage available.

Brand History

1921 Reuben Mattus, founder of Häagen-Dazs, helps in his mother's ice cream business selling fruit ice pops from a horse-drawn wagon in the bustling streets of the Bronx, New York.

1940s 1940s Ice cream becomes a year-round treat due to improved refrigeration. Mattus expands the product line to include pints, quarts, half-gallons, bulk ice cream and novelty items.

1950s Mattus introduces innovations including color-coded packaging, year-round retail distribution and round pint containers.

1960s The original Häagen-Dazs range launches with three flavours: Chocolate, Vanilla and Coffee.

1961 The Häagen-Dazs name is registered by Mattus to market the single best ice cream available and Häagen-Dazs super-premium ice cream starts to be sold in gourmet shops in New York City.

1990 Häagen-Dazs opens a flagship store in Leicester Square, London and begins retail distribution.

1992 A new manufacturing facility in Arras, France is established.

2013 The new Salted Caramel ice cream launches, which quickly rises to become a top five flavour for the brand in the UK.

2016 Häagen-Dazs becomes the official ice cream of Wimbledon.

2017 Häagen-Dazs launched its new brand positioning 'Everyday Made Extraordinary' marked by a impactful and disruptive new packaging and campaigns.

In 1910 an **18 year-old JC Hall** stepped off a train with nothing to his name but two shoeboxes full of picture postcards, **big dreams and an entrepreneurial spirit**. More than 100 years and billions of good wishes later, Hallmark remains the **world's largest supplier** of greeting cards.

Market

Since 1910, when JC Hall started out, the vision has been to create a world-class product that encompasses creativity and a way to bring people together. His passion for design, innovation and quality has been the foundation of everything Hallmark puts its name to. It continues to be the driving spirit that has made this family business the iconic international brand it is today.

Even in the digital age, sending a 'physical' card remains a cornerstone of British life. Be it birthdays, special occasions, or just to say hello, the British public sends more than £1bn worth of cards every year and the greeting cards market is larger than tea, coffee or biscuits.

In the 100 years since JC Hall established Hallmark Cards many things have changed, but Hallmark's passion for quality and creativity has not. Working with key high street retailers and grocers as well as more than 1,500 independent card shops across the country, Hallmark leads the way in category expertise as well as nurturing the best creative talent in the industry. The designers programme sponsored by Hallmark has helped more than 50 graduate designers come into the industry since it began and it was the first greetings card company to sponsor New Designers, nearly 20 years ago – the UK design degree showcasing over 3,000 of the best in graduate design talent.

DID YOU KNOW?

Compiled over a 100 years, **Hallmark has over 10 million digital assets** at its disposal.

Product

Hallmark operates in more than 100 countries worldwide, employing some of the world's best designers, creating over 10,000 new cards per year.

The company believes in partnering with the very best brands and licenses to give its customers more choice. The offerings include ranges from Star Wars™, Disney™ and Marvel™ to Warner Bros™ and The Simpsons™, to name but a few.

The Forever Friends brand, which celebrated its 30th birthday in 2017, continues to be one of the most loved and commercially successful brands within the portfolio. The same year also saw the growth of the global collectable sensation, Itty Bitty's, with family favourite Disney added to the line-up of famous faces. The Itty Bitty family has, since its launch in 2014, seen the collection grow to nearly 100 characters across 11 licenses including Star Wars, Disney and Peanuts.

Hallmark believes in creating the very best mix of products at the right prices. Despite operating in a challenging market with cheaper product alternatives, Hallmark ensures that 100% of its products use certified, well-managed or recycled materials.

Brand History

1910 Joyce Clyde Hall successfully sells postcards in Kansas City. His brothers Rollie and William then join him and Hall Brothers is formed.

1928 Hall Brothers becomes Hallmark Cards.

1958 Hallmark UK opens for business in its London offices.

1966 Hallmark International is set up in the UK to co-ordinate all activities outside of the US.

1972 Fine Arts is established in Ireland to print all of Hallmark's requirements in Europe.

1994 The company acquires The Andrew Brownsword Collection and bring Forever Friends and Country Companions into the Hallmark portfolio.

1998 Hallmark Cards UK forms – merging all the previous acquisitions into one business.

2001 Hallmark Cards plc is formed.

2016 A bespoke card for the Queen's 90th birthday is designed.

2017 Marks 30 years of the Forever Friends Hallmark property and 100 years since the Hall Brothers invented decorative gift wrap

Achievements

As category leaders, Hallmark is continually striving to be first to market, with a track record of innovation that has been recognised by the industry with 24 Henries awards (given by the Greeting Card Association and voted for by industry buyers). 2017 saw the latest award added to the collection within the Best Traditional Words & Sentiments category for the Heart Story range.

Recent Developments

In a world where consumer needs are changing, Hallmark has always led the way in trend analysis and innovation. From its 2,000 strong team in the US to local designers in Yorkshire, right back to its Kansas roots in 1910. In 2017 Hallmark celebrated just that, marking a century since the Hall brothers invented decorative gift wrap. In 1917, at the peak of the Christmas season, the Hall Brothers ran out of the tissue traditionally used to wrap gifts. They improvised with paper designed for use in envelope linings. It was an instant hit and the decorative gift wrap business was born.

Promotion

Hallmark is continuing to connect with consumers through social media, which has meant a renewed relevance to younger generations. The launch of a brand new website in 2016 also now offers consumers a new way of engaging with the brand through exciting and relevant content. This includes a design and inspiration zone to share creative ideas as well as its 'Gifted' programme to attract new talent to the creative studio.

Hallmark's brand awareness remains at over 90%, making it one of the only recognised card brands in the industry.

DID YOU KNOW?

Hallmark's Cards are distributed in more than 100 countries worldwide.

Brand Values

By producing the very best to help people communicate and connect, Hallmark has established a brand that is synonymous with caring and quality, creativity and innovation. Its brand essence 'Leave your mark' is underpinned by a simple promise that for moments that matter, Hallmark cards will help leave an enduring mark. Today's brand statement brings together all these values, at the same time as connecting it to the original dictionary definition of the word 'hall-mark', a sign of distinctiveness and quality.

ESTD
HARDYS
1853

The **world's leading Australian wine brand** and the number one selling wine in the UK, Hardys was established in Australia in 1853 by Thomas Hardy. From humble beginnings, Hardys is **now sold in more than 100 countries** and is into the **sixth generation** of the Hardy family.

Market

Hardys has long been one of the most successful wine brands in the competitive UK market where well-known brands bring much needed reassurance and familiarity to a fragmented and, at times, confusing category. For the last five years, Hardys has maintained its position as the UK's market-leading wine brand with retail sales worth in excess of £275m per annum (Source: ACNielsen 52 Weeks to 12.08.2017).

Product

Throughout its 160 years of winemaking history, Hardys has built a tradition of great endeavour in winemaking. A succession of winemakers have followed in the footsteps of the founder, Thomas Hardy, whose vision was 'to produce wines which will be prized in the markets of the world by showcasing innovation and resourcefulness, directed at making wines of quality and character.'

The brand continues the great Australian blending tradition, between regions and varieties, to make wines of character and complexity with the positive landmarks that the world has come to expect from Australia.

DID YOU KNOW?

In the last year, Hardys **sold** more than **60m bottles of wine** in the UK.

Hardys' pioneering spirit and passion is at the heart of the outstanding range of wines that Hardys has to offer. The portfolio is extensive, spanning a variety of price points and wine varietals.

These include the well-known Hardys VR, Hardys Stamp and Hardys Crest core sub-brands – all of which have been available in the UK market for over two decades.

Achievements

Hardys is proud of its illustrious history. Four years after planting his first vines in 1853, Thomas Hardy, the founder of Hardys, produced his inaugural vintage and became one of the initial exporters of Australian wine. In 1882, he then made history by producing the first Australian wine to be awarded the prestigious Gold medal at the International Wine Show in Bordeaux.

Fast forward some 136 years and the brand has gone on to win more than 7,500 wine awards worldwide.

Hardys' longevity not only reflects the quality but also the familiarity that consumers have with the brand. When asked to name a wine brand, UK consumers mention Hardys more than any other (Source: Wine Brand Tracker Wave 2; Research Now For Accolade Wines; May 2017). This, combined with being the most trusted wine brand in the UK, (Source: Wine Brand Tracker Wave 2; Research Now For Accolade Wines; May 2017) helps Hardys sell over 60m bottles a year, in the UK alone.

DID YOU KNOW?

At 168 years old, Hardys is older than Coca-Cola and Louis Vuitton.

Recent Developments

In 2014, Hardys became the Official Wine of England Cricket. This successful partnership with the UK's number one summer sport is set to continue for another three years. 2017 saw the brand reinforce its number one brand position in the UK with a new creative that showcases the brand's core range whilst also reflecting its strong ties to England Cricket.

Promotion

Hardys' 2017 commitment to a further three years of partnering with England Cricket will be integral to Hardys promotional strategy moving forward, with the opportunity to leverage a refreshed set of assets and media, along with access to the cricket players themselves. Notably, brand ambassador, Stuart Broad, will continue in his role, using his high profile to bring the brand closer to the sport's fans.

Brand History

1850 Thomas Hardy leaves Devon for Australia.

1853 Thomas establishes Hardys.

1857 Thomas produces his first vintage and becomes one of the first exporters of Australian wine.

1870 Thomas purchases the Tintara vineyards and winery in McLaren Vale.

1882 Thomas' wines become the first in Australia to be awarded two prestigious Gold medals at the International Wine Shows in Bordeaux.

1912 Thomas dies, passing the business on to his son, Robert Burrough Hardy.

1988 The Hardys Stamp of Australia range launches at the World Exposition in Brisbane.

1990s The Crest range is launched.

2013 The entire Hardys range is revitalised with new packaging design.

2014 Hardys announces a major three-year sponsorship deal and becomes Official Wine of England Cricket.

2016 The 30th anniversary of the production of the first Eileen Hardy Chardonnay is marked.

2017 Hardys commits to a further three years of partnering with England Cricket.

As well as marketing in cricket grounds during 2017, Hardys ran an on pack promotion where consumers could win cricket tickets every 24 hours. This was communicated with a limited edition cricket front label and promotional neck flag as well as being supported by a social media campaign.

Indeed, social media has seen an increase in focus in supporting the Hardys cricket partnership and the latest campaign of videos reached more than 2.5m people.

Outside of cricket, the next three years are very important for the Hardys brand with a greater focus on customer marketing. Through consumer insight research, the brand has identified that each range within the Hardys portfolio communicates to different consumers, which needs to be thoughtfully reflected in both the packaging and marketing of each.

Brand Values

Hardys has built a tradition of great endeavour in winemaking. Thomas Hardy's vision was to produce wines that would be prized in the markets of the world by showing outstanding innovation and resourcefulness, directed at making wines of quality and character. The expertise and devotion, driven by the Hardy family since 1853, is in every sip of wine.

Heathrow

Heathrow is the UK's gateway to the world. Last year the airport helped **78 million passengers travel across the globe,** more than any other airport in Europe. Providing **world-class shopping and a wide range of services is key** to Heathrow's success with passengers choosing it for **travel, adventure, business and leisure.**

Market

As the UK's only hub airport, Heathrow flew to 204 destinations in 85 countries in 2017. It is the largest airport in Europe by passenger volume and the second largest airport for passengers travelling to international destinations. The airport handles around 210,000 passengers each day with more than a quarter of these connecting between flights. In June of last year, Heathrow recorded its busiest day with 259,917 passengers flying through.

Product

Heathrow aims to give its passengers the best airport service in the world. The priority is to offer a convenient and memorable journey to passengers from the moment they leave home. This includes a seamless journey to and from the airport, navigation around all four terminals and arriving at their destination on time.

The quality and variety of the extensive shopping and food offering is also of great importance. Personal Shopper appointments, terminal transfers for shopping, Shop & Collect, Reserve & Collect as well as Home Delivery are all part of the range of services available to travellers. In addition, Passenger Ambassadors, who collectively speak over 49 languages, are on hand to help along the way.

Lounges are also available in every terminal, both in arrivals and departures for travellers to relax, refresh and prepare for their flight. Some lounges even offer spa facilities, games rooms and bedrooms. The airport also regularly hosts exhibitions, activities for children and other special events.

Achievements

Last year, passengers voted Heathrow the 'Best Airport in Western Europe' for the third successive year and the 'Best Airport for Shopping' globally for the eighth consecutive year at the 2017 Skytrax World Airport Awards.

Heathrow continues to deliver high quality passenger service with 83% of passengers

LITTLE MISS EXPLORER

Roger Hargreaves

DID YOU KNOW?

Heathrow's **most popular destinations** in 2017 were **New York, Dubai, Dublin, Amsterdam** and **Hong Kong.**

in 2017 rating their Heathrow experience as 'Excellent' or 'Very Good'. Heathrow also achieved a record service quality score of 4.16 out of 5.00 in the Airport Service Quality (ASQ) survey, the airport's strongest performance to date.

Furthermore, as testament to its commitment to service, Heathrow received recognition from the International Airport Review in November 2017 by winning the category of 'Best Airport Security' worldwide.

Recent Developments

The Government announced its support for a third runway at Heathrow in 2016 and work is now underway for the consultation phase. 2017 marked a year of retail innovation for Heathrow, which included digital storefront

fit-outs, experiential firsts, and a refresh of many of its restaurants. Highlights included the launch of a new augmented reality treasure hunt for families, a life-sized interactive Burberry-branded hot air balloon installation in Terminal 2 as well as innovative use of space via pop-ups for several big name brands, including Rolex, Bvlgari and Kate Spade.

In addition, a new pre-order app for selected restaurants in terminals was another big innovation in 2017 as well as partnering with Apple to improve Heathrow's digital maps, which can be accessed on mobile devices. The retail team continued to increase its luxury offering with new Gucci, Yves Saint Laurent, Louis Vuiton, Valentino and Bottega retail spaces, as well as improving the permanent space offered to brands such as SuperDry and Dixons, contributing to major improvement in Terminal 3.

Promotion

Last year, Heathrow's marketing team continued to build an emotional connection with its passengers. The summer campaign focused on the excitement of travel and the world of opportunity flying from Heathrow opens up. The winter campaign saw the welcome return of Edward and Doris Bair, two teddy bears who tugged on the nation's heartstrings and featured in a number of prominent top 10 Christmas advertising round-ups. The team behind the ads also won – and were shortlisted for – a number of prestigious industry awards.

To enhance the experience for its younger passengers, Heathrow's very own Mr. Men character, Mr. Adventure, was joined by a new sidekick, Little Miss Explorer, who is also exclusive to Heathrow. A free augmented virtual reality app was created using these characters to keep younger travellers entertained. The fun treasure-hunt style game offers virtual badges that can be redeemed for real badges at the airport's information desks. The marketing campaign that launched the app won the 2017 Most Effective Augmented Reality Campaign in the Effective Mobile Marketing Awards.

Brand History

1946	London Airport opens on the current site.
1966	The British Airports Authority is created and London Airport is renamed Heathrow Airport.
1977	The London Underground reaches Heathrow.
1977	The Terminal 5 public planning inquiry – the longest in UK history – comes to an end.
1998	The Heathrow Express rail service begins.
2008	Terminal 5 opens and the first commercial A380 flight arrives at Heathrow.
2010	Terminal 2 is demolished and work starts on its £1bn replacement.
2012	Heathrow welcomes the world as Host Airport for the 2012 Olympic Games and Paralympic Games.
2014	Terminal 2: The Queen's Terminal opens in June.
2015	Expansion of Heathrow is recommended by the Airports Commission.
2016	Heathrow celebrates its 70th birthday and the UK Government announces that Heathrow is its preferred option for airport expansion.
2017	With the younger travellers in mind, Mr. Adventure is joined by the new exclusive character, Little Miss Explorer.

Emirates Skywards, Miles & More, Royal Brunei Royal Skies, Singapore Airlines KrisFlyer and Virgin Atlantic's Flying Club.

The improved Rewards programme won the best loyalty programme at the loyalty 360 awards 2017 and was 'highly commended' in the Moodie Davitt Digital Awards 2017 and was also a finalist in the loyalty magazine awards in 2017.

Brand Values

A fleeting impression when connecting. A last look before departure. An emotional welcome home. Heathrow wants every experience of its airport to be the best it can possibly be for each of its 78m passengers. That is why Heathrow does everything it can to make it an uplifting experience, aiming to deliver to its passengers the best airport service in the world.

Heathrow Rewards, the company's loyalty programme, had over 1.1 million members on its marketable base in 2017. It continued to strengthen member benefits which included fast download speeds with free wifi and Instant Rewards, which can be redeemed at a range of stores including Dixons Travel, Jo Malone, Ted Baker, Thomas Pink and World Duty Free. Rewards can also be converted to air miles or Avios points with Heathrow's travel partners; AerClub, Avios Travel Rewards Programme, British Airways Executive Club, Eithad Guest,

heathrow.com

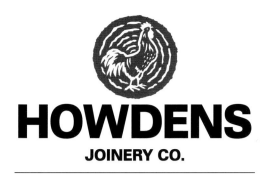

HOWDENS
JOINERY CO.

MAKING SPACE MORE VALUABLE

The **Howdens story began in 1995** with a commitment to provide kitchens
and joinery to trade customers from local stock at best local price.
Today, **Howdens is the UK's largest supplier** of fitted kitchens and associated products,
offering quality products and services to local builders and kitchen fitters nationwide.

Market

In 2016, Howdens supplied 350,000 kitchens, 775,000 appliances and 2.5m doors to trade professionals, generating sales of approximately £1.3bn through nearly 650 depots across the country. Howdens' products are installed in homes of all kinds and sizes, both owner-occupied and tenanted. Howdens' success has allowed the business to continue to invest in its prospects and in its products, services, people and brand.

Howdens is a decentralised business. Local depot managers are authorised to hire their own staff, build their own customer base, manage relationships with local builders and swap items on the spot if required. Howdens' nett monthly account and in-stock model mean builders can complete every project on time and get paid for it before they have to pay Howdens.

Product

When it comes to kitchens, Howdens is the number one choice for trade professionals, with one of the highest rates of brand awareness amongst tradespeople. Builders choose Howdens because of its local, in-stock model, together with the service it offers them and its varied product range.

With more than 70 different kitchen designs available in a variety of colours and finishes, Howdens has kitchens to suit every home, budget and lifestyle. By staying at the forefront of design trends and technology, the business can continue to introduce new products and develop its range.

DID YOU KNOW?

**Howdens' distribution
fleet covers around
24.5 million** miles each year.

A kitchen is more than just its cabinets, and Howdens supplies everything needed to create a complete kitchen – from worktops and flooring through to sinks, taps and lighting. Lamona appliances are exclusive to Howdens, and come with a two-year guarantee. Builders can also buy all of the hardware, tools and fixings they need to complete each job, direct from their local depot.

To help bring a new kitchen to life, Howdens also offers a free home survey and kitchen planning service that builds on its market-leading design expertise. Each depot has its own experienced designers, who work closely with builders and their customers to create a 'home to be proud of'.

Achievements

Customers are in prestigious company when they choose a Howdens kitchen. In January 2015, Howdens was granted a Royal Warrant as a Supplier of Fitted Kitchens By Appointment to Her Majesty the Queen.

Sustainability is important to Howdens. All of its cabinets, laminate worktops and breakfast bars are British-made in factories in Howden, East Yorkshire and Runcorn, Cheshire, where 98% of the waste produced is recycled. In 2016 the business used 225,000 cubic metres of chipboard and 33,000 cubic metres of MDF, all of which came from FSC® (Forest Stewardship Council®) certified sources. All of the products manufactured by Howdens hold the FSC chain of custody certification.

Howdens runs apprenticeship programmes that offer a range of worthwhile futures to young people across the country. There are currently around

300 apprentices in training in a variety of roles including manufacturing, engineering, logistics, sales, kitchen planning and design.

Howdens understands that motivating and supporting every employee is key to its continuing success. In 2017 Howdens was chosen for the third time as one of The Sunday Times, 30 Best Big Companies to Work For.

Recent Developments
In 2016, Howdens celebrated the 12th anniversary of its partnership with Leonard Cheshire Disability (LCD), which supports people with disabilities and works for a society where everyone is equally valued. Last year, through this partnership, 27 adaptable, inclusive Howdens kitchens were planned, donated and fitted in LCD homes. Howdens also supports LCD's 'Can Do' initiative, which offers local volunteering opportunities for young disabled people that help them build confidence and develop important life skills.

Howdens has designed numerous innovations to make life easier for the builder, including a new, heavy-duty cabinet leg that requires no screws.

This was introduced in 2017, and now all rigid cabinets come with the new leg as standard, making fitting faster and easier.

Promotion
Direct, local marketing reflects the principles on which Howdens is founded. Each depot manager has the autonomy to tailor local promotions and advertising to appeal to local builders, who rely on Howdens to provide a service of value, based on the right combination of range, quality, availability and price.

Local promotions are supported by a range of informative material, covering all product categories that builders can share with their customers, either in print or online. This material showcases Howdens' inspirational kitchen designs and the breadth of choice available, helping the builders customers to explore the many possibilities for their home.

Brand Values
Howdens helps builders to simplify the complex task of kitchen installation, supplying them with expertly designed kitchens and joinery from local

Brand History

1995	Howdens is founded by Matthew Ingle and starts trading with 14 depots.
1999	The 100th depot opens.
2007	Lamona, Howdens' own appliance brand, is launched.
2011	The 500th depot opens in Gosport, Hants.
2014	Howdens reports £1bn of sales in the UK.
2015	Royal Warrant of Appointment to Her Majesty the Queen.
2016	The 1,000,000th Lamona appliance is sold.
2017	The number of depots trading in the UK reaches 650.

stock at best local prices. Whichever depot they visit, builders and their customers can find a wide choice of product, a first-class planning service and knowledgeable advice they can trust. And most importantly, there are no ordering delays – every product is always available in their local Howdens depot.

INVESTORS IN PEOPLE

Investors in People believe that **organisations succeed when they realise the potential of their people**. In turn, individuals perform at their **best when they are led and supported well by their employer.** The Investors in People accreditation is the **sign of an outperforming place to work and a clear commitment** to sustainable growth.

DID YOU KNOW?

IIP's values are to be **ambitious, driven, collaborative, empowered** and always improving.

DID YOU KNOW?

Since 1991, more than **10 million people** have worked in an **organisation recognised by Investors in People**.

Market

Investors in People (IIP) was launched in 1991 to raise the performance of UK businesses relative to international competitors. Today, the world of work and business is transformed. Workforces are becoming more diverse, the parameters between work and personal life are blurring and organisations must understand their responsibility to protect the wellbeing of their employees. More than ever individuals, employees and customers desire to work with sustainable, ethical organisations that align societal, individual and business objectives. The Investors in People framework defines what it takes to lead, support and manage people well for sustainable results.

For employees – An Investor in People commits to giving its employees a voice. Individuals can expect to work within a culture of trust and gain recognition for doing a good job.

For employers – Investors in People enables organisations to listen to their employees, to be recognised as an employer of choice, as well as providing recommendations for areas of improvement to drive the organisation forward.

For the community – Investors in People's mission is to shape a better standard for people management, highlighting excellence and sharing best practice across a diverse community.

Product

The Standard is underpinned by the Investors in People framework that sets out the criteria to achieve Investors in People Accreditation. The framework reflects the latest workplace trends and is constantly updated by world leading academics, practitioners and other industry experts.

The Investors in People framework enables organisations to measure and recognise their success, as well as highlighting areas for improvement and progression.

A key product feature is the online survey, a powerful tool for giving employees a voice. The survey offers detailed benchmarks at industry, sector and engagement driver level, providing insights to compare performance to the very best organisations.

Achievements

As a brand, Investors in People has maintained significant awareness amongst UK businesses, and retained its position as the dominant B2B people management accreditation. In 2017 Investors in People was established as a Community Interest Company, a move to enhance the organisation's ability to deliver for employees, businesses and communities.

At the 2017 Princess Royal Training Awards, four IIP Platinum accredited companies achieved recognition for investing in the training and development opportunities within their organisations. The Awards honour employers who have created outstanding training and skills development programmes, which have resulted in tangible business benefits. The fact that 10% of the Princess Royal Training Award winners were IIP Platinum organisations demonstrates the dedication across the IIP community to ensuring that people are supported and businesses are high performing.

Recent Developments

In July 2017 Investors in People was cited in the government commissioned report 'Good Work: The Taylor Review of Modern Workplace practices.' IIP was highlighted as a key

Brand History

1990 The Employment Department is tasked with developing a national standard of good practice for training and development; Investors in People is born. The following year, the first 28 Investors in People organisations are celebrated at the company's formal launch.

1993 Investors in People UK forms as a business led, non-departmental public body. The first review of the Standard occurs and an operation is established in Australia.

2004 Investors in People launches the latest version of the Standard and the Champions programme is introduced.

2007 Investors in People 'Interactive', a free online support tool, launches.

2008 7,771,357 employees are in organisations working with Investors in People. The following year an extended framework introducing Bronze, Silver and Gold recognition launches.

2010 The Health and Wellbeing Good Practice Award is launched and ownership of the Investors in People trademark transfers to the UK Commission for Employment and Skills.

2012 Investors in People operates in 80 countries worldwide. The following year Investors in people undergoes a brand refresh.

2015 Investors in People launches the sixth generation Standard at The Bridgewater Hall in Manchester.

2017 Investors in People is established as a Community Interest Company, with a key objective to raise the standard of people management for the benefit of employees, employers and communities. Also, Investors in People is mentioned in the Government commissioned 'Good Work: The Taylor Review of Modern Workplace practices and four IIP Platinum accredited companies are recognised by Princess Royal.

stakeholder in encouraging 'employee voice' in UK workplaces. IIP's CEO, Paul Devoy, was invited to speak about this important agenda at a House of Lords Luncheon, stressing the vital role of employers in safeguarding the wellbeing of their employees.

Also in 2017, Investors in People joined the 'Beyond the Badge' campaign and are proud to be working with other standard setting bodies sharing common values and principles such as the Living Wage Foundation, the Trust Mark and the Ethical Consumer Best Buy Label. All partners are united by a common focus of setting and overseeing robust, credible and transparent standards for businesses.

Promotion

2017 saw the largest Investors in People global member awards held at the iconic Old Billingsgate, hosted by comedian Rob Beckett. Hundreds of businesses from across the globe came together to recognise and celebrate the people that make their organisations great. In 2018, Investors in People will host its fifth awards ceremony, to be held at Camden Roundhouse, with the addition of a new category focusing on organisations that demonstrate putting the health and wellbeing of employees first, the evening will celebrate the very best of the Investors in People community.

In 2018 Investors in People launched its annual employee sentiment poll, revealing major trends across the UK workforce. The annual job exodus survey tracks the likelihood that people are looking to move jobs, the reasons for doing so and the most attractive benefits that employers offer. In 2018 the campaign saw press coverage across major news outlets including Sky News, The Telegraph

and The Independent. Exploring issues such as gender discrimination and wellbeing in the workplace, Investors in People's annual polls will provide more insightful trends in 2018 and beyond.

Investors in People have also recently featured in the Business Reporter within The Telegraph, with IIP's CEO Paul Devoy offering an interesting insight into the world of work in 2030.

Brand Values

As a community interest company Investors in People's vision is to ensure every community prospers through investing in people.

IIP's brand values underpin the success of an organisation's purpose to help organisations succeed by realising the potential of their people.

IIP's values are to be ambitious, driven, collaborative, empowered and always improving.

Kingspan is **renowned for innovation, product performance, technical support** and its outstanding commitment to responsible practice. From the drive to become **net zero energy, to the positive environmental impact of its products,** and the astute acquisitions that have secured financial security, Kingspan epitomises the business case for sustainability.

Market

Today's market demands many things of its buildings – fire safety, energy efficiency, healthy environments, ease of construction and durability. Kingspan products have been developed, tested and proven to meet each of these requirements, without having to compromise on the rest.

Product

The Kingspan Group now has five operational divisions: Insulated Panels, Insulation, Environmental, Access Floors, and Light + Air. Each division offers a wide range of products for the built environment, backed by high levels of customer support, including design technical services, Building Energy Modelling (BEM), U-value calculations, field services, compliance advice, waste take-back schemes, after sales, and comprehensive product guarantees.

Achievements

Kingspan's aggregate renewable energy use was 57% of its total energy use in 2016, beating its interim target of 50%, and placing it firmly on track to hit its goal, set in 2011, of operating at Net Zero Energy (NZE) by 2020. Furthermore, Kingspan was named for the third year in a row on The Climate 'A List' by CDP, the international not-for-profit organisation that measures the environmental impact of thousands of companies around the world.

Kingspan Insulated Panels' continual commitment to responsible business practices has been recognised with the achievement of BES 6001: Responsible Sourcing of Construction Products certification. This Division was also recognised with the Excellence in Sustainability Award at the Irish Construction Industry Awards, and was shortlisted in the Responsible Large Business category at the Wales Business In The Community Awards 2017.

DID YOU KNOW?

Kingspan products have been **passing large scale fire tests since 1995.**

The health and safety of all employees is a top priority, and Kingspan Insulated Panels has consistently been awarded a top-level Gold RoSPA (The Royal Society for the Prevention of Accidents) Safety Award, since 2008. Reflecting Kingspan's commitment to its workforce, a total of 20 staff from Kingspan's Environmental Division recently graduated from the Outstanding Managers programme.

In addition, Kingspan Insulation was crowned Manufacturer of the Year at the 2017 Herefordshire & Worcestershire Chamber of Commerce Business Awards, and was shortlisted within the Excellence in Customer Service category. The Division has also been shortlisted for a Queens Award for Innovation, results pending.

Recent Developments

BENCHMARK by Kingspan has launched Dri-Design – a ground-breaking rainscreen system which offers outstanding aesthetics, tested fire performance and limitless design options in a simple-to-install package.

Kingspan Insulation announced the launch of two new products to join its innovative Kooltherm K100 Range, designed to deliver lower U-values

with a minimal construction thickness. This Division also released over 500 new flat roof BIM objects, helping to streamline the specification process.

At the start of 2017, Kingspan became a sponsor of the International Master of Science in Fire Safety Engineering (IMFSE). The IMFSE is a two-year full time Masters degree, set up in the Erasmus+ framework, which promotes close international collaboration. The sponsorship funds full or partial scholarships, supporting the highest calibre students, regardless of their background or circumstances.

A new global website which was rolled out over 2017, provides a single platform from which customers can access the full wealth of the Kingspan offering. Kingspan Insulation division has launched a free online education centre: Kingspan Insight. Users can choose from a range of interactive multi-unit courses, covering key industry topics, and earn points towards their CPD. In addition, both Insulation and Insulated Panels divisions have been running regular CPDs on the fire building regulations, tests and standards as well as on the fire performance of their products.

A new Kingspan office was opened in Singapore with expectations for significant future growth in the Asia-Pacific region and a 51% controlling share was acquired in the Brazilian company,

Brand History

1960s Founded by Eugene Murtagh, the Kingspan Group, a small engineering business, starts up with the manufacture of steel frame buildings.

1970s The business moves into the small-scale manufacture of environmental products.

1980s A number of plants are established in Ireland and the UK, manufacturing Insulated Panels and Insulation products.

1990s Expansion and diversification into Europe takes place, establishing facilities and sales teams in Benelux, Germany, Poland, Hungary and the Czech Republic.

2000s The network is broadened and strengthened with the Group's global presence expanding across Europe, North America, Australia, and South East Asia. Further acquisitions lead to the creation of two new Divisions – Access Floors and Environmental.

2010s Continued growth through investment in acquisitions, plant and product development takes place as well as the creation of new Division – Kingspan Light + Air.

Isoeste Construtivos Isotérmicos S.A. (Isoeste), the leading insulated panel manufacturer in Brazil with forecast sales of approximately €134m for 2017. Furthermore, Kingspan Insulation in North America commissioned a new $25m GreenGuard XPS manufacturing line.

Kingspan Light + Air acquired CPI Daylighting, marking its first step into the façade space and further enhancing its offering both within the US and globally. The division has also launched Day-Lite Kapture – a precision engineered rooflight with outstanding light diffusion.

Kingspan Insulation has announced it is investing €17m in two state-of-the-art, low waste production lines at its facilities in Derbyshire and North Yorkshire: a prototype Continuous Process Line 3 (CPL3),

DID YOU KNOW?

Kingspan is one of only two **Irish companies** to make the Climate 'A List'.

which is the latest evolution in the firm's Queen's Award winning CPL technology, and a 2,400 m² manufacturing line for Kingspan Styrozone insulation.

Promotion
The new Kingspan website represents a major investment, providing a central hub for all stakeholders to find information about the

business, whether as an investor, supplier, customer sourcing products or specifier seeking technical guidance. It showcases the scale and breadth of the Kingspan offering, whilst enhancing brand consistency across the whole Group.

Brand Values
Whether it is tackling climate change or fuel poverty, providing healthy buildings or social value, the Kingspan ethos is about helping people to make things better. It does this through high performing products, innovation, technical expertise, education and support. As a brand, it represents quality, service, and corporate responsibility, and it strives always for excellence.

LEVC are the **manufacturer and retailer of iconic vehicles** that set the standard in their class. From **purpose-built taxis, the iconic black cab,** to LEVC's future offering of **commercial and public service transport**, its aim is to create and build true icons of industry.

Market

Taxis, also known as taxicabs and cabs, are distinct from public transportation such as buses, trams or Underground systems in that they offer greater privacy, comfort, convenience and safety by conveying small groups of private passengers directly to a precise location of their choice. In this respect, they can be viewed as a more upmarket alternative to mass transit methods; particularly in urban environments.

Although there are similarities, the taxi industry is varied not only by country, but in each city and is influenced by a multitude of historic and current factors, such as geography, climate, population, tourism and industry, public transport infrastructure, economic factors, legislation as well as the passenger car market. In general, taxis can be grouped into three distinct categories: Hackney carriages also known as public hire, hailed or street taxis; Private hire, also known as minicabs which are licensed for pre-booking only, via telephone, online or via apps, such as Uber; and Limo Services, contract cars that are chauffeur driven, catering to special occasions and an upmarket audience, with higher fares.

Product

As the leading global manufacturer and retailer of purpose-built taxis, LEVC is universally acknowledged for creating the world-renowned black cab. Following substantial investment by parent company Zhejiang Geely Holding Group (Geely) in 2013, the company has developed an all-new electric taxi to aggressively target new expansion opportunities, both within the UK and internationally.

Built in a state-of-the-art facility in Ansty near Coventry the cutting-edge TX electric taxi combines a fully electric powertrain with range-extender, pioneering aluminium architecture and unrivalled levels of comfort and quality to create a new generation of premium taxi, which is still unmistakeably a black cab.

LEVC drew on 60 years of expertise and engineering to create the new vehicle from the ground up and

DID YOU KNOW?

The **Internet Movie Cars Database** has recorded black cabs featuring in over **2,000** films in the past **80 years**.

develop the ultimate zero-emissions capable taxi for today's cities. From passengers, pedestrians and legislative bodies to the most important people of all, owners and drivers, the new electric taxi is as compelling as its iconic predecessor.

Achievements

LEVC has sold the archetypal black cab to more than 40 countries across the world for 70 years, so has a wealth of experience and expertise to build upon.

The official opening of LEVC's new state-of-the-art, vehicle plant in Coventry sees the UK's first car plant dedicated solely to the production of electric vehicles and is where the world's first purpose-built, mass-market electric taxi will be built. The investment and expansion in the new site and the next-generation London taxi has helped create more than 1,000 new jobs, including 200 engineers and 30 apprenticeships.

When at full capacity, LEVC will be able to build more than 20,000 vehicles per year, designed for, and dedicated to one task: to be the best ultra-low emission commercial vehicles in the world. The taxi vehicle uses proven Volvo Car electric powertrain system technologies and components comprising a new EV lightweight platform, while retaining the iconic design heritage, which is recognised around the world. Further derivatives of this new EV architecture will follow.

Plans are also in place for the second vehicle to come off the line, an electric light commercial van (LCV). This all-new, highly flexible, commercially competitive electric vehicle will help fleet owners lower their running costs, improve air quality and support cities in tackling the pollution crisis in urban areas.

In 2017 LEVC won Manufacturer of the Year at the Low Carbon Vehicle Partnership Awards. A second award came later in the year at the Next Green Car Awards where LEVC was the winner of the Innovation Award 2017.

Recent Developments

In December 2017, LEVC's electric TX taxi became fully certified to carry fare-paying passengers. This marked a revolution for passengers who should expect unrivalled ride comfort, class leading wheelchair accessibility, air conditioning, phone charging and a much more spacious cabin, with six seats. Features are in abundance and include wide opening coach doors, power sockets for laptop and phone charging, fast on-board wifi, contactless card machines as well as an expansive panoramic roof.

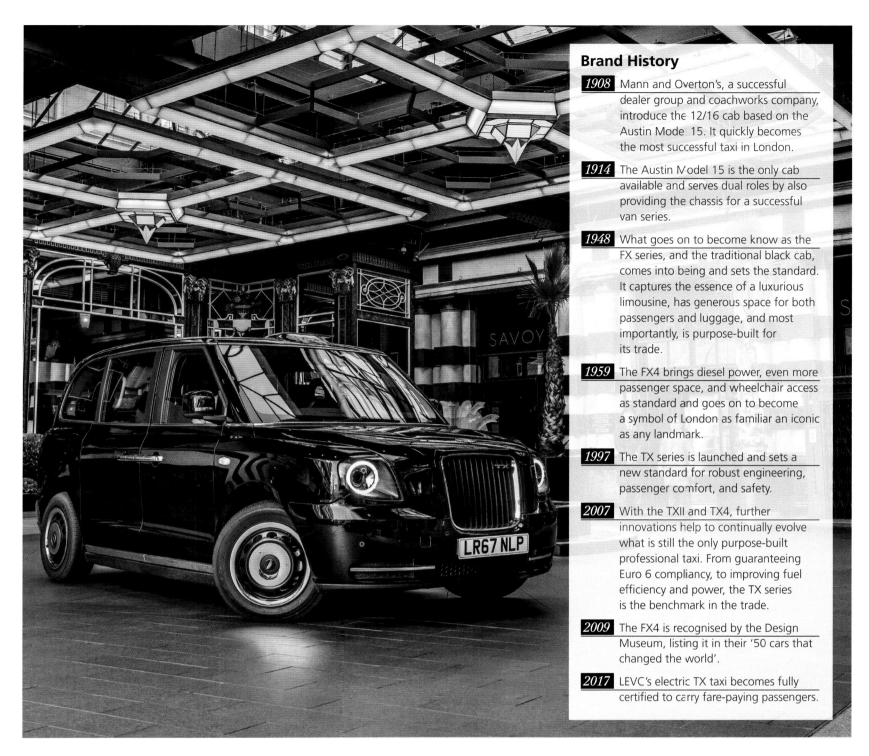

Brand History

1908 Mann and Overton's, a successful dealer group and coachworks company, introduce the 12/16 cab based on the Austin Mode 15. It quickly becomes the most successful taxi in London.

1914 The Austin Model 15 is the only cab available and serves dual roles by also providing the chassis for a successful van series.

1948 What goes on to become know as the FX series, and the traditional black cab, comes into being and sets the standard. It captures the essence of a luxurious limousine, has generous space for both passengers and luggage, and most importantly, is purpose-built for its trade.

1959 The FX4 brings diesel power, even more passenger space, and wheelchair access as standard and goes on to become a symbol of London as familiar an iconic as any landmark.

1997 The TX series is launched and sets a new standard for robust engineering, passenger comfort, and safety.

2007 With the TXII and TX4, further innovations help to continually evolve what is still the only purpose-built professional taxi. From guaranteeing Euro 6 compliancy, to improving fuel efficiency and power, the TX series is the benchmark in the trade.

2009 The FX4 is recognised by the Design Museum, listing it in their '50 cars that changed the world'.

2017 LEVC's electric TX taxi becomes fully certified to carry fare-paying passengers.

The TX has been heralded as "the forefront of green transport technology" by Shirley Rodrigues, Deputy Mayor for Environment and Energy, who also stated that the vehicle "will play a transformational role in the Mayor's plan to phase out diesel and clean up the transport network, which will help to accelerate improvements to London's toxic air."

LEVC will also be introducing the TX into Europe. In December 2017 it announced that Oslo-based Autoindustri has been chosen as the importer for the new electric taxi. This marks the second agreement to export the TX electric taxi to Europe, following a deal signed with Dutch mobility firm RMC, which was announced earlier this year. 2018 will also see many more similar announcements in cities across Europe and the rest of the world.

Over the last two years, the London EV Company (USA) LLC, has been designing and developing bespoke prototype delivery vehicles for the United States Government. These exciting new prototype vehicles are seeking to become the leading commercial delivery vehicle for the US Government. If the trials are successful, the vehicles will be built in the US bringing with it significant investment and job creation.

Promotion
Due to the transformational power that the TX taxi can bring, it is in a fortunate position of gaining interest from all corners of the media as well as MPs and environmental groups raising the profile of the product.

Furthermore, within the next two years, the next step in LEVC's journey as a vehicle manufacturer will be realised, with the launch of a light commercial vehicle, based on the latest evolution of the taxi, which will undoubtedly create more attention, interest and support around LEVC and its innovative products.

Brand Values
LEVC is a progressive, forward-looking company that continues to invest in developing technologies for cleaner, greener vehicles – with the aim of becoming 'The Urban Commercial Vehicle Provider of Choice'.

It keeps the vision of its founders in mind – 'to make vehicles that are the defining statement in their class'. LEVC remains committed and true to this concept, but also to growing its reach and brand across global markets.

This vision comes with a renewed responsibility to the environment with its vehicles meeting the strictest emission standards in the world. Through the use of integrated EV technology and advanced materials, even the iconic black cab has gone green.

Note: The London Taxi Company was the brand voted on in the 2018 Superbrands voting process but has subsequently rebranded to LEVC.

LLOYD'S

The world's specialist insurance and reinsurance market. Lloyd's is the foundation of the insurance industry and the future of it. Led by expert underwriters and brokers who cover more than 200 countries and territories worldwide, Lloyd's develops the essential, complex and critical insurance needed to underwrite human progress.

Market

With revenues of £29.9bn, Lloyd's works with a global network to grow the insured world and has been able to retain its pre-eminent position in global insurance due to a combination of reputation, scale, governance, a unique working culture and continuing commitment to innovation and boldness.

Lloyd's is a unique insurance market with an unrivalled concentration of specialist underwriting expertise. The market is comprised of more than 50 leading insurance companies, over 200 registered brokers and a global network of over 3,800 approved coverholder office locations who operate in and bring business to Lloyd's. Much of the business at Lloyd's works by subscription, where more than one insurer takes a share of the same risk. As the insurance and re-insurance market changes, so too must Lloyd's, and its vision aims to ensure that Lloyd's remains the global centre for specialist insurance and re-insurance.

Product

Lloyd's provides a platform for individual commercial businesses to thrive. At Lloyd's, customers have the access to the combined scale, expertise and capacity of the entire market, not just a single insurance company. Underwriters in the Lloyd's market know that standard policies don't always meet the needs of their customers so they are able to develop specialised, well-priced solutions in response.

Lloyd's is a varied market, containing large international organisations as well as smaller niche businesses. Lloyd's insurers cover risks that are often too complex for other insurers, including categories such as shipping, aviation, pandemics, nuclear, political risk and cyber. Lloyd's pioneered the first cyber liability policy back in 1999 and today there are over 70 insurers in the Lloyd's market providing coverage for cyber risks.

LLOYD'S PAID ON AVERAGE £46M OF CLAIMS PER DAY IN 2017

Lloyd's not only provides the market with infrastructure and transactional support, but oversees the operations of its participants, holds licenses with governments to write insurance in over 75 countries worldwide and manages a central fund designed to guarantee policies underwritten in the Lloyd's market, should any Lloyd's insurer be unable to meet its commitments.

Lloyd's has constantly sought to respond quickly to events and lead change in the industry, whether it be following the historic loss of HMS Lutine, whose bell hangs in the atrium of the Lloyd's underwriting room today, or the natural disasters that blighted 2011.

Lloyd's is proud of its reputation for paying valid claims and in the last five years alone, Lloyd's has paid £62.8bn in claims.

Achievements

While insurance is seldom seen as exciting, the specialist cover Lloyd's provides plays a crucial role in advancing social progress. Lloyd's does not reduce risk, but as our world changes from economic, environmental, geopolitical and technological shifts, the breadth, depth and cover offered by the Lloyd's market gives customers confidence to move forward in the face of change.

Lloyd's is uniquely constituted to consider extremely risky proposals that other parts of the insurance market are unable to. Originally created to insure shipping ventures 330 years ago, Lloyd's has covered Arctic explorers, international aid organisations and space missions, as well as key current global risks such as cyber and terrorism. Face to face negotiations between brokers and underwriters has stood the test of time for over 300 years with the judgment of its expert underwriters helping brokers to come up with innovative solutions to risks.

As the world becomes more interdependent, the fall-out from risk is far-reaching. Lloyd's is well placed to meet the needs of the global economy with significant operations in Singapore, Shanghai, Beijing, Tokyo and Dubai. Its business is continuing to expand in Latin America with offices in Mexico and Colombia alongside an established operation in Brazil and most recently commenced operations in India in 2017.

Brand History

1688 Lloyd's coffee house is recognised as the place for obtaining marine insurance.

1774 The modern Lloyd's is born as it moves to the Royal Exchange and leaves the coffee business for good.

1904 Lloyd's writes its first motor policy, cementing its reputation for innovation.

1906 Faced with the devastation of the San Francisco earthquake, Lloyd's underwriter Cuthbert Heath instructs prompt payment: "in full, irrespective of the terms of their policies."

1911 Lloyd's writes its first policy for aviation.

1965 The first space satellite insurance is placed at Lloyd's and in 1984, Lloyd's launches a successful salvage mission to reclaim two rogue satellites, sending a shuttle and five astronauts into orbit in order to retrieve them.

1986 The new Lloyd's building at One Lime Street, designed by Richard Rogers, was officially opened by Her Majesty The Queen.

1999 Lloyd's Asia opens in Singapore as part of its commitment to develop the insurance industry in new and emerging markets.

2001 The events of 9/11 changed the world's perception of risk forever. It was also Lloyd's largest-ever single loss, impacting many different classes of business.

2015 Lloyd's launches its global City Risk Index which found that nearly half the economic risks faced by 301 cities around the world were linked to human made threats.

2016 Lloyd's expands its award-winning diversity festival across its global network of offices and is recognised as leading the field in encouraging open, inclusive cultures across the insurance industry.

2017 Lloyd's commences operations in India and the market's claims payments support recovery in the US and Caribbean, following hurricanes Harvey and Irma.

UK Chancellor Philip Hammond said "Lloyd's decision to expand into India is a perfect example of the role Britain's world-leading financial services sector plays in supporting growth both at home and abroad. It will help Indian insurance firms increase the resilience of the Indian economy to catastrophic events and boost Britain's ties with one of the world's most exciting economies, underlining our status as a truly global, trading nation."

Recent Developments

Lloyd's has helped customers around the world withstand shock, recover and rebuild and it is proud to continue that service today. The challenges facing Lloyd's are varied and complex and a far cry from the days when almost everything insured was marine. Now, Lloyd's is responding to the risks of cyber-attack, climate change or pandemics.

Lloyd's uses its central position as a marketplace to catalyse discussion and action on the issues and megatrends that will impact the future of the global economy.

Lloyd's continues to support businesses at the cutting edge of development and technology,

new companies that are shaping the way we live and work. Lloyd's insures a huge range of risks from the latest rocket technology and the sharing economy to terrorism and cyber risk – Lloyd's is now the world's largest cyber insurer. By insuring their risks, Lloyd's gives these companies the confidence to drive forward social and economic development and by doing so enables human progress.

Promotion

With expertise earned over three centuries, Lloyd's is a name that resonates beyond its market. As well as communicating to the specialist insurance and reinsurance market, it also looks outward towards the markets in Latin-America, South-East Asia and India as well as its more traditional markets in the UK, Europe, and North America.

Lloyd's helps to keep the market on the front line and customers on the front foot by regularly publishing Emerging Risk reports that scan the horizon for issues and trends likely to affect the insurance market. Recent reports include analysis on the insurance implications of technology, cyber, climate change and urban resilience.

Brand Values

Lloyd's key brand values are Trust, Modernity, Innovation, Expertise and Global. Lloyd's is clear about its aim to be the global centre of specialist insurance and reinsurance; meeting the challenges of a changing world and accessing the major overseas territories and emerging markets. It is a market where innovation is encouraged and entrepreneurs can thrive.

Marshalls

Creating Better Spaces

Marshalls is the UK's leading manufacturer of hard landscaping products, and has been supplying superior natural stone and innovative concrete products to the **construction, home improvement and landscape markets since the 1890s.** Marshalls strives to create products that improve landscapes and create better environments to develop happier and healthier communities.

Market

In the public sector and commercial markets, Marshalls focuses on developing products that help architects, local authorities and contractors to make better spaces, whether it is landscape furniture, natural stone paving, stone cladding and facades, block paving, water management, or landscape protection products.

Marshalls' domestic customers range from homeowners to professional landscapers, driveway installers and garden designers. Sales continue to be driven through the Marshalls Register of Accredited Landscapers and Driveway Installers.

Marshalls has an established and growing presence in the Middle East, Northern Europe, North America, and China.

Product

Marshalls is committed to producing new products that better any existing market offering, and to make

them from the best materials it can source. Over the years, Marshalls has continued to develop and expand its products and services to both the commercial and domestic markets.

In the public sector and commercial market, Marshalls satisfies the needs of a diverse commercial customer base, which spans local authorities, commercial architects, specifiers, contractors and house builders. It offers them unrivalled technical expertise, manufacturing capability and an enviable product range, including superior natural stone, innovative concrete hard landscaping products, water management solutions, rail products, landscape protection products, landscape furniture, and natural stone cladding as well as facades.

Marshalls' domestic customers range from DIY enthusiasts, to professional landscapers,

OVER 14.5 MILLION
MINUTES OF MARSHALLS' YOUTUBE VIDEOS HAVE BEEN VIEWED

driveway installers and garden designers, and Marshalls specialises in helping them to create beautiful, yet practical outdoor spaces that families can enjoy for years to come. Marshalls' extensive product ranges are designed to inspire, combining quality, elegance and durability in both traditional and cutting-edge designs, with products to suit every taste and style.

Achievements

Environmental responsibility has been key to Marshalls for many years. Indeed, by 2009 more than 2,000 of Marshalls' commercial products had a Carbon Trust Carbon Reduction label. Sustainability remains at the heart of everything Marshalls does, and the company remains at the forefront of sustainable business. As the first company in its sector to belong to the Ethical Trading Initiative

(ETI), Marshalls is committed to the implementation of the ETI Base Code, pioneering the ethical sourcing of natural stone paving from India and China, and has remained a signatory of the United Nations Global Compact since its acceptance in 2009. Marshalls was first awarded The Fair Tax Mark in 2015 and has now been accredited with the mark for three consecutive years, and also as a Living Wage Employer in recognition of the business' commitment to transparent tax processes and responsible pay respectively.

Recent Developments

Following on from a successful charity partnership with Prostate Cancer in 2016, Marshalls chose Mind as its corporate partner charity for 2017. Marshalls was committed to fundraising for this worthy cause throughout 2017 via various different events, initiatives and challenges.

In 2016 Marshalls published its Modern Slavery Statement, furthering its commitment to corporate social responsibility and 2017 saw

Marshalls partner with anti-slavery organisation Hope for Justice. Marshalls is taking huge steps in order to identify and eradicate slavery from its supply chains, and in recognition of this, the company was shortlisted for the 2017 Thompson Reuters Foundation Stop Slavery Award. Additionally, Marshalls was the first organisation to achieve the BRE Global Ethical Labour Sourcing Standard Verification (BES 6002).

Furthermore, Marshalls launched a range of artificial grass as a new addition to its domestic product range. Three types of grass are available which compliment an already extensive range of landscaping products.

Finally, 2017 saw Marshalls join the Made in Britain movement – a not-for-profit organisation that aims to unite all British manufacturers and promote British manufacturing. Marshalls Group Marketing Director, Chris Harrop, is also Chairman of the organisation.

Promotion

Across the group of businesses, Marshalls continues to invest heavily in communications. The 2017 domestic advertising campaign, Not all driveways/ patios are created equal, was used to promote the business' landscape products to trade and consumer audiences.

The commercial business focused on highlighting the ethical risk of specifying natural stone products, and ran an integrated campaign for the newly launched Ethical Risk Index, which aims to highlight potential issues when it comes to stone sourcing in a number of well-known countries. The Ethical Risk Index (ERI) uses a bespoke, independently audited scoring framework and gives a genuine insight into the ethical challenges facing stone procurers to allow for more informed decision-making.

Alongside this, the commercial business also launched a Housebuilder product package that contains a complimentary suite of products that have all been designed with housebuilders in mind. The package ensures that all products supplied are cohesive and provide an attractive aesthetic on any housing scheme.

Furthermore, Marshalls continues to lead the way in thought leadership, and has been featured on a number of BBC news programmes discussing the importance of Landscape Protection products in light of recent terror attacks, and how they can be attractively integrated into landscapes without compromising on a design's aesthetic or affecting pedestrian movement and interaction.

Brand Values

Marshalls' shared values of Leadership, Excellence, Trust and Sustainability underpin the company and are important to the continued success of the business.

Marshalls aims to be the supplier of choice for every landscape architect, contractor, installer and consumer, and for the brand to remain synonymous with quality, innovation and superior customer service.

Brand History

1890 Solomon Marshall starts to quarry in Southowram, Halifax, and in 1904 establishes S. Marshall and Sons Ltd in West Yorkshire.

1947 A second production site is opened, manufacturing lintels, steps and fence posts. In 1948 an engineering division is established.

1964 Marshalls becomes a plc, with shares quoted on the London Stock Exchange.

1972 New product development sees the introduction of block paving and the famous 'Beany Block' that combines drain and kerb.

1988 Brick manufacturer George Armitage & Sons is acquired, becoming Marshalls Clay Products.

2004 Marshalls acquires Woodhouse, expanding its product offering to include design-led street furniture, lighting and signage.

2011 Marshalls announces a European venture, Marshalls NV.

2012 Marshalls is an official supplier to the London 2012 Olympic Park. In addition, an office is opened in Xiamen, China.

2014 Marshalls is accredited by the Living Wage Foundation.

2017 Marshalls acquires precast concrete manufacturer, CPM.

MoneySuperMarket **strives to provide unrivalled services and products for households across the UK. It exists to help customers grow, save and manage their money. In 2017, when the cost of living rose and wages remained largely stagnant, MoneySuperMarket helped British households to save billions on their household bills.**

Market

Since it was founded in 1999, MoneySuperMarket has helped create and develop the UK price comparison market and remains a dominant website in the sector.

The company acts as a virtual market place, showcasing the products of over 900 UK brands in a digital one-stop shop where consumers can compare, buy and save across a range of financial services and household bills.

Products range from insurance to banking products, and from gas and electricity tariffs to broadband contracts.

Today it is one of the five largest brands in the sector along with a profusion of smaller players.

Product

MoneySuperMarket compares numerous insurance brands, across current account, savings, credit card, mortgage, energy and personal loan providers. Ease of use and transparency are to the fore and the company is committed to putting its customers first.

Central to the customer-first ethos is having the best possible site. In 2018, MoneySuperMarket's shift to a single technology platform is allowing customers to have an improved and consistent journey, irrespective of the device they use or the product they are looking for.

Tools, calculators and personalised onsite content also allow customers to feel empowered and informed when they compare products and make a purchase.

In addition to this, MoneySuperMarket's app allows users to run car insurance quotes, purchase policies and keep on top of all-important diary dates via policy expiry reminders and MOT and road tax renewal prompts.

DID YOU KNOW?

The He-Man and Skeletor Dirty Dancing campaign received 25m organic views on Facebook.

Achievements

MoneySuperMarket's groundbreaking, stand-out campaigns have achieved considerable recognition from the creative community in recent years. These include four Campaign Big Awards, three D&AD awards and the coveted Campaign of the Year Award for 'Strut', which featured a man in denim hotpants.

However, it is the public's response that really counts to MoneySuperMarket and here the

campaigns have succeeded in capturing the imagination. There have been numerous spoofs of the Skeletor and He-Man ads, people have baked cakes in their honour, and one man even got a tattoo of the He-Man and Skeletor Dirty Dancing lift.

Recent Developments

In 2017 MoneySuperMarket started a two-year partnership with the homeless and housing support charities Shelter and Shelter Cymru (the company has offices in England and Wales). Through a series of fundraising events, MoneySuperMarket has raised over £70,000 for these worthy causes.

The money raised by the group has helped Shelter Cymru's online advice service help 220,000 users (85% above the users predicted) and facilitated 25% of all webchats from April to December 2017 on the Shelter England and Scotland website.

MoneySuperMarket takes great pride in supporting the work of these charities and, by providing funding towards online advice and support, the aim is to help millions who every year struggle with bad housing or homelessness.

Brand History

1993	Mortgages 2000 launches in Chester as an offline mortgage listings business.
1999	MoneySuperMarket is established online.
2000	Credit cards, personal loans and insurance comparison expand the range of products on offer.
2007	MoneySuperMarket is listed on the Stock Market with an offer price of 170p.
2012	MoneySavingExpert joins the MoneySuperMarket Group.
2013	My Profile launches, enabling customers to have a single log-in and create a personal account.
2014	The start of a £50m+ three-year technology investment programme to step change the customer experience begins.
2015	The in-house digital team win three UK Search Awards, three Drum Search Awards, two European Search Awards and two Drum Digital Trading Awards.
2016	The MoneySuperMarket app launches.
2017	Mark Lewis joins as CEO.

Promotion

The MoneySuperMarket brand has long celebrated the 'mental fist-pump' that comes when money is saved on household bills. In 2017, the company looked to find a new expression of this feeling.

The brand went looking for a cultural touchpoint that could bind its broad 35yrs+ audience together. Research showed that they shared a common bond as new or experienced parents, together with a sentimental view of their own childhoods and an associated shared nostalgia for the 1980s.

The search was on for characters who could not only tap into '80s nostalgia but also take the MoneySuperMarket 'epic' feeling to a new level. So, it was decided to enlist the services of Masters of the Universe characters, Skeletor and He-Man. The first campaign demonstrated that even the eternally-doomed Skeletor could 'feel epic' when he saved money on his car insurance. Such was his delight that he was soon dancing through the streets to Irene Cara performing Fame.

For the second campaign, the intention was to ratchet it up a notch with the 1980s cult classic, Dirty Dancing. What could be more delightful than watching two famous arch enemies, Skeletor and He-Man, put their differences aside to perform that 'epic' dance lift? It created

the perfect expression of 'feeling epic' having saved at MoneySuperMarket.

Engaging the audience emotionally, however, wasn't enough. MoneySuperMarket also appealed to their pockets by proving afresh that it offers superior value. This was achieved via a tactical strand of retail promotions across the brand's product range, supported across TV, print, digital and social channels.

The initiative led to an unprecedented increase in awareness for products such as home insurance, gaining over £1m of incremental revenue for that channel alone.

MoneySuperMarket's 2017 campaign is among the most engaging ads ever recorded by Millward Brown and was AdWatch's most recalled and liked ad in May of that year. This positive engagement has also led to a 13% increase in brand trust.

Brand Values

MoneySuperMarket's vision is to help every household make the most of their money.

Innovating for tomorrow, listening as well as understanding, and living the brand are at the heart of MoneySuperMarket's values.

MORE TH>N®

MORE TH>N was founded 15 years ago as a **fresh, customer-focused alternative to traditional insurers** and has gone on to become one of the UK's best known insurance brands.

Market

MORE TH>N's launch in 2001 was a response to the perceived negativity surrounding the insurance industry. Research revealed that many customers saw insurance companies at best as apathetic, at worst dishonest – hiding behind confusing jargon and technical loopholes to avoid paying out.

While the rise of price comparison sites brought consumers greater choice and transparency, it also had a commoditising effect, inadvertently encouraging many insurers to prioritise upfront price at the expense of product and service quality.

These factors reinforced the opportunity for a radically new, service-led approach. MORE TH>N's mission was simple: build a new type of insurance company. One committed to going beyond just about good enough and consistently delivering more than consumers expected.

Product

MORE TH>N prides itself on bringing this approach to a wide range of products including home, motor, pet, landlord, travel and small business insurance.

MORE TH>N's home insurance comes with 24hr Emergency Assistance as standard and if a customer has a no claims bonus of four years or more, MORE TH>N car insurance allows this to be protected – no matter how many claims the customer makes. Its pet insurance includes access to vetFone – a Freephone pet helpline, with expert vet nurses working 24/7 to answer pet health or behavioural questions.

All three main products were highly rated in 2017; MORE TH>N's upgraded home insurance has a 5* Moneyfacts rating, while premier pet insurance and comprehensive car insurance both have 5* Defaqto ratings.

Achievements

In 2017, MORE TH>N added to its collection of awards for its quality cover including Your Money's Best Online Pet and Travel insurance provider, Consumer Intelligence's winner for claims as voted for by drivers and Personal Finance's Best Overall Car Insurer.

Additionally, MORE TH>N won at the Insurance Marketing and PR Awards two years in a row. 2017 saw it win PR Campaign of the Year for the #PlayMore art exhibition for dogs, whilst in 2016,

its Happy Dog Project won Digital Marketing Campaign of the Year.

MORE TH>N continuously push the boundaries of insurance marketing through innovative use of social formats and imaginative campaigns. A particular hit was the addictive, mobile-friendly SM>RT WHEELS game – arguably the world's only video game to be based on an insurance policy. Players were rewarded for driving safely and with the chance to win £1,000. This social campaign delivered 11.3m views.

MORE TH>N is a proud partner of the RSPCA. From an initial donation of £150,000 and 50p donated for every single pet policy sold, MORE TH>N has raised over £1m for the animal charity.

Recent Developments

MORE TH>N is the only insurer currently working in partnership with PitPat – a canine version of a 'fitbit'. The dog activity monitors were issued for free to customers who signed up to participate in a trial to track the exercise levels of their dogs. The data is being used to understand the relationship between pet activity and health, acquiring learning to shape a wider wellbeing pet insurance proposition in the future.

Promotion

2017 saw the successful launch of a major new marketing campaign, bringing to life the brand in a positive and entertaining way.

TV spots focused on fictional founder Mordenn Suren's mission to relieve pressure on modern families, highlighting features like Home Emergency cover and SM>RT WHEELS rewards.

The campaign continued across high-impact outdoor advertising, radio, digital, social, PR and customer communications.

2017 also saw MORE TH>N become the first insurance brand to hero in MoneySuperMarket's epic Skeletor television campaign, with a cashback offer on home insurance.

Brand Values

At the heart of MORE TH>N's approach are four customer promises that underpin all areas of the business. These are defined in the following way:

On Price: More Honest. More Open. More Value.

On Claims: Listen First. Act fast. A More Personal Service.

On Cover: More Clear. More Confidence You're Covered.

On Service: Effortless. However You Get In Touch.

To embed these promises into its culture, MORE TH>N has a strong focus on internal engagement – its internal brand mantra is 'We're more than on it, we're #ALLOVERIT.' MORE TH>N has its own '#ALLOVERIT crew' – a team of volunteers from across all its office locations who are ambassadors for the Brand and help to sprinkle a little bit of '#ALLOVERIT magic' across all of the MORE TH>N sites. The focus on employees is reflected in MORE TH>N's latest internal survey, which shows 77% of staff feel proud to work for the company.

Pet insurance with 24/7 vetfone.
Health wisdoms for the beloved family fur.

WE DO > MORE TH>N®

Since its launch in 2000, **npower has established itself as one of Britain's leading energy companies.** It is part of the innogy group, one of Europe's leading electricity and gas companies, and **serves around five million residential and business accounts.** The company **employs around 6,700 people** in the UK.

Market
Energy is an essential service, key to every aspect of modern life. British households spend around £30bn on gas and electricity each year. Businesses, charities and public bodies spend an extra £20bn each year.

Product
npower is one of the largest energy suppliers in the UK. Its main priority is making sure its customers get the energy they need, in a way that minimises environmental impact. It also has a focus on enriching society, using its presence in millions of UK homes to help clubs, organisations and those in need.

Achievements
npower is the only energy company to have received triple certification to the Carbon Trust Standard for achievements in reducing carbon, water and waste from its offices.

In addition, it was recognised at the Third Sector Awards 2017 as the Corporate Partnership of the Year for its work with Macmillan Cancer Support.

Recent Developments
As the energy sector continues to evolve, npower has been exploring ways to innovate in the market.

npower is providing financial backing to Powershop, a new challenger in the household power supply market, which is changing the way customers engage with their bills, enabling them to buy only the electricity they have used.

DID YOU KNOW?

Customers submit an average of 20,000 meter readings on npower's digital channels every day.

A Powershop app also allows customers to monitor their electricity usage via mobile or desktop, with or without a smart meter, incentivising them to make changes to reduce their energy bills.

Promoting green energy and sustainability is an integral part of npower's future plans. The Go Green Energy Fix tariff, launched in September 2017, was, at the time of launch, the only tariff of its kind offered by any of the major energy suppliers. As well as market-leading green credentials the tariff was supported by a partnership with Trees for Cities, who committed to planting two trees for every dual fuel sale of the product.

Promotion
npower prides itself on its consistent involvement with sports in England. Early in its existence, it recognised the value and importance of sports

sponsorship in developing grass-roots skills, delivering major events and getting the brand to new audiences.

Over the past decade, npower has been involved in the Football League, Test cricket, Wembley Stadium and even the 2018 bid to host the football World Cup in England. In 2017 npower confirmed its sponsorship of Wigan Warriors and Wasps Rugby Club.

As part of a strategy to promote npower as a company that can help simplify family lives, npower created a campaign that focused on what's important to customers – their families.

The Family Super Powers campaign showcased the hidden super powers of the UK, and introduced some new ones from npower. Beyond advertising, npower brings its brand to life through a programme of community partnerships centred on families.

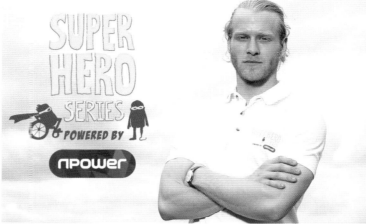

Brand History

2000	The npower brand is launched.
2001	npower launches its first home service products.
2002	RWE purchase Innogy.
2003	Innogy is renamed RWE Innogy.
2004	RWE Innogy is officially renamed RWE npower. It also becomes a Business Superbrand and the npower and Macmillan partnership launches. Also, npower sponsors the English Test cricket.
2009	npower sponsors the Football League.
2010	npower joins the bid to host the 2018 football World Cup in England.
2016	The npower Fuel Bank™ initiative launches and the renewable, network and retail businesses of RWE, which includes npower, are spun off into a separate entity, innogy SE.
2017	npower becomes the title partner of the Superhero Series, the first disability sports event for 'Everyday Superheroes' and their families.

As the UK's only mass participation sports event exclusively for families living with disability, npower's partnership with the Superhero Series has made disabled sport not just more visible, but more accessible for everyone.

Together with the Superhero Series, npower set out to champion its brand position of 'empowering families' by launching a targeted social media campaign to encourage people with disabilities to take part in the event.

A total of 1,750 participants joined the triathlon, including some of the UK's best known para-athletes. More than 7,000 people attended and Channel 4 aired a one-hour long highlights programme about the event.

npower has a longstanding partnership with Macmillan. Although cancer is a very familiar illness, the financial impact of keeping warm is less commonly discussed. Those living with cancer spend on average £177 a year more on their energy bills as a direct result of their illness and treatment.

npower's partnership with Macmillan began in 2004, and through npower's Macmillan Fund it has helped cancer-affected customers with their energy bills. npower has also committed a further £4m over the next three years, so that together they can help those living with cancer concentrate on the recovery process.

In 2017 npower and Macmillan launched the world's first interactive hologram in aid of Macmillan Cancer Support. People across the UK were encouraged to use the hologram, called Light Sky, to send messages to loved ones,

while raising funds for the charity. The Light Sky transformed each message into a 3D holographic animation, infused with a Christmas theme, and projected it above London's skyline.

In 2015, npower Fuel Bank™ was created in response to the increase in the number of people having to make the agonising choice between 'heating or eating'. With the UK seeing a rise in the number of people seeking help from food banks, npower saw the need for additional help with the cost of fuel as well as the provision of food.

The scheme is currently available in many food-bank locations across the UK, and provides a top-up voucher for approximately two weeks'

worth of fuel to clients with a prepayment meter and who have been deemed as in 'crisis need' by an independent food-bank referrer. Fuel Banks™ have so far helped around 35,000 people and npower is committed to growing the scheme, pledging to provide at least £2.25m by March 2018.

Brand Values

npower continues to be a company that puts people at the heart of everything it does, with the aim of making society a better place for all involved. With so many exciting changes on the horizon, the future of the company is full of opportunity.

P&O FERRIES
YOUR TRIP. YOUR SHIP.

P&O Ferries is a **leading pan-European operator** with in excess of 20 ships. **Every year with 27,500 sailings**, it carries more than **10 million passengers and 2.2 million freight units**. With P&O Ferries people get **flexibility to have more adventurous holidays**. The brand also has a sister logistics company P&O Ferrymasters.

Market

P&O Ferries operates eight main routes between Britain, France, Northern Ireland, Republic of Ireland, the Netherlands and Belgium. Its core audience are car passengers, though it also services freight, coach and foot passengers. The ferry market is complex, with varying passenger and competitor profiles.

Across the English Channel, P&O Ferries runs up to 46 sailings a day between Dover and Calais.

On the Irish Sea, P&O Ferries operates the fastest and shortest crossing, running between Cairnryan and Larne. Here it helps those travelling to see friends and family, students, or business people.

On the North Sea, it operates a daily overnight sailing from Hull to either Zeebrugge or Rotterdam as well as minicruises.

Outbound, it takes many British passengers to Europe for their holidays. Inbound, it brings many EU passengers to Britain for holidays, especially from France, Germany and the Netherlands.

DID YOU KNOW?

In an **average week** a P&O ferry will travel **the length of a football pitch 25,000** times.

Across all its routes, P&O Ferries competes with other ferry companies, train operators and airlines. However, it has the highest brand awareness scores in the UK ferry market. The English Channel is its busiest route and on it P&O Ferries has a 60% share of all ferry passengers.

Product

P&O has been around for over 180 years, but the ferry side of the business began in the 1960s, when it pioneered this mode of travel.

In 2006, P&O Ferries was acquired by Dubai based DP World. With new leadership the innovative spirit has continued, driven by the brand's customer-centric ethos – to 'Recognise and Respond'. P&O Ferries strives to be more than a means-to-an-end travel option by bringing freedom, flexibility and choice to each passenger.

P&O Ferries offers a full range of tickets, including a Standard Flexi, which allows customers to sail on any crossing up to four hours earlier or later than originally booked, at no extra cost.

Its onboard experience has something for everyone. From complimentary champagne in the Club Lounge to delicious meals in the Brasserie Restaurant, Starbucks coffee on the sundeck to cocktails in the live jazz Sunset Bar.

P&O Ferries has an award-winning website that helps customers book tickets, add accommodation and research destinations.

Achievements

Along with being nominated as a Consumer Superbrand for the last six years, P&O Ferries is very proud to have held Best Ferry Operator

for the last 10 years running, from the respected and prestigious British Travel Awards. P&O Ferries also currently holds Best Ferry Booking Website and Best Ferry Minicruise Operator, both of which the brand has won year-on-year since the awards introduced these categories. In 2018, P&O Ferries was also delighted to again secure the public vote for Favourite Ferry Company and was also awarded Best Ferry Company, at the 2018 Globe Travel Awards.

DID YOU KNOW?

P&O Ferries has worked with the Magical Taxi Tour for the last 24 years, taking over 4,000 children with life-threatening illnesses to Disneyland.

Recent Developments

Since 2014, P&O Ferries has been developing a brand platform, brought to life with a new vibrant look and feel. It focuses on promoting adventurous and flexible holidays via a relaxing and personalised travel experience.

P&O Ferries' new identity has modernised the brand, injecting colour, charm and energy. It has delivered a much-needed thread that runs across all brand activity, increasing its emotional appeal, visibility and branded attribution.

P&O Ferries has also aligned more closely with the main holiday decision-making process in December and January to get ferry-enabled holidays on the consideration list, widening the pool of prospects. The brand has been working in partnership with tourist boards, especially Visit Britain, to inspire audiences to explore the UK and also began developing product propositions across customer journeys in order to have a wider role in its customers' lives, including travel money and insurance.

Promotion

To achieve the brand focus of attracting new audiences, P&O Ferries has tapped into the insight that many people today aspire to be 'travellers', not just holidaymakers. The brand uses this insight

to showcase the authentic, adventurous and active trips that P&O Ferries enables through the freedom of taking a car on holiday.

The brand has drawn inspiration from children's pop-up books, creating a 'paper world of adventure' that has proved highly effective across numerous channels. In 2017, the brand focused its messaging on older couples.

P&O Ferries reached out to 'empty nesters', by animating an emotional journey in which a typical couple break free from their dull monochrome world – by taking a holiday that starts with a P&O ferry journey. Once abroad, the couple's world transforms into one of vibrant colour, as they rediscover wonderful places and reconnect with each other.

The idea that P&O Ferries helps put the colour back into people's lives was further enhanced by using a catchy remix of a track drawn straight from the soundtrack of their youth – Joe Jackson's, Steppin' Out.

Brand Values

P&O Ferries aims to put the excitement back into travel. It does this by inspiring people to enjoy the freedom of an independent, car-based holiday and creating a more flexible and relaxing travel experience. The result? P&O Ferries is uplifting, optimistic and charming in tone, and its brand values are Inspirational, Insightful, Trustworthy, Reliable, Simple and Direct.

Since opening the **first PizzaExpress restaurant in London's Soho in 1965**, **great food, evocative music, and distinctive design** have remained at the heart of the brand's DNA. This is one recipe that has never changed, and the brand still promises '**good food and good times**' for millions of customers every year.

Market

PizzaExpress was the pioneer of a now £5.7bn (Source: MCA Restaurant Market Report) branded restaurant market in the UK and has changed the way we dine out in the UK and in Ireland (under the Milano brand). This market is set for continued growth against a backdrop of sector wide pressures including business rates, pay rates and food inflation.

Product

Not resting on its laurels, PizzaExpress continues to innovate and evolve its menu in line with consumers' ever-evolving needs, tastes and dietary demands, paying particular attention to customer feedback and ideas shared through its restaurant teams, direct from customers and through social channels. A vegan mozzarella alternative was launched in June 2017, responding to the growing trend in customers opting for vegan lifestyles and is available for customers to swap out the mozzarella used across the menu.

The iconic Dough Balls continually prove to be a true crowd pleaser for diners, and the now annual return of the Snow Ball Dough Balls onto the menu over Christmas has furthered their popularity. The addition of the Leggera range has provided increased choice for consumers looking for a lighter option, while the Pollo Ad Astra has been voted by customers as their favourite pizza.

PizzaExpress' extension in to the Grocery channel has delivered increasing share of the total pizza market, complemented by a range that includes branded dressings and those infamous Dough Balls.

DID YOU KNOW?

In both 2015 and 2016, the **PizzaExpress Jazz Club** was named '**Venue of the Year**' in the London Lifestyle Awards.

Achievements

Attracting a diverse audience across a range of occasions, from family dining, first dates and providing for those on special diets, PizzaExpress has received wide ranging recognition.

It regularly wins 'gold' awards from Mumsnet for being 'family friendly', with its extensive children's menu and welcoming approach to families.

In 2014 PizzaExpress won 'best restaurant chain' in the Free-From Eating Out awards, reflecting its commitment to meeting special dietary requirements, and offers a range of gluten free products across the menu from its pizza bases

and Dough Balls to gluten free beer, all certified by Coeliac UK. In the same year, Men's Health voted it 'the best place to go on a date'.

It has also been recognised by the Good Housekeeping Institute as the UK's 'favourite high street restaurant', and by Which? magazine for being the 'healthiest and tastiest pizza on the high street'. Furthermore, the Leggera range has received praise ranging from Marketing Week to Rosemary Conley.

PizzaExpress has won marketing awards for its innovative use of technology as well as its entertainment venues, its work with schools and 'good cause' related activities.

Its chatbot won The Caterer's 'Best Use of Technology' award in 2017 and enables customers to book through Facebook Messenger as well as play games and win prizes. The PizzaExpress Live 'diner-tainment' brand won London Lifestyle Awards 'Hall of Fame' award for outstanding contribution to lifestyle in the city of London for the third year in a row.

The brand is currently working in partnership with Macmillan Cancer Support, with one simple goal: to bring people together so that no-one faces cancer alone and has raised over £500,000 over the last 18 months through sales of their

Brand History

1950s Peter Boizot travels through Europe, eventually arriving in Rome where he works as a reporter for the Associated Press and selling postcards from a barrow in St. Peter's Square.

1965 On his return to the UK, Peter is shocked to discover that, unlike in Italy, great tasting pizza is nowhere to be found. This gave him the idea of bringing the spirit and taste of an Italian pizzeria to England.

1965 The first PizzaExpress opens its doors in London's Soho for what is, at this time, a radical venture.

1967 Renowned Italian designer Enzo Apicella joins forces with Peter to open a second restaurant on Coptic Street, in London's Bloomsbury. He then goes on to design 85 PizzaExpress restaurants.

1969 Embracing his passion for jazz, PizzaExpress Jazz Club in Dean Street, Soho opens. t goes on to host a wealth to talent from Van Morrison and Tony Bennett, to Amy Winehouse, Norah Jones and Ed Sheeran.

2009 The Leggera range of lower-calorie pizzas is introduced in UK restaurants.

2011 The PizzaExpress Snowball Dough Balls make an appearance on the menu for the first time.

2014 PizzaExpress wins 'best restaurant chain' in the Free-From Eating Out awards, reflecting its commitment to special dietary requirements.

2017 The brand now has more than 500 restaurants in 13 countries around the world.

Padana Pizza and team members taking on their own personal challenges, including everything from a 10km run to a five peaks trail.

Promotion

PizzaExpress believes in simplicity and creativity as the recipe for remaining relevant for millions of customers after over 53 years and sets high standards for itself in continually innovating to improve its customers' experiences within and beyond the four walls of its restaurants.

Its marketing mix broadly consists of its physical presence on the high street, a well-developed partnership strategy, as well as building advocacy through a sizeable database of fans, its network of 10,000 plus employees and through thoughtful social based content, based on human truths. PizzaExpress is the single biggest restaurant brand in the UK with a growing international presence in over 13 countries. Its focus on simplicity is an important aspect of ensuring customers can enjoy their favourite pizza wherever they are, adding credibility and authenticity to its brand in the eyes of consumers.

Experiential activities have included PizzaExpress Boxed at Barclaycard British Summertime festival in Hyde Park, ensuring music lovers did not go without their favourite PizzaExpress pizza, and sponsorship of the Live Jazz stage at the Henley Festival. The PizzaExpress Live brand has played host to such talents as Gregory Porter, Amy Winehouse, Brian May, Will Young and Morcheeba as well as, more recently, an array of comedy acts and intimate 'audience with' events including Guy Chambers, Michael Palin and football stars such as Paul Merson.

Brand Values

PizzaExpress still works to its founding principles of providing 'great food, evocative music, and distinctive design'. It aims to be an inclusive brand, welcoming a cross section of the population, from those on special diets, families with children to city dwellers needing some 'me time'.

'People first' is the keystone of the brand's philosophy and pride is taken in offering a high standard of hospitality to create unforgettable experiences, in all of the brand's restaurants, from London's Soho to the heart of Mumbai, the vibrancy of Hong Kong to the cultural district of Beijing or the glitz and glamour of Dubai.

Polypipe

Polypipe is one of **Europe's largest manufacturers of piping, water management solutions,** underfloor heating and energy-efficient ventilation, developing and manufacturing products that enable **solutions for a sustainable and resilient built environment.**

Soakaway solution for Jebel Ali Hills, Dubai

DID YOU KNOW?

Polypipe has a **wide range of water management solutions** to make space for water, for **projects around the world.**

With its leading edge design expertise, innovative technology, detailed understanding within its sectors and products backed by industry standard accreditations, Polypipe is able to provide systems that are engineered to perform – meeting the industry challenges of today and for the future.

Achievements

Polypipe's people are its most valuable assets and as it continues to grow and the industry adapts to the challenges of progress, so too does its investment in people. Perhaps that is why its Nuaire division won Employer of the month for Januay 2017 with Educ8. Polypipe also received an apprentice award from the Engineering Employees Federation (EEF)

Interactive House

Polypipe's polymer recycling and processing plant at Horncastle

Market

Having built its business around the residential, commercial, civils and infrastructure markets, Polypipe has a detailed understanding of the applications in which its systems are used – including the activities of the New Build and Repair, Maintenance and Improvement (RMI) sub-sectors.

Product

With over 24,000 product lines, a fleet of over 400 vehicles and over 3,000 employees, Polypipe has the capability to design, manufacture and deliver a wide range of innovative systems including above and below ground drainage, plumbing and rainwater systems, cable protection, water management and climate solutions including energy-efficient ventilation and underfloor heating systems. As plastic solutions are lighter in weight, its products are well-placed to compete with traditional materials such as concrete, clay and copper.

and has the FORS Silver Driver's Award for best practice for commercial vehicle operators – covering safety, efficiency and environmental protection. Furthermore, investing heavily in the right technology and people to develop its own recycling and processing plant, it has been able to recycle 17,500 tonnes of plastic waste. With complete control of all material that passes through, Polypipe guarantees only the highest grade recycled material is used where appropriate. By utilising recycled material in this way provides consistency in supply – both in quality and structure. Very little, if anything, goes to waste; Polypipe reuses any wastage during the recycling process, for example, and it has even adopted a scrap reduction programme to minimise materials.

Recent Developments

Polypipe has always been a company of innovators, problem solvers and solution providers, which is why it continues to invest in new manufacturing technology at its factories

DID YOU KNOW?

Polypipe Systems enable solutions for a **sustainable and resilient** built environment.

in Horncastle. At Loughborough, its team of Apprentices have designed and manufactured a brand new RXL Tanks and Chambers display area – and, although slightly avant garde, it has supplied RXL pipes to Paris – for a 'live' art installation at La Place Vendôme. The launch of its new boiler and SMART control manifold for its underfloor heating range provides an additional heating source to complement existing heating boilers so underfloor heating can be installed as a further heating solution. Its new double-skinned below ground drainage pipe enables recycled material to be used where appropriate. Polypipe has seen large growth in its fabricated soil stacks, engineered off-site, providing minimal disruption on-site.

Promotion

By working with its customers and understanding the key market sectors, Polypipe strives to deliver campaigns that highlight its innovation and technical advances with concepts and messaging that 'speaks their language'. Polypipe launched its 'Below Ground Drainage' campaign – a 'One' concept that used 3D images of products used by the residential as well as civils and infrastructure sectors, to create a concept message of 'One Range, Endless Solutions'. Through further developing its 'SMART Controls' campaign, Polypipe brought its concept to life in a scale model 'House'. The interactive house featured at national exhibitions and shopping centres such as The Trafford Centre in Manchester.

Throughout its history, Polypipe has been at the forefront of surface water drainage innovation. With perpetual change in climate and urbanisation, it has been pushing its customer-focused research to develop water management products and systems that make space for water to include important Green Infrastructure. Polypipe will be launching its new innovation in 2018 to help towards making its urban environments – and the people who live in them – more resilient.

Brand Values

Polypipe understands the challenges the industry faces and it grows and innovates with it, moving forward to meet those challenges. It understands its specific needs and provides solutions to satisfy key market drivers. Trust. Support. Experience. Innovation. Polypipe views these not simply as words but as a philosophy and it aims to stand by this thinking throughout each and every project that it undertakes – enabling it to maintain the market-leading position for creating surface water drainage technology and sustainable products that are intelligently engineered for a more resilient future for all.

Ridgistorm-XL for a Scottish hydroelectricity project

Brand History

1980	Polypipe is formed in Doncaster.
1988	A full range of plastic drainage products for the residential construction market launches.
1996	Polypipe moves into mainland European construction market manufacturing.
1997	Entry into the civils and infrastructure market takes place.
1998	Plastic hot-and-cold-water plumbing and heating systems are launched.
2000	Polypipe's underfloor heating range is launched and Polypipe enters the Italian market.
2004	A new range of SuDS products and solutions are launched.
2007	Polypipe Water Management Solutions team is launched.
2007	Entry into Commercial market takes place.
2007	Polypipe Gulf is formed.
2008	Ridgistorm-XL large-scale engineered pipe system is launched.
2012	Carbon-Efficient Solutions is launched.
2013	PolyMax is launched adding to the UK's largest range of plastic plumbing systems.
2014	Polypipe is admitted to the London Stock Exchange.
2015	Polypipe Underfloor Heating makes its TV debut.
2015	The acquisition of Nuaire Ventilation business takes place.
2016	A Middle East Training facility is launched.
2017	A new continuous corregator and factory unit is launched.

Fed up with all the processed food on the market, **Julian Metcalfe and Sinclair Beecham** started Pret A Manger to make the food that they craved but couldn't find – handmade, using fresh ingredients. Thirty years on, Pret has **over 500 shops in six countries,** serving more than 435,000 customers every day.

Market

The UK Eating Out market was expected to grow by 1.7% in 2017, reflecting lower growth than recent years due to uncertainty around Britain's departure from the EU and weaker consumer demand resulting from price inflation. The UK Food to Go market segment was, however, expected to outperform the overall Eating Out market with anticipated growth of 3.8% (Source: MCA Food to Go, 2017). A key consumer trend of 2016 was 'healthier eating' (Source: MCA Eating Out Report, 2016) along with increasing prevalence of low meat diets (7% to 10% over the last five years) across all age groups and increasing veganism in the 18-34 years age category (2% to 5%). These are trends that Pret is well placed to respond to with its fresh food and product innovation.

Product

Pret is committed to serving handmade food and organic coffee. It continues to adapt its menu to meet an ever growing demand for healthy

options. In 2017, Pret launched several dairy-free products to engage with the growing numbers of customers who do not eat or drink dairy. A new Coconut Porridge recipe delivered 11.3% sales growth across the porridge category. Two new dairy-free desserts included the Chocolate Chia Pot and Mango Chia Pot – the latter selling 50% more than Pret's previous best selling dessert, its Chocolate 'Moose'. In the hot drinks category, Pret introduced a rice-coconut milk alternative which drove total coffee and hot chocolate sales from 10.8% to 14.5% year on year.

DID YOU KNOW?

Pret's **most popular** product worldwide is the **croissant** – it is the best seller in the UK, US, France and China, with **more than 16 million** purchased each year.

Indeed, coffee remains an important area of growth for Pret, selling 1.7 million cups a week globally. Pret staff also handed out over one million free hot drinks last year as part of the company's alternative loyalty scheme, which is based on the concept of 'random acts of kindness'.

Achievements

The Pret Foundation Trust was established to help alleviate homelessness in the UK. Thanks to the donation of 10p from every soup sold, 50p from the sale of every Christmas sandwich and baguette, plus donations collected in each shop's charity box, the Pret Foundation Trust is able to support local, grassroot charities with financial support. Through its fleet of charity vans and volunteer collections, Pret's unsold food is delivered to shelters and hostels across the UK every

night. The Pret Foundation Trust also runs the Rising Stars scheme to help get people from homeless backgrounds back into full-time, paid employment. Since it started, the scheme has helped support and train more than 350 people.

In 2017, Pret's London Heathrow T5 shop was the global winner for the Airport Food To Go Offer of the Year at the FAB Awards.

Recent Developments

Having opened its first vegetarian-only shop in 2016, Pret continued its commitment to vegetarian and vegan recipes with its second and third Veggie Pret shops, both located in London. It also ran a nationwide campaign, Not Just for Veggies, which saw green fridges installed in each shop to highlight the vegetarian and vegan menu.

The importance of sustainability within the wider market continues to increase. In 2016, to help encourage a reduction in the number of paper cups

Brand History

1986 Pret is founded by entrepreneurs Julian Metcalfe and Sinclair Beecham. The first shop, 75B Victoria Street, serves more than 7,000 customers per week in its first year.

1995 Pret sets up the Pret Foundation Trust which goes on to distribute millions of unsold sandwiches every year to people on the streets and gives countless donations to help homeless charities and shelters.

2000 Pret opens its first international shop on Broad Street, New York City.

2001 McDonald's buys a minority stake in Pret, although it has no direct influence over what is sold or how.

2008 Bridgepoint, a European private equity firm, acquired a major share in Pret, bringing an end to its relationship with McDonald's.

2014 Having had a successful business in Hong Kong for 15 years, Pret opens in Shanghai, China.

2016 Pret becomes the first ever major food retailer to open a vegetarian only shop in London.

2017 Pret reaches a milestone by opening in Cheltenham, its 350th shop in the UK.

2017 Pret launches its new mobile app in the US.

it used, Pret trialled an initiative that offered customers a 25p discount if they used a reusable cup. The trial proved a success and in 2017 the offer was rolled out to all of the UK shops. Continuing the desire to reduce the amount of packaging, Pret has also begun a trial of selling reusable water bottles. Started in its Veggie Pret shops, it has now launched in the Manchester area along with in-shop water taps that all customers can use free of charge.

In 2017, Pret launched a new app in the US. Designed to provide customers with a quick and simple payment solution, the app also offers a customisable menu based on dietary preferences. Within six weeks of launch, the app had reached over 50,000 downloads and provides Pret with a further channel to engage and communicate with its customers.

Promotion

Pret's philosophy is to communicate with its customers without the aid of traditional marketing budgets. It doesn't use mass media and direct marketing, instead focusing on investing in its staff

59% OF SALES NOW FALL OUTSIDE OF LUNCHTIME

As eating habits shift to healthy snacking and more meals being eaten out of the home.

and the quality of its food, and using relevant communication channels that allow for quality engagement with customers. Importantly, this engagement is utilised to encourage a genuine conversation with customers, listening to feedback and acting upon it, as highlighted by the inception of the first Veggie Pret in 2016. Furthermore, the shops and packaging are used as channels through which the brand – known for its use of humorous and quirky images of food – is promoted.

Brand Values

Pret's success relies on the pride its staff have in their work, a culture fostered from within. The egalitarian hands-on approach filters down from the CEO to shop assistants and emphasises the importance Pret places on training and retaining good staff. The brand personality is underpinned by its core values – a passion for food, a passion for people and a commitment to doing the right thing within the communities in which it operates.

Ryman

2018 marks 125 years since the opening of the first Ryman store
on Great Portland Street, London, by Henry Ryman. Famous for customer service,
Ryman is the leading stationery specialist on the high street, offering an extensive range,
expertise and value for money via its chain of stores and website.

Market

Since opening in 1893, Ryman has had a longstanding history of product innovation and customer service. The epitome of 'multi-channel', Ryman combines a strong high street presence with a website offering an extended range of products.

Ryman's core product range and multi-channel approach is further enhanced by in-store services such as DHL (international courier service), Western Union (international money transfer service) and a variety of other services including photocopying, printing, design, binding and, more recently, personalisation of products such as notebooks and pens. Underpinned by Ryman's values, these additional services allow Ryman to be innovative whilst ensuring that it is meeting the ever-changing needs of its individual customers as well as businesses.

Indeed, Ryman recognised that businesses, of all sizes, represent a significant percentage of its customer base and has tailored an offer to suit their needs. Small businesses have access to an in-store and online discount card as well as an enhanced range of products, designed to suit their business needs. Larger businesses, benefit

from this range as well as a personally managed credit account with free next day delivery and a bespoke price list.

The Ryman Business segment has grown significantly leading to further range diversification, allowing Ryman to offer a full service solution including cleaning products and refreshments as well as office furniture, bulk deals on paper and large format print.

Striving to develop existing business support services, 2016 saw Ryman build on the success of its Business Accounts by making inroads into the education sector with the introduction of Ryman Education, giving schools, colleges and universities access to an enhanced range of stationery products with credit facilities and discounts for bulk orders.

RYMAN SELLS 7.8 MILLION ML OF PRINTER INK PER YEAR ENOUGH TO FILL 10,400 WINE BOTTLES

In 2017, Ryman further enhanced its business and education offering with the launch of a new dedicated business website, which focuses on products and services relevant to the business and education sectors. This has been complimented by the publication of a new Ryman education catalogue.

The breadth of Ryman's range and the wide appeal of stationery and office supplies means that Ryman has a significant, and growing, number of competitors, ranging from 'traditional' stationery retailers to emerging fashion stationery retailers, to supermarkets and discounters who have broadened their range to include stationery supplies. There are also a number of business

focused stationery and office supplies operations that Ryman compete with. Despite this competitive landscape, Ryman continues to be successful in growing its market share.

Product

Ryman sells a comprehensive range of stationery and office supplies, ranging from writing equipment, paper and filing solutions to printers and ink to office furniture and tech products, including large capacity hard drives and accessories for smart devices.

A range of business support services are offered both in-store and from its Retail Support Centre in Crewe. These services include product personalisation, print, design support, DHL and Western Union money transfer service.

Working with all of the best known brands in the stationery and office supplies sector including HP, Epson, STAEDTLER and Newell, Ryman has more recently introduced premium brands to the range, such as Moleskine and Leuchtturm.

In addition, Ryman has a large own label range across many of its categories, that is well renowned for its high quality and value for money. This reputation has led to strong sales growth in own label products which now represent a significant percentage of Ryman's overall sales.

Brand History

1893 Henry J Ryman opens his first store on Great Portland Street, London.

1970s The family business is sold. Over the next 20 years its owners include Burton Group, Terence Conran, Jennifer d'Abo and Pentos.

1995 Ryman is acquired by Chancerealm Ltd (later known as Ryman Group Ltd), in which Theo Paphitis is the controlling shareholder.

2001 Ryman acquires Partners the Stationers, comprising 86 stores.

2007 Ryman acquires 61 Stationery Box stores, which are rebranded to Ryman by October 2008.

2009 Ryman partners with Red Nose Day, raising more than £500,000 for Comic Relief through colleague fundraising and the sale of exclusive product.

2014 Ryman becomes headline sponsors of the National Enterprise Challenge, a challenge designed to help children to leave school 'work ready'.

2016 Ryman acquires London Graphic Centre.

2017 Ryman launches its new 'business' specific website enabling business and education account customers to shop online.

Achievements

2017 marked nine years of Ryman's partnership with Comic Relief. Each year Ryman Colleagues raise money by selling the Official Comic Relief pen as well as taking part in fancy dress days and other activities to raise more than £4m for the charity.

As in previous years, supporting charities and education initiatives remains a focus area for Ryman. It continues to support The Ryman National Enterprise challenge for a further year and will be once again supporting Comic Relief in 2019.

Recent Developments

2016 saw Ryman acquire the iconic London Graphic Centre, the 7,000 sq ft Covent Garden store, which is widely regarded as a stand out destination in the world of arts and graphics.

December 2017 saw the launch of Ryman's new Business website, which allows business customers to reap the benefits of their credit account and discounts online whilst also being presented with a product set that is representative of their order history.

2017 was also an important year for the Ryman Print Service Team, with print solutions being extended to all in-store customers as well as the addition of a personalisation service, enabling customers to order personalised notebooks, gift wrap and canvases as gifts. 2018 is going to see further development for this team with the introduction of 'web to print' which is expected in the first quarter of the year.

Promotion

Ryman has a strong promotional programme, which offers customers deals on branded and own label products throughout the year. The offer is targeted locally so offers are most relevant to the market served by an individual store's location and demographics, from inner city to market town to University campuses. In addition, Ryman offers further discounts to higher education students.

Charity fundraising and supporting education initiatives has, and will continue to be, a central part of Ryman's culture. Supporting the likes of Comic Relief, Sport Relief and Royal Manchester Children's Hospital 'Many Hands' business initiative as well as sponsoring the Ryman National Enterprise Challenge, encouraging young people to be work ready.

Brand Values

Ryman is synonymous with quality, value and reliability. Famous for customer service, Ryman is the market-leading stationery specialist on the high street, offering expertise and value for money via online and its nationwide chain of stores.

These core values are further underpinned by Ryman's reputation for investing in, and supporting, its people as well as its continued support of both charitable and education initiatives.

From its beginnings, **128 years ago** in Manila, San Miguel has spread its **optimistic and adventurous spirit** worldwide and has become a truly global brand. It is the **second largest world beer brand in the UK** and sells the equivalent to over **176 million pints to UK consumers each year**.

Market

San Miguel is part of the World Beer segment of the beer market alongside other key players Peroni, Corona, Heineken, Birra Moretti and Estrella Damm. San Miguel holds 19% of the volume share of the Total World Beer category, which makes it the number one Spanish World Beer and the number two World Beer overall in the UK (Sources: CGA OPM, Nielsen Scantrack,

data to 04/12/2017, Total Brand Level). San Miguel is part of an elite club of only eight beer brands in the UK, selling over one million hectolitres per year, since 2016 (Source: Internal sales data and CGA OPMS Data to 04/11/2017, Nielsen Scantrack).

Product

San Miguel is a premium world lager available in draught and packaged formats. The brand's portfolio also includes an alcohol-free variant, San Miguel 0,0% as well as a gluten free offering, San Miguel Gluten Free, which has been available in the UK since September 2017.

San Miguel is brewed using a special mashing process, which gives the beer a fuller and slightly sweeter flavour. The unique recipe and San Miguel's yeast then come together to deliver a refreshing, full-bodied beer. San Miguel is a pilsner style lager, with a rich golden colour and a characteristically generous white creamy head.

Achievements

In 2017, the distinctive San Miguel taste was recognised when it won 'best alcoholic drink' in the Sainsbury's magazine Food & Drink Awards. It also received the Best Newsbrand Campaign for the San Miguel Rich List at the Newswork Planning Awards for showing what jury member, Zaid Al-Qassab described as, "meticulous planning, real collaboration and clear and meaningful metrics".

Recent Developments

In addition to the development of its Rich List campaign, San Miguel extended its UK portfolio in 2017. In September it launched San Miguel Gluten Free, with a view to appeal to more people on more occasions as well as responding to health and wellbeing consumer trends. Mintel research has found that many UK consumers are drinking less alcohol so expect more out of the times that they do. In line with the continued trend of premiumisation, in April 2018, San Miguel will further extend its portfolio and launch San Miguel Selecta.

This super-premium 6.2% variant is brewed with a selection of three malts, three hops and matured in cellars, ideal for consumers who are looking to treat and indulge themselves.

Promotion

San Miguel's advertising has been built around the key insight that consumers, particularly millennials, are increasingly more likely to value experiences over material possessions (Source: Goldman Sachs,

Brand History

1889 The renowned businessman, Don Enrique María Barretto de Ycaza y Esteban, applies for a royal grant from Spain to establish a brewery in the Philippines.

1890 The brand is founded in Manila, with the help of Germany's top master brewer. On the feat day of San Miguel, in the district of San Miguel, they inaugurate the first brewery in South East Asia.

1903 A brewery is established in Hong Kong.

1930 San Miguel is launched in the US.

1957 San Miguel returns to Spain.

1965 San Miguel launches in Africa.

1967 The brand first appears in the UK.

2001 San Miguel launches its 0.0% beer in Spain.

2015 San Miguel 0,0% is launched in the UK.

2016 The San Miguel Rich List is launched.

2017 San Miguel Gluten Free is launched in the UK.

2018 San Miguel launches San Miguel Selecta in the UK.

Millennial Research). According to ZenithOptimedia Millennial Research, this contrasts with the parents of millennials, who were more inclined at this age to equate material wealth with happiness.

These findings led to the creation of The San Miguel Rich List, a list featuring people who have lived rich lives and share the brand's values. As an international premium brand, San Miguel's belief is that experiences are 'the new riches' and its communications reflect the view that true wealth is found in experiences rather than material possessions. It sees its beer

as a p oduct of the brand's own rich experiences and its journey around the globe. This is why San Miguel celebrates those who have the same thirst for adventure and exploration; who pursue richer ife experiences, above all else.

Members of the San Miguel Rich List are selected based on four different categories – trailblazers, legacy makers, artisans, and collectives – reflecting the brand's history and values. By sharing the amazing stories of these people, San Miguel wants to inspire consumers to get the most out of life and encourage them

to have more experiences themselves, whether this means going on an incredible journey or simply enjoying a San Miguel beer in a great setting with friends.

Brand Values

San Miguel aims to be welcoming, genuine and playful, celebrating and enabling those with an optimistic and adventurous spirit to experience more of what life has to offer, inspiring and enabling people to have 'richer experiences'.

the Luxury Included® holiday

By offering **luxury, innovation and choice**, Sandals and Beaches Resorts have been at the **forefront of the Caribbean all-inclusive travel sector for 36 years**. In an industry brimming with new contenders, the **combined knowledge and experience** of Sandals' management team and resort staff has maintained its **market-leading position**.

Market

In recent years the concept of luxury travel has steered away from conservative, off-the-shelf five-star packages towards tailor-made holidays. Sandals Resorts sets itself apart by placing an emphasis on personal choice, always aiming to offer more for the price of the holiday.

Sandals Resorts' prices include 5-Star Global Gourmet™ specialty restaurants, premium brand drinks, tips and taxes, in addition to land and water sports such as golf and complimentary scuba diving*. There are 16 Sandals resorts created exclusively for 'two people in love' located in Jamaica, Saint Lucia, Antigua, the Bahamas, Grenada and Barbados. Its sister brand, Beaches Resorts, currently comprises three resorts in Jamaica and Turks & Caicos. Beaches Resorts caters for families, groups, couples and singles.

*price includes two dives per day for certified divers

Product

In March 2017, Sandals Resorts launched 12 Over-the-Water Honeymoon Butler Bungalows and five Over-the-Water Villas at Sandals Royal Caribbean Spa Resort & Offshore Island in Jamaica. This was followed by the opening of nine Over-The-Water Honeymoon Butler Bungalows at Sandals Grande St. Lucian, Saint Lucia in May 2017. These lavish bungalows are the first of their kind in the Caribbean and feature an over-water hammock for two, expansive sundeck, Tranquility Soaking Tub™ and glass floor panels that provide views of the marine life below. The Tahiti-style private villas are larger than the bungalows and feature an infinity pool and two outdoor showers, amongst other high-end, luxury features.

Sandals recently unveiled the first Over-the-Water wedding chapels in the Caribbean. Both Sandals South Coast in Jamaica and Sandals Grande St. Lucian in Saint Lucia feature Over-The-Water Serenity Wedding Chapels complete with 360-degree, panoramic water views with a glass aisle bottom.

DID YOU KNOW?

Sandals Resorts is home to **38 Over-the-Water Suites**, with 17 at **Sandals Royal Caribbean**, 12 at **Sandals South Coast** and nine at **Sandals Grande St. Lucian.**

The award-winning Sandals Whitehouse European Village & Spa was relaunched as Sandals South Coast in Jamaica in 2016. Recent renovations include a dedicated Over-the-Water bar, Latitudes°, with hammocks suspended above the Caribbean Sea; a new Italian Village comprising 112 ocean-facing rooms and suites as well as new 5-Star Global Gourmet™ dining options such as Sushi on The Sand, Jerk Shack (an open-air seating restaurant serving authentic jerk dishes) and Schooner's (a restaurant which serves Caribbean fare).

Achievements

In 2017, Sandals received an array of Travel Trade awards including Hotel & Resort Operator of the Year at the TTG Travel Awards (for the ninth consecutive year) as well as a Selling Travel Agents Choice Award. The Luxury Included® resort company also won 11 awards, as voted for by consumers at the World Travel Awards. For the 22nd consecutive year, Sandals Resorts was recognised as the Caribbean's Leading Hotel Brand, demonstrating its continued commitment to the excellence of the brand and its resorts.

Sandals Resorts International has a philanthropic arm, The Sandals Foundation. Since its inception in 2009, it has aimed to unite the region with one common goal: to elevate its people and protect its delicate ecosystem under the pillars of community, education, and the environment. Eight years later, the Sandals Foundation has implemented projects and programmes worth over $28m including training over 1,100 teachers and impacting more than 227,000 people through healthcare initiatives.

Recent Developments

Sandals Resorts welcomed its second Luxury Included® resort to Barbados in December 2017, just in time for the winter season. Sandals Royal Barbados offers 222 concierge and butler-level suites as well as being home to a number of Sandals firsts. A four-lane bowling alley, a men's barbershop and an exclusive rooftop infinity pool, complete with the French restaurant, La Parisienne and poolside bar, are a selection of the innovations that are debuting at the new Sandals Royal

Barbados resort. Rooms include Sandals' signature Rondovals, Millionaire Butler Suites and Skypool Suites, along with an extensive Crystal Lagoon Pool Complex including Swim-Up Suites. For guests in select top category suites, Sandals Royal Barbados offers chauffeured Rolls-Royce airport transfers.

Following a series of Over-the-Water additions at Sandals Resorts, the recently renamed Sandals South Coast resort opened 12 Over-the-Water bungalows in December 2017. These offer luxuries such as an expansive patio with a Tranquility Soaking Tub™, a hammock for two that sits above the water and an outdoor

THERE ARE AS MANY AS 21 DIFFERENT CUISINES FROM AROUND THE WORLD AT EACH SANDALS RESORT

shower. The interior boasts 'sea-through' glass floors, a king-size bed, and a spacious, spa-style bathroom. Guests can also benefit from personalised butler services and 24-hour room service.

Beaches Turks & Caicos was also re-opened in December 2017, post Hurricane Irma. New additions include a new Sky Rooftop Restaurant, combining fine dining with spectacular views of Grace Bay; and Bombay, offering the finest authentic Indian cuisine. This brings the total number of restaurants at Beaches Turks & Caicos to 21.

In 2016, Sandals and Beaches Resorts opened a £1.5m dedicated retail store in Chelsea, London. The 5,000 sq ft interactive store further cements Sandals' status as industry leader and innovator, as the first overseas hotel brand to have a stand-alone high street outlet in the UK. The Sandals store has hosted an array of events with media partners in 2017.

Promotion

Sandals Resorts' advertising campaigns support the efforts of travel agents and tour operators to market the Sandals Resorts and Beaches Resorts brands. Sandals' visual brand identity is evolving to suit global markets, in particular the expansion into Europe, ensuring the brand is more sophisticated and lifestyle-focused. Sandals Resorts and Beaches Resorts operate a sophisticated customer relationship management programme, which includes a loyalty scheme, Sandals Select. The Sandals Select Rewards Programme has recently launched six new tiers each offering a range of superb offers, new pre-travel items and a simplified enrolment process.

Brand Values

Sandals continues to build on its strong position in the Caribbean hotel industry with innovations such as the Luxury Included® concept.

Brand History

1981 Sandals Montego Bay, the flagship resort, opens.

1985 Sandals Inn opens in Montego Bay.

1986 Sandals Royal Caribbean opens becoming the only resort in Jamaica with a private island.

1989 Sandals Ochi makes its debut in 'Butch' Stewart's hometown.

1991 Sandals Grande Antigua – the first destination outside of Jamaica to have a Sandals presence – opens.

1994 Sandals Halcyon in Castries, Saint Lucia opens.

1996 Sandals Royal Bahamian opens in Nassau, Bahamas.

1997 Sandals introduces its first family resort in Jamaica, as Beaches Negril opens its doors. Beaches Turks & Caicos opens in Providenciales, becoming the second family resort.

2002 Both Sandals Grande St. Lucian, Saint Lucia and Beaches Ocho Rios, Jamaica open.

2005 Sandals South Coast, Jamaica opens.

2008 Grand Pineapple Beach Resort opens in Negril, Jamaica.

2009 The Sandals Foundation is announced.

2010 Sandals Emerald Bay, Great Exuma, Bahamas opens.

2013 Sandals LaSource Grenada opens and Sandals Barbados is acquired.

2015 Sandals Barbados opens following an extensive renovation project.

2016 Sandals opens its first ever dedicated high street retail experience, Sandals Luxury Travel Store, in Chelsea, London.

2017 Sandals Royal Barbados opens.

Savills is a **global real estate services provider with an international network of more than 700 offices** and associates throughout the UK and continental Europe, the Americas, Asia Pacific, Africa and the Middle East. Its **32,000-strong workforce combines entrepreneurial spirit and a deep understanding of specialist property sectors** with high standards of client care.

Savills also returned to The Times Top 100 Graduate Employers list in 2017, rising 11 places to 83rd. The firm continues to be the only real estate agent to make the list, which ranks UK businesses across all sectors and geographies.

Savills won the coveted 'Residential Adviser of the Year' for a second consecutive year at the 2017 Estates Gazette Awards and at the Property Week Awards 2017, the team was crowned 'Industrial Agency Team of the Year'.

Savills is one of the founding members of Changing the Face of Property, an initiative run by a number of major property firms, which focuses on tackling diversity. In November 2017, Savills signed Real Estate Balance's 'CEO Commitments for Diversity' pledge, which was launched at the British Property Federation annual dinner. The industry-wide initiative saw over 50 business leaders commit to promoting an inclusive, gender balanced workforce. The 10 commitments in the pledge are designed to change how gender, as well as all other aspects of diversity, are delivered across the property sector.

Market

Savills is the largest multi-service property advisory business in the UK, providing more sector specialisms than any of its competitors across the commercial, residential, rural and energy sectors. With 138 strategically located offices throughout the UK, Savills has the largest national footprint rivalling its competitors.

Savills continued to demonstrate its strength as a global advisor when it advised CC Land Holdings Limited a Hong Kong-based investment holding company, on the purchase of The Leadenhall Building, in the City of London, acknowledged as one of London's most iconic office buildings. The deal was the second largest single asset ever to trade in the UK in 2017.

Product

During its 163-year history, Savills has grown from a family firm of chartered surveyors into an international property services group. Servicing all aspects of the residential, rural and commercial property markets, the firm continues to adapt its offer to cater for its diverse client base.

Achievements

Savills is The Times Graduate Employer of Choice for the 11th consecutive year, a position that the firm has held since the category's inception in 2007.

WITH A NETWORK OF 138 OFFICES SAVILLS HAS THE LARGEST UK NATIONAL FOOTPRINT RIVALLING ITS COMPETITORS

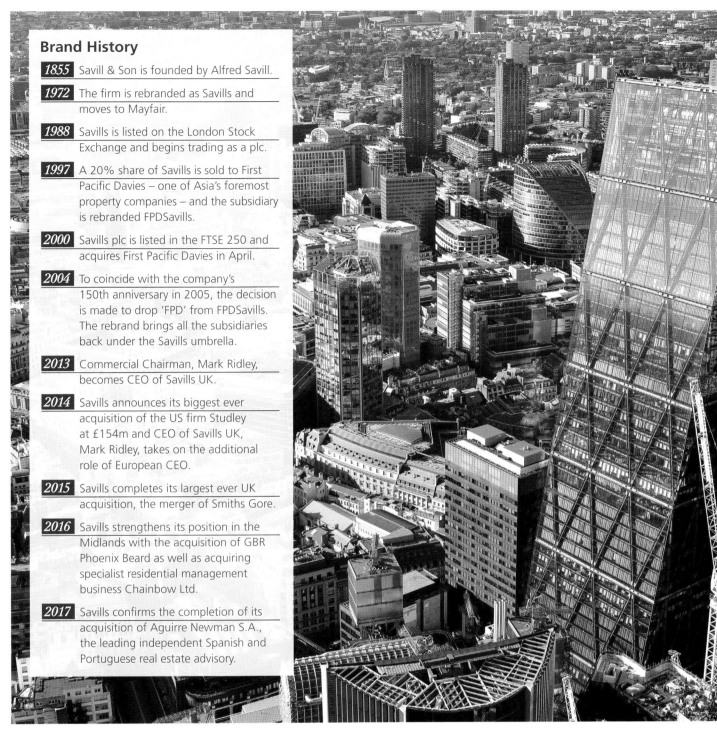

Brand History

1855 Savill & Son is founded by Alfred Savill.

1972 The firm is rebranded as Savills and moves to Mayfair.

1988 Savills is listed on the London Stock Exchange and begins trading as a plc.

1997 A 20% share of Savills is sold to First Pacific Davies – one of Asia's foremost property companies – and the subsidiary is rebranded FPDSavills.

2000 Savills plc is listed in the FTSE 250 and acquires First Pacific Davies in April.

2004 To coincide with the company's 150th anniversary in 2005, the decision is made to drop 'FPD' from FPDSavills. The rebrand brings all the subsidiaries back under the Savills umbrella.

2013 Commercial Chairman, Mark Ridley, becomes CEO of Savills UK.

2014 Savills announces its biggest ever acquisition of the US firm Studley at £154m and CEO of Savills UK, Mark Ridley, takes on the additional role of European CEO.

2015 Savills completes its largest ever UK acquisition, the merger of Smiths Gore.

2016 Savills strengthens its position in the Midlands with the acquisition of GBR Phoenix Beard as well as acquiring specialist residential management business Chainbow Ltd.

2017 Savills confirms the completion of its acquisition of Aguirre Newman S.A., the leading independent Spanish and Portuguese real estate advisory.

Charitable activity is strongly encouraged across the business. YoungMinds, the UK's leading charity championing the wellbeing and mental health of young people, was chosen by Savills graduates as the charity of choice for 2017 and organised a number of fundraising events throughout the year. Savills employee Harry Wentworth-Stanley, and his teammates, completed the 3,000-mile trans-Atlantic Talisker Whiskey Challenge in 2017. This resulted in donations exceeding £550,000 – a race record – which will fund James' Place, a series of non-clinical crisis centres designed to offer support for those with depression. Harry and his friends undertook the challenge to raise awareness of anxiety, depression and suicide after his brother ended his life, age 21, in 2006.

Recent Developments
Within Europe, Savills successfully opened an office in Prague, in order to support the company's continued expansion across Central and Eastern Europe. As 2017 came

to a close, Savills confirmed the completion of its acquisition of 100% of Aguirre Newman S.A., the leading independent Spanish and Portuguese real estate advisory. The newly combined business located in Spain and Portugal will be re-branded Savills Aguirre Newman.

Promotion
In the residential sector, which is undergoing huge disruption, Savills, as a premium brand, needed to actively differentiate itself from the rest of the market. Through market research the firm uncovered a real insight about consumers – that they have relationships with their homes which are akin to those they have in real life. Savills used these findings in its TV adverts and through a number of other channels in an engaging and humorous way to reach new audiences in new markets.

Savills also launched Workthere, a new venture introduced to help growing businesses find flexible, co-working and serviced office space

across Europe, America and Asia-Pacific. The concept was formed by Cal Lee, a former graduate and development surveyor within the business.

Brand Values
Savills focuses on attracting the best individuals within its market. Through careful selection and the preservation of a unique culture, it provides a global platform from which its talents and expertise can not only benefit clients but also the wider community.

The firm's vision is to be the real estate adviser of choice in the markets it serves.

Savills does not wish to be the biggest, just the best (as judged by its clients). Its values capture commitment not only to ethical, professional and responsible conduct but also to the essence of real estate success; an entrepreneurial, value-embracing approach.

Securitas gives complete peace of mind. Blending people, technology and knowledge to deliver total protection to keep people, property and assets safe. No other security provider layers six Protective Services: On-site, Mobile, Electronic Remote Security, Fire & Safety and Corporate Risk Management to provide intelligent pro-active security.

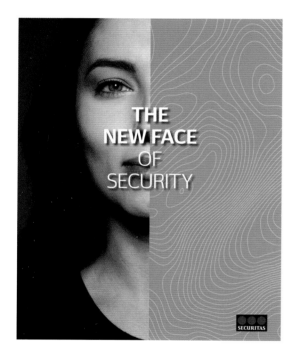

THE NEW FACE OF SECURITY

Market

Securitas is the leading global security services provider employing more than 335,000 people in 54 countries, throughout North America, Australia, Europe, Latin America, Africa, the Middle East and Asia.

In the UK, Securitas employs over 11,000 people, providing Protective Services to a wide range of clients from small local businesses, to national and global corporations, and even international airports.

Securitas' focus is on security and its ability to offer real value through its six Protective Services, including Fire and Safety. Unique within the industry, its focused service offering is a key differentiator in all the markets in which it operates.

With its global footprint, Securitas is at the forefront of innovation, moving the industry towards predictive security by harnessing 'big data' to provide intelligent, pro-active solutions.

Product

Technology and customer needs are evolving. Security no longer simply involves a lone security officer with a torch, nor the passive gaze of a security camera.

In Securitas, the security of the future focuses on a combination of people, technology and knowledge; moving from a traditional guarding and transactional commodity approach, to providing value driven, predictive, total security solutions.

With a greater focus on security as a specialisation, substantial investment in new technologies and a global approach to corporate risk management, Securitas provide intelligent security solutions, using client and industry data to analyse risks by geography, sector and customer.

Achievements

The state-of-the-art Securitas Operations Centre (SOC), monitors tens of thousands of system signals every day and was the first UK SOC to receive European accreditation to BS EN 50518 and the industry leading NSI Gold Standard.

The Securitas Learning and Development Academy was awarded City & Guilds training centre status in 2015 (another industry first), for delivery of its multiple training and development solutions including e-learning, portfolio, classroom based, NVQ-style modules, on-site and blended learning.

No other organisation offers the level of training and development of its people that Securitas does, providing tangible qualifications for its Protective Services Officers.

In 2016, Securitas UK became the first Home Office approved training provider to deliver Project Griffin counter terrorism awareness training to its staff.

Ranked amongst the UK's top 400 companies by Bloomberg in 2016, Securitas UK won the TQ

Employer of the Year Award (TQ are one of the UK's leading education and training providers).

Securitas UK relaunched Security Trained Assistance and Reception Services (STARS) in 2017 – highly professional and presentable front of house receptionists with SIA security qualifications.

In 2017 Securitas UK successfully achieved British Approvals for Fire Equipment (BAFE) accreditation. Certified to ISO 9001 and BAFE SP101 standards in the maintenance of portable fire extinguishers, Securitas UK is also listed on the official BAFE Register.

Securitas is the UK's first and only government-certified canine security provider, achieving Free Running Explosive Detection Dog (FREDD)

Brand History

1934 Erik Philip-Sörensen founds Hälsingborgs Nattvakt in Halsingborg, Sweden. It quickly expands as Sörensen acquires a number of other security companies in southern Sweden.

1935 Securitas Alarm is founded in Sweden to meet the demand for alarm technology as a complement to the guarding services.

1936 All companies owned by Erik Philip-Sörensen are gathered under the collective name Securitas. The logotype of three red dots – for Integrity, Vigilance and Helpfulness – quickly becomes a well-known symbol, first in Sweden, then internationally.

1981 Securitas AB is listed on the Stock Exchange.

1985 Investment AB Latour becomes Securitas' new owner and a focus is placed on security – a new strategy is outlined and the concept of multi-service is left behind. Also, Securitas purchases Reliance Security Services and Chubb Security Personnel.

2015 Securitas announces Vision 2020, focusing on providing protection through six Protective Services; blending people, technology and knowledge.

2018 Securitas UK first City & Guilds certified Protective Services Officers graduate.

certification in 2017 – the EU standard for the use of dogs in aviation cargo security.

Recent Developments

More recently, Securitas UK announced its accreditation as the 100th Recognised Service Provider, working closely with the Living Wage Foundation (LWF). The only global security company currently accredited by the LWF, Securitas UK has made a commitment to offer a Real Living Wage option alongside every tender opportunity to all prospective and current clients.

Promotion

In 2017 Securitas relaunched its UK Experience Centre; an interactive, hands-on experience for new and existing clients. With live demonstrations, augmented and virtual reality applications and interactive case studies, the Experience Centre showcases the very latest in intelligent security technology.

With a focus on digitalisation, Securitas UK has replaced its printed marketing collateral using

DID YOU KNOW?

Securitas is the only security company to provide truly national mobile coverage in the UK.

a digital e-zine format which is available to clients via the website and to Protective Services Branch Managers through an online app.

Securitas LEAD, a showcase augmented reality app (with booklet), brings each of the six Securitas Protective Services to life, engaging the reader in a unique hands-on experience.

Stay Ahead, Securitas UK's monthly digital e-zine, encourages readers to think about the security landscape in the face of a changing world and ever increasing security threats.

Brand Values

The relaunch of the Experience Centre in early 2017, coincided with a global rebrand, introducing Securitas as the New Face of Security.

Keeping people, property and assets safe lies at the very heart of Securitas. As a trusted advisor Securitas is modern, true and straightforward. The new brand design and direction harnesses these elements to empower customers to invest in total security solutions.

The Securitas UK brand style reflects the Securitas global 'one company, one brand, one story' positioning and builds on the 'one brand makes us stronger' concept.

No other security provider layers six Protective Services to deliver total protection: 335,000 Securitas colleagues in 54 countries are making the world a safer place, every day.

The secret to a great night's sleep

Silentnight is the **UK's largest manufacturer of branded beds, mattresses and sleep accessories.** With a wide consumer profile, Silentnight's **mission is to use its passion, product knowledge, exceptional quality and sleep expertise** to provide sleep solutions for all the family.

Market

The UK retail bed and mattress market is worth around £1.98bn (Sources: Mintel, Conlumino, NBF Sales Statistics). Silentnight is the UK's favourite bed and mattress manufacturer (Source: GfK data) and remains well known, with strong brand recall and consideration from consumers, in particular the brand's iconic Hippo & Duck characters.

Product

Founded in 1946 in North Yorkshire, Silentnight's factory and offices have remained in Lancashire and, in 2016, the brand celebrated 70 years of quality and innovation. Over the years it has developed a strong core product offering to cater for the mass market, with families being the key audience. Products include a wide selection of mattresses using its exclusive Miracoil® and Mirapocket® advanced spring system technologies, bases with different storage options and a comprehensive children's proposition. Silentnight is also available across bed frames, sleep accessories such as pillows and duvets, a range of heating and cooling products and even pet beds.

As the UK's leading bed and mattress manufacturer, Silentnight is committed to working to the highest quality standards for its customers. All its mattresses

and upholstered beds are handmade in its UK factory. The products and raw materials are rigorously tested in its in-house SATRA-approved testing lab, established in 1980. Experienced staff, proficient in materials testing, structural testing of finished products and flammability testing, ensure customers can sleep safe in the knowledge that their bed or mattress meets all safety, quality and flammability standards.

DID YOU KNOW?

One in five homes in the UK have a **Silentnight** product.

Achievements

Silentnight has been awarded a Which? Best Buy for its mattress-now® Memory 3 Zone rolled mattress for four years running. In May 2016, the 1200 Mirapocket® mattress was recognised by Which? for the second year running as being "one of the best value mattresses we've tested". Furthermore, in June 2017, the brand gained

its third Which? Best Buy with its Studio medium mattress, which was the 'Top scoring bed-in-a-box mattress'.

Silentnight Beds is a member of the Furniture Industry Sustainability Programme, having shown commitment to social, economic and environmental sustainability across its business. In 2011, Silentnight achieved Forest Stewardship Council certification for all the timber used in the production of its divans and headboards. In 2017, Silentnight was also recognised for its commitment to the environment, being awarded The Furniture Makers' Company Sustainability Award.

Recent Developments

Silentnight is committed to new product innovation in its drive to give consumers the best sleep experience possible and to remain at the forefront of the market place. Studio by Silentnight continues to appeal to consumers. One mattress that is available in three comforts, Studio by Silentnight is designed with the reassurance of Silentnight, but offering a fresh, contemporary experience and can be rolled and boxed for the consumer's convenience.

Another product innovation, only available in the UK to the Silentnight Group is Geltex®, a high-performance gel-infused foam which offers unparalleled breathability, ideal pressure relief and optimal body support for a truly restful night's sleep. Silentnight has placed emphasis on increasing the use of Geltex® across its range. The latest innovation to the brand is the mini-spring 'Ultraflex'. Working in harmony with the brand's spring systems to provide enhanced comfort and increased breathability, it aims to take sleep to the next level.

Promotion

Silentnight's new advertising campaign, 'Sleep, your way', demonstrates that when it comes to sleeps, everybody is different and the brand understands that. The multi-channel campaign covers a variety of the brand's leading product ranges including its Which? Best Buy

Brand History

1946 In Skipton, North Yorkshire, Tom and Joan Clarke form a new company under the name Clarke's Mattresses Limited.

1948 Tom and Joan register Clarke's Mattresses Limited and rent their first shop, moving operations to a bigger site a year later, due to huge demand.

1951 Clarke's Mattresses changes its name to Silentnight Limited.

1961 The business continues to expand and moves to its current premises in Barnoldswick.

1986 Silentnight launches its 'Ultimate Spring System'. To demonstrate its unique no-roll-together properties, Hippo and Duck are introduced.

1990s The unique spring system is improved and renamed the Miracoil® Spring System.

2002 Hippo and Duck catch the nation's attention in an animated TV commercial, set to a reworked version of Hot Chocolate's 'You Sexy Thing' (I Believe In Miracoils).

2003 Silentnight begins production of beds and mattresses for the children's market.

2008 Mattress-now® – the first Silentnight 'convenience' rolled mattress is launched.

2010 Silentnight sponsors American Idol and launches the Best for Bedsteads range.

2012 Safe Nights and Healthy Growth ranges are launched. A refreshed brand identity is rolled out, with Hippo and Duck still central to communications.

2013 The next generation sleep technology – Geltex® inside collection is launched.

2013 Silentnight is awarded two Which? Best Buys for mattresses and the Safe Nights Memory Wool cot-bed mattress wins a number of parenting awards.

2016 Silentnight celebrates its 70th anniversary and launches Studio by Silentnight.

2017 Silentnight launches its mini-pocket system, Ultraflex.

Mirapocket® 1200 and Studio products as well as the exclusive Geltex comfort layer. Adverts are also dedicated to smart storage solutions, and the stylish upholstered bed frames the brand has just launched. The campaign has run across television, press, digital, social and PR with plans well underway to continue the campaign into 2018.

Brand Values

Silentnight's mission is to help everyone in the family find their perfect sleep solution. To ensure Silentnight remains an authority in sleep expertise, it invests in continuous research into sleeping habits, building the latest scientific developments and technical innovations into its products.

THE BEST START IN LIFE

Founded in 1877, **Silver Cross is one of the world's leading premium nursery brands.** Loved and **trusted by millions of parents across the globe,** it is recognised for producing beautifully crafted and **innovative products to give babies the best start in 'life.'**

Market

Silver Cross is a leading name in the baby and nursery market.

For more than 140 years, the brand has been dedicated to the highest standards of craftsmanship, designing products which are both beautiful and innovative.

This commitment to quality is the reason Silver Cross has been trusted from one generation to the next over so many years. For many parents, grandparents and great-grandparents, Silver Cross has always been part of the family.

The company's success story continues apace and its products are now sold worldwide. In addition to its UK headquarters, it has offices in Hong Kong, Shanghai, Melbourne, Dubai and Barcelona. It also has three successful flagship stores in Hong Kong, Shanghai and Moscow.

Product

Silver Cross believes in purity of design, timeless beauty and an obsessive attention to detail. Key to every product is excellent design and premium quality.

The company has an award-winning team of in-house designers, engineers and product development specialists based at its Yorkshire head office.

Thanks to its long and unique heritage, the Silver Cross product range is unrivalled. It continues to produce the beautiful and iconic Balmoral and Kensington coach prams, a masterpiece of design and engineering and the only prams still hand-crafted exclusively in the UK.

DID YOU KNOW?

Silver Cross founder **William Wilson** is credited with **inventing the baby pram** concept.

A hallmark of every Silver Cross pram is the famously smooth ride – a quality that continues in its outstanding range of innovative and contemporary travel systems and pushchairs. Combining the latest advances in technology with modern and stylish design, it is at the forefront of the baby travel market.

In addition, Silver Cross has a successful home and nursery division featuring beautifully crafted furniture sets and exquisite baby bedding.

Achievements

Silver Cross continues to impress industry experts and parents alike with its products, winning the most prestigious awards from parenting websites and magazines.

Wave, the new One plus One pram system launched in 2017, has proved a huge success both in the UK and internationally and is already the proud owner of eight awards, including a Best Buy from independent consumer association Which? and a Gold from Mother & Baby, the UK's leading pregnancy and baby magazine.

A strong, evolving product range is key to the company's success, while an uncompromising approach to quality and unrivalled experience have helped Silver Cross become a global brand, loved and trusted by millions of parents worldwide.

Recent Developments

To meet the demands of today's families, Silver Cross continually drives forward its product range, with a series of stylish, practical and beautifully crafted products.

In 2017 it acquired stroller brand Micralite, marking a new period of growth for the company. It has also launched successfully in the US,

Brand History

1877 Silver Cross is founded by William Wilson, who invented the first-ever baby carriage.

1950-1870s Silver Cross is crowned the number one baby carriage for royalty.

1980s New manufacturing techniques for lightweight pushchairs are developed and The Wayfarer is launched. It becomes Britain's best-selling pushchair.

2002 Led by CEO Nick Paxton, Silver Cross develops a new approach to innovation and product development.

2006 Silver Cross goes global, forging partnerships with distributors around the world.

2017 Growth continues in the UK, Asia, Middle East, Europe and the US. The company also continues to invest in product, people and customer service.

where it continues to go from strength to strength and expand the product range.

Silver Cross enjoys an ongoing successful collaboration with Aston Martin, uniting two iconic and premium British brands.

It has already seen the launch of the Surf Aston Martin Edition – the world's most exclusive pram system – but new for 2018 is the Reflex Aston Martin Edition, a luxury stroller, plus the Aston Martin Cot and Fine Linen Collection, offering the ultimate in exclusivity for the nursery.

Another key launch for 2018 is a new collaboration uniting Silver Cross with luxury children's wear designer, Princess Marie-Chantal of Greece.

The Princess' passion for classic, elegant and timeless design is shared by Silver Cross and

provides the inspiration for this exclusive range of luxury prams, nursery furniture and bedding. Each elegantly crafted piece features the utmost attention to detail and high-end fabric, offering the perfect balance of beautiful design and baby comfort.

Promotion

The brand's values of being authentic and open are reflected in its communications – a theme that runs through all of its consumer touch-points. Silver Cross' strong brand values of quality, innovation, design and heritage remain at the forefront of its appeal.

The brand's strongest marketing tool, however, has always been word-of-mouth and endorsement from those who have first-hand experience of Silver Cross products.

Online activity remains a key tool to communicate and engage with consumers around the world. Silver Cross has a global website, while social media channels allow the brand to hold direct conversations with its consumers.

Brand Values

More than 140 years after it was founded, Silver Cross continues to develop the most innovative products, with a focus on design excellence and premium quality. Its long heritage shapes its future and its mission is to be loved by parents and babies alike. Silver Cross is proud to say millions of parents all over the world have trusted its products to give their baby the best start in life.

SOPHOS

Security made simple.

Sophos makes IT security simple with **next-generation solutions** that **protect networks, servers, and devices, wherever they are.** Today, **more than 100 million users in 150 countries and a global network of channel partners trust Sophos** to deliver simple solutions to complex security challenges.

SEEING THE FUTURE
IS THE FUTURE
OF CYBERSECURITY.

Market

The threat of cyber-attacks continued apace in 2017. Outbreaks such as WannaCry have hit headlines all over the world, and has led to growing market interest in next-gen anti-ransomware solutions. The threat landscape is growing increasingly complex as today's criminals inject more creativity and sophistication into attacks than have ever been seen before – from seamlessly branded phishing to ransomware that spread automatically using exploits stolen from the NSA. Working 24/7/365 SophosLabs receives and processes approximately 400,000 previously unseen malware samples each day, to meet the challenge head on and deliver advanced security protection to customers and partners that is simple and reliable.

Focused on innovation and backed by a global network of SophosLabs threat intelligence centres and industry-leading support, Sophos delivers solutions that are simple to deploy, maintain and manage, enabling organisations to focus on performance and growth.

Sophos is a dedicated market leader committed to delivering advanced IT security that is simple and reliable. Over the past year, Sophos has seen significant interest in its leading next-gen anti-ransomware solutions, with awareness raised by global attacks such as WannaCry and NotPetya.

Product

Sophos' security solutions offer the best next-generation protection against complex threats and data loss, which are simple to deploy, manage and use and span encryption, endpoint security, web, email, mobile and network products built with innovative technology.

Sophos protects millions of users globally by removing the complexity from IT security, with products that continue to be recognised by leading analysts, including Gartner.

DID YOU KNOW?

Sophos Intercept X proactively protected its customers from the WannaCry ransomware attack, which hit the UK in 2017.

Sophos Synchronized Security has pioneered an innovative approach to network and endpoint threat intelligence enabling the automatic isolation of infected endpoints before the threat can spread, slashing incident response time by 99.9%.

With the threat of ransomware on the rise, Sophos Intercept X has seen strong market interest and been a tremendous success for Sophos due to its anti-ransomware technology, which stopped the NotPetya, WannaCry as well as Bad Rabbit ransomware strands. Sophos Intercept X is a next-generation endpoint security product that stops zero-day malware, blocks all exploit techniques known today and includes an advanced anti-ransomware feature that can stop both known and unknown ransomware variants within seconds. Intercept X can be installed alongside existing endpoint security software from any vendor, immediately boosting endpoint protection by stopping malicious code before it can infect an entire network. As threat complexity continues to evolve, Intercept X delivers deep learning capabilities that leverage an artificial neural network to build a model used to make predictions with speed, scale, and judgements that exceed human capabilities.

Achievements

Sophos products and solutions have been recognised as industry leaders for the past decade. In 2017, Sophos was named a Leader in the Gartner MQ for Endpoint Protection Platforms and UTM, Gartner also awarded Sophos as a Visionary for Enterprise Network Firewalls and Enterprise Mobility Management. This recognition speaks to Sophos' strong portfolio that is underpinned by Sophos'

DID YOU KNOW?

Sophos (SOPH) was the largest technology IPO in 2015 on the London Stock Exchange.

Synchronized Security strategy and cloud-based, centralised Sophos Central management platform.

Sophos has also been recognised at numerous awards for various products over the years, with Intercept X recently winning Innovation of the Year at the Computing Security Excellence Awards, for the integration of deep learning technology. In addition to its products, Sophos has also been recognised by CRN for its dedication to the channel, and in 2015 Sophos (SOPH) was the largest technology IPO in 2015 on the London Stock Exchange.

Recent Developments

Sophos is now leading a new wave of security innovation though the integration of deep learning into its products. With cyber criminals now using artificial intelligence and machine learning to facilitate their attacks, security providers need to remain one step ahead. Innovation continues to be a key driver within Sophos. It was the first vendor to launch Synchronized Security, and continues to have an aggressive product roadmap to effectively protect its customers against sophisticated and zero day threats. Sophos is doing something that has never been done in the IT security market – succeeding at being a leading provider of both end user and network security.

Promotion

Using the same innovative security that protects businesses, in an easy-to-use consumer package, Sophos Home was launched in 2015 to offer free home security for Mac and PC users. As online threats continue to grow Sophos wanted to offer consumers access to the same award-winning technology that IT professionals trust to protect their businesses.

Sophos Home protects every Mac and PC in the home from malware, viruses, ransomware and inappropriate and malicious websites and was awarded a Which? Best Buy Award in 2017. Consumers can manage security settings for the whole family – whatever their location.

Brand History

1985 Sophos is founded in Oxford, England.

2015 Sophos launches its free home security tool, Sophos Home as well as Synchronized Security with Security Heartbeat. In addition, an IPO on London Stock Exchange (LSE) in July (SOPH) takes place.

2016 Sophos becomes Gartner Magic Quadrant Leader in both Network and Endpoint. Intercept X is also launched, which is recognised for protecting customers from NotPetya and WannaCry.

2017 Invincea, machine learning based, next-generation antivirus is acquired.

Brand Values

Security made simple is at the core of everything Sophos does. Its mission is to be the best in the world at delivering innovative, simple, and highly-effective cyber security solutions to IT professionals and the channel that serves them. Sophos' focus on innovation and simplicity goes hand-in-hand with its commitment to a channel-first, channel-only sales model.

Established in 1977, **Speedy is the UK's leading tools, equipment and plant hire company,** also providing **training, testing inspection and certification services, as well as product and consumables sales.** Speedy operates **in the UK construction, infrastructure, industrial, utilities, events and facilities management markets,** and in the Middle East and Kazakhstan.

Market

The £4.5bn UK equipment hire market (Source: AMA Research) is highly fragmented with the top five companies managing circa 30% of the market, alongside hundreds of local and specialist operators. Speedy is one of the UK's market leaders in the provision of equipment for rental, with a circa 12% share of its addressable market.

Product

From large, multi-site corporate businesses through to small, family-run enterprises that all need the right equipment and services for the job, Speedy offers a full end-to-end solution to enable customers to successfully deliver its projects. Speedy's services include the hire of equipment from large powered access booms through to cordless drills, on site training, equipment testing and consumables sales. Speedy has one of the largest, national networks in its sector with more than 200 depots across the UK and Ireland. It operates a hub and spoke model with a National Distribution Centre, Multi Service Centres and approximately 40 superstores. It is known for its wide range of fully certified, tested and competitively priced products, all compliant in line with the highest Health and Safety standards.

Speedy's hire fleet of approximately 300,000 assets or circa 5,000 product lines encompasses tools, plant, access, lifting, survey, safety, rail and power generation. It also offers additional products through a comprehensive range of supplier partnerships. Training courses include PASMA and IPAF certification, with over 200 training courses, delivered across 32 depots. Testing Inspection and Certification services for on-site equipment such as cranes and lifting systems are offered through its Lloyds British business. Customers can opt to purchase any plant/equipment alongside on-site consumables.

Innovation is a priority and Speedy works closely with customers and suppliers to develop new products. With over 70 'Green Option' products, independently tested in the market

DID YOU KNOW?

Lloyds British, a Speedy business, tested the Titanic's chain and anchor.

for their environmental credentials, customers can manage challenges around noise pollution and dust management. Speedy developed the fPod® in partnership with suppliers to provide a single refuelling point for any site, reducing on-site vehicle movements and fuel containers, offering environmental, safety and cost benefits to all users. Fitted with an intelligent monitoring system, the tank is monitored and refilled to ensure constant fuel supply and productivity on site.

Speedy's award winning, revolutionary, unmanned, self-service hire 'depot', the ePod®, provides a specialist, secure storage solution for customers, who work on remote sites or who do not operate in traditional business hours.

Achievements

Speedy's commitment to safety, sustainability and innovation is at the heart of everything it does and has led the way to receiving many accolades in recognition of this. It promotes solutions to hazards through its online Intelligent Safety portal and continues to be the safest hire provider in the industry, based on accident and injury rates (seven day +, specified and RIDDOR injuries). Its carbon footprint is the lowest in the industry. Speedy is accredited to ISO 9001, 14001, 18001 becoming the first company in the sector to achieve ISO 50001 accreditation for energy performance in 2017.

Also in 2017, Speedy gained a Considerate Construction Award in London and was awarded the RoSPA Gold Medal for safety performance for the third year running. Speedy is accredited to gold standard under the Fleet Operator Recognition Scheme (FORS) and has won awards for its vehicle fleet including Fleet Van Operator of the year (Motor Transport Awards) 2017. The Group operates a fleet of award winning electric i3 vehicles which enhance its energy efficient credentials.

Brand History

1977 The first depot opens and John Brown forms Livesey Hire in Wigan.

1993 The first centralised, national call centre in the hire sector, Hire Direct, is launched.

2001 The company name is changed to Speedy Hire Plc.

2007 Speedy becomes the only UK hire company to offer bio-fuel generators.

2009 Through the Construction Site Solutions Consortium, Speedy wins the contract with the Olympic Delivery Authority to provide hire equipment, building supplies and training to companies working on the 2012 Olympic Games.

2015 A new pioneering National Distribution Centre, eight Multi-Service Centres and 38 Superstores are launched.

2016 Rail overhead line equipment specialist, Rail Hire UK, is acquired and industry leading Smart Device technology is launched to track customer deliveries. Speedy becomes the first company in the sector to achieve the ISO 50001 accreditation for energy saving.

2017 The acquisition of powered access specialists Prolift Access Limited and Platform Sales & Hire Limited takes place and Speedy's biggest Annual Expo event, the largest UK private hire show, takes place. Speedy's 40th birthday is also celebrated.

Recent Developments

Speedy has grown rapidly, in part due to acquisitions. The purchase of Lloyds British, Rail Hire UK and more recently Prolift and Platform Sales & Hire, have strengthened its proposition and established the brand as a credible supplier of specialist equipment and solutions.

In 2016, Speedy acquired Lloyds British, a company recognised as a leader in a testing, inspection and certification of products, tools and equipment. Lloyds is a major partner of BSi and works with other major UK companies to ensure equipment on site is accredited and safe.

These acquisitions position Speedy not just as an equipment hire company but as a full end to end services company, delivering a range of customer projects, from annual events such as Glastonbury, to multi-site and national infrastructure projects such as the Olympics, Crossrail and Hinckley Point, as well as multi-site training projects for national customers.

Speedy recently relaunched its mission, which is 'to provide safe, reliable hire equipment and services to enable the successful delivery of customers' projects'. Delivering service excellence to customers is a key priority and ensuring equipment is provided to customers where and when they need it, is monitored closely through the Group's reporting systems. Customers are independently surveyed regularly at the point of order, delivery and collection. Based on these surveys 90% of customers are satisfied or very satisfied with the Speedy's service.

Promotion

Speedy has always built and developed strong client relationships. As Speedy has added more services to its portfolio, it has seen its customer base grow to more than 55,000 customers across all segments of the market. Speedy uses a range of integrated, targeted, promotional activities combining digital, social media and content-led campaigns with customer and industry events to promote Speedy's hire and service offerings. This enables social media, retargeting and SEO improvements enable Speedy to target a much wider audience with greater ROI. Recently Speedy launched a service promise to all customers within the M25 where all orders before 3pm will be delivered the same day, or Speedy provides the product free for a week. This integrated campaign has already attracted significant interest.

Brand Values

Speedy's vision is to be the best company in its sector to do business with, and to work for. The mission is to provide safe, reliable hire equipment and services to enable the successful delivery of customers' projects. These objectives are achieved through three principal goals, providing excellent customer service, innovating and differentiating from the competition, and cultivating strong client relationships. The brand has been repositioned over the last few years to be associated with excellent customer service and a strong service ethic. Underpinning the customer service ethos within the business is a commitment to keeping its people and customers safe, and creating an empowered culture.

Speedy has four key values: Safe – the first priority in everything it does; As One – working together to collectively achieve its goals; Innovative – to continuously improve; Driven – to deliver first class customer service.

STAEDTLER®

Designing and manufacturing premium quality writing instruments since 1835,
STAEDTLER offers a comprehensive range of stationery and craft products for the school,
home and office, including instantly recognisable classics such as the Noris pencil.
Innovation remains key to the company's success with regular breakthroughs
in design, performance and manufacturing.

Market

In a competitive marketplace, STAEDTLER is the market leader for blacklead pencils, coloured pencils and fineliners. It is also number one in colouring felt pens, targeted at teenagers and adults, in the retail market (Source: GfK data, 2016). STAEDTLER supplies retailers, the education sector, B2B markets as well as having other independent trade customers.

The brand has a presence in 150 countries worldwide and is the largest manufacturer of wood-cased pencils, OHP pens, erasers, mechanical pencil leads and modelling clays in Europe.

Ongoing innovative product development to explore new colours, techniques and trends drives the brand forward. For example, the increasingly popular adult colouring sector was pioneered by STAEDTLER.

Product

The STAEDTLER product range has evolved over centuries to encompass a vast selection of premium quality writing and drawing instruments for the school, home and office. Its stationery range caters for every age group, starting with learner pencils for very young children. Alongside this, STAEDTLER also offers an extensive craft range including the popular FIMO polymer modelling clay.

STAEDTLER is renowned for producing high quality products and its iconic, market-leading Noris pencil has a market-share of more than 53%. Amongst its other internationally recognised classics are the Mars plastic eraser and the Lumocolor marker.

Achievements

Quality, reliability and design innovation, together with a clear environmental pledge, are at the heart of everything STAEDTLER does. This standpoint has helped to maintain the brand's position as one of the top three brands in the UK writing instruments market.

DID YOU KNOW?

STAEDTLER sells over 65 million wood-cased pencils in the UK – that's **one for every man, woman and child.**

Over the years, STAEDTLER has won numerous accolades for marketing excellence, product innovation as well as customer supplier awards.

In 2017, STAEDTLER received 'Initiative of the Year' at the BOSS Awards for pioneering the lucrative adult colouring sector. It was also awarded, Best Toy for ages 8 - 11 years, in the Mums Choice Awards for its FIMO Kids, Form and Play sets.

Recent Developments

Consistent commitment to new product development has led to regular breakthroughs in product design, performance and manufacturing. Recent innovations include the award-winning triplus range of triangular writing instruments; Anti-Break-System (ABS), the revolutionary break-resistant protective coating for coloured pencils; WOPEX, a ground-breaking production process that maximises the usage of raw materials; as well as Noris colour, an eco-friendly, premium quality coloured pencil.

In early 2015, STAEDTLER identified the start of the adult colouring trend and accurately predicted its massive future potential. The brand partnered with the world renowned artist and adult colouring pioneer, Johanna Basford, to provide customers with a special edition range of beautifully packaged adult colouring essentials, bearing her image and endorsement. As STAEDTLER foresaw, a huge surge in demand for colouring products in the UK, from both children and adults alike, ensued. This led to a complete change in the way in which stationery products were perceived. No longer merely a functional necessity, stationery products became viewed as cool, 'must-have' items. STAEDTLER was well positioned to harness and promote this new energy and excitement in the industry. All challenges prompted by the boom were successfully converted into business opportunities, allowing the brand to flourish within this dynamic sector.

With the continued growth of the STAEDTLER brand, investment is being made into the creation of the company's own plantation in Ecuador. This is a forward-looking step both from an ecological and economic point of view. The aim is to create a more efficient manufacturing process, with a lower rate of raw material consumption, reduced CO_2 emissions and,

DID YOU KNOW?

Almost **three-quarters** of total production is in Germany.

ultimately, less waste. With wood being a vital material in pencil production, overseeing every stage of the process, from the species of tree used, will ensure that the existing flora and fauna around STAEDTLER's 1,800-hectare site is taken into consideration. Over the next 10 years, STAEDTLER will be investing around seven million Euros in the project.

Promotion

The promotional activity of STAEDTLER is tailored to meet the requirements of the various channels that it sells into. In addition, it is also strongly promoted to consumers through carefully targeted, high profile campaigns including TV and cinema advertising. One such TV campaign won a CANMOL award at the Wales Marketing Awards, which was hosted by the Chartered Institute of Marketing. An impactful campaign is also planned for 2018 to further increase brand awareness.

Brand Values

With its impressive heritage and international reputation, STAEDTLER remains committed to pioneering new product development and attaining the highest possible standards of quality and reliability. At the same time, the company's 'efficient for ecology' pledge ensures that the premium quality product range is produced in the most efficient, environmentally friendly way with consideration for both natural resources and everyone involved in the process.

In 2012, STAEDTLER (UK) Ltd was proud to achieve 'Investors in People' status, independent accreditation that officially recognises its policy of actively encouraging and fostering ongoing personal and professional development for all personnel. The company is also committed to a CSR programme within the local community, working with schoolchildren in particular.

Brand History

1662 Ancestor of the STAEDTLER founder, Friedrich Staedtler, works as a pencil maker in the German city of Nuremberg.

1835 Johann Sebastian STAEDTLER sets up his pencil manufacturing plant in Nuremberg.

1866 STAEDTLER employs 54 people, producing more than two million pencils annually.

1966 In the UK, STAEDTLER acquires the Royal Sovereign Pencil Company.

1968 Approximately 275 people now employed at the UK factory.

1973 The STAEDTLER (UK) Ltd company name is introduced.

1977 Royal Sovereign-STAEDTLER Ltd becomes a wholly owned subsidiary of STAEDTLER Noris GmbH.

2016 STAEDTLER (UK) Ltd celebrates its 50th anniversary in the UK with a year-long programme of activities.

2017 STAEDTLER has 21 manufacturing and distribution subsidiaries globally, employing more than 2,100 people and announces plans for its own plantation, to maintain the highest ecological standards of production.

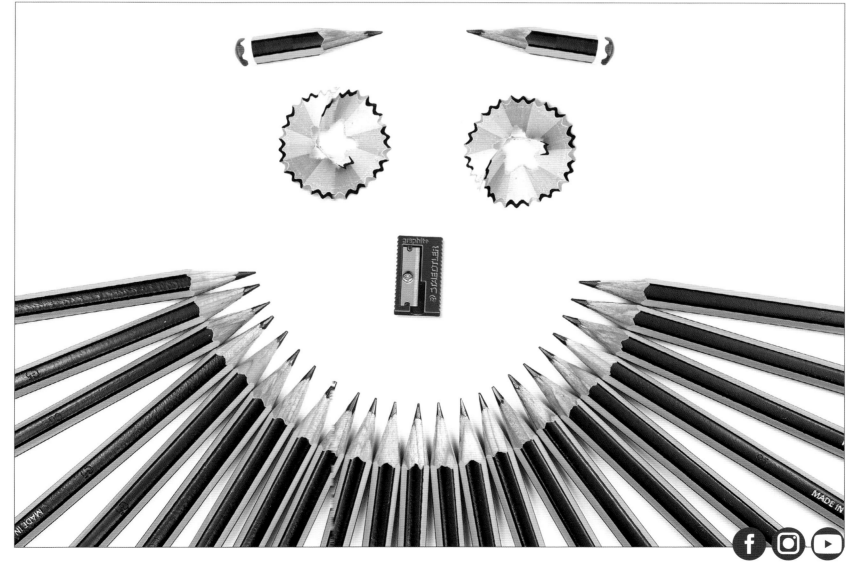

Stobart Group is an **entrepreneurial business** that uses its logistics and customer service expertise to **own and manage a range of key infrastructure** sites and operating divisions. The Group is focused on **delivering support services** to the energy, aviation and rail and civil engineering sectors.

Market

Stobart Group is one of the UK's leading and best-known infrastructure and support service businesses. It is listed on the London Stock Exchange and operates in the renewable energy, aviation and rail and civil engineering sectors. It also has investments in a national property and logistics portfolio, including the Eddie Stobart business and brand.

The company's vision is to deliver superior growth and shareholder returns by enhancing and realising its Infrastructure and Investments assets, and by creating new growth platforms in energy, aviation and rail.

Stobart Group aims to stand out from its peers by using its business development capabilities, logistics heritage, capital and the credibility of its brand.

Product

Stobart Group is made up of three operating divisions: Stobart Energy – the number one supplier of biomass in the UK, sourcing and supplying fuel to biomass plants under a mix

DID YOU KNOW?

Stobart **owns and operates all aspects of London Southend Airport** from the train station to baggage handling.

of short and long-term contracts; Stobart Aviation – which owns and operates London Southend Airport, Carlisle Lake District Airport, regional airline Stobart Air, and aircraft leasing company Propius, as well as an aviation services business; Stobart Rail and Civils, is one of the UK's leading providers of rail and non-rail civil engineering projects, and a Tier 2 Partner to Network Rail.

Achievements

Stobart Group's Energy business established a renewable energy supply chain to deliver and process two million tonnes of biomass by the end of 2018, and in 2017 reported improved EBITDA per tonne.

Stobart Aviation's key asset – London Southend Airport – has seen passenger numbers increase 25% year on year and, for the fourth year in succession was rated Best UK Airport in the Which? customer satisfaction survey.

Stobart Rail and Civils won Network Rail's Best On-track Plant Suppler Award for its innovative approach, and became a Tier 1 supplier on Network Rail's National Vegetation Management Framework.

The Stobart Infrastructure and Stobart Investments divisions achieved a £120m increase in book value and generated £112m in cash following the partial disposal of its investment in Eddie Stobart Logistics, in which the Group retains a 12.5% stake.

Recent Developments

In early 2018, Stobart Aviation launched its new executive Jet Centre at London Southend Airport, offering a seamless and speedy route into London. In addition, the new World Duty Free Store and Bourgee Champagne Bar offers passengers an enhanced experience at the airport.

Brand History

1960s Founder, Eddie Stobart, goes into business as an agricultural contractor.

1970s The business incorporates, becoming Eddie Stobart Limited.

1980s The business expands significantly, opening depots across the UK. Andrew Tinkler forms WA Tinkler Building Contractor.

1990s WA Tinkler Building Contractor becomes WA Developments, growing its turnover to over £20m a year.

2001 William Stobart leaves Eddie Stobart Limited to become a shareholding Director in WA Developments.

2004 WA Developments International acquires Eddie Stobart Limited.

2005 Eddie Stobart wins its first Tesco Distribution Centre contract and introduces a striking new livery.

2007 The LSE-listed Stobart Group is formed.

2008 Stobart Group acquires London Southend Airport and Carlisle Lake District Airport is acquired the following year.

2010 Stobart Biomass Products is formed to source and transport sustainable biomass. 'Eddie Stobart: Trucks & Trailers' airs on Channel 5.

2013 Stobart's London Southend Airport is voted best in the UK, an achievement upheld for the next four years. Also, Stobart Fest attracts 20,000 people.

2014 Stobart sells its Transport and Distribution division as part of a strategic partial realisation.

2015 Stobart Aviation moves more than one million passengers.

2016 Stobart enters an agreement with the Environment Agency to provide flood response services.

2017 Eddie Stobart floats on the AIM; 11 new routes launch from London Southend Airport; Stobart Capital is established; and Warwick Brady takes over as CEO from Andrew Tinkler, who remains an Executive Director.

Stobart Aviation Services was created to shake up the baggage handling market in the UK, using Stobart's proven expertise in logistics, systems and customer service. In addition, Stobart Aviation has acquired a regional airline and an aircraft leasing company.

Promotion
Stobart Aviation continues to implement comprehensive sales and marketing campaigns which focus on a first-class passenger experience and a lower overall journey time.

Stobart uses its strong association with horse racing to leverage brand awareness. As the second biggest spectator sport in the UK, Stobart Group established an innovative sponsorship agreement with the Professional Jockey Association, sponsoring the Stobart Jockeys Championship's for Jump and Flat racing in the UK and Ireland.

The Stobart Shop and Club continues to florish, attending events such as TruckFests which allow fans to get up close and personal with the Stobart trucks.

Brand Values
Quality, service, performance and sustainability are values inherent to the Stobart Group brand, and exemplary employment and environmental practices are amongst its core principles.

Superdrug is the **UK's second-largest beauty and health retailer**, currently operating over **800 stores in the UK, with more than 200 in-store pharmacies**. Its purpose is to be the best in everyday accessible beauty and health and is **committed to bringing innovation as well as the latest styles and trends** to every high street.

Market

Superdrug is committed to bringing innovation and the latest styles and trends to every high street in the UK and Republic of Ireland, at competitive prices. As well as some of the best beauty and health brands, its range also encompasses a host of exclusive products that aren't available anywhere else.

Superdrug currently has more than 800 stores and employs 14,000 colleagues. A total of 200 Superdrug stores have pharmacies with pharmacy consulting rooms and over 20 stores have nurse clinics that offer health checks.

A key element in the success of the Superdrug brand is ensuring that its team is trained to provide customers with good customer service. Through Superdrug's retail academy, team members are given the skills, confidence and knowledge to offer customers some of the best beauty and health advice on the high street.

Superdrug has an inclusive attitude towards its customers and caters for a wide range of customer types, celebrating and campaigning for what is important to them. It also believes that it's the brand's personality that sets it apart from other beauty and health retailers on the high street.

Superdrug caters for a broad range of customers' needs, from beauty and health essentials to the latest beauty trends from the catwalk as well as being a destination store for essential cosmetics and toiletries at the lowest prices.

Product

Superdrug offers a combination of world-class global brand names and exclusive brands that customers won't find anywhere else, both in Superdrug stores and on superdrug.com. While the product mix has evolved over the years, the product mission remains the same – to offer a unique combination of makeup, perfume, skincare and personal care, toiletries and babycare items as well as health and wellbeing products.

DID YOU KNOW?

Superdrug **sells over one million bottles** of own brand **nail polish remover** a year.

Recently Superdrug has expanded its operations internationally, by shipping direct to customers who place orders on Superdrug.com firstly to Republic of Ireland, and then in 2017 to Finland, Sweden and Denmark. The rise of the international appeal of UK beauty bloggers has seen global demand for Superdrug's fast beauty makeup and beauty products continue to rise and shipping to Scandinavian countries has made Superdrug more accessible to millions more customers.

Achievements

Since 2010 all of Superdrug's own brand beauty products have carried the leaping bunny symbol of Cruelty Free International. In addition, Superdrug has banned microbeads from its own brand products and has requested that all of its suppliers remove microbeads from branded products on sale in its stores.

Superdrug aims to offer products that are suitable for as many customers as possible, which is why it launched the B. range. This isn't just cruelty free and high quality, but also 100% vegan. It is therefore ideal for those avoiding animal by-products in their makeup, skincare and male grooming products whether for religious, ethical or lifestyle choice reasons.

It is not however just about products, Superdrug is keen to give something back to the community every day and works with Marie Curie to raise funds to support the charity's nurses through fundraising in store as well as the sale of special products. In 2017 colleagues across the country continued to support Marie Curie nurses by taking part in collections, marathons, walks and swims as well as organising fundraising events in store.

While working with Marie Curie over the last five years Superdrug customers, colleagues and suppliers have raised £3.7m for the charity, enough to fund over 180,000 hours of vital Marie Curie nursing hours.

Superdrug is committed to the development of its colleagues. The business runs training

Brand History

1964 Superdrug is founded by the Goldstein family.

1966 The first Superdrug store opens in Putney High Street, followed two years later by stores in Croydon and Streatham.

1971 US company, Rite Aid Corporation, acquires a 49% stake in Superdrug.

1981 The 100th store opens in Manchester.

1983 Superdrug is floated on the USM stock market in February.

1984 Bishop Auckland becomes the company's 200th store.

1992 Superdrug launches its No Animal Testing Charter.

1996 The number of in-store pharmacies increases to 60.

2000 Superdrug launches Superdrug.com.

2007 A £46m investment programme launches giving 440 stores a facelift. The following year, its travel health clinics open.

2010 Superdrug Own Brand beauty and toiletry products are accredited as cruelty free and carry the BUAV symbol.

2011 Superdrug launches BeautyCard, its first customer loyalty card.

2013 That Superdrug Feeling campaign launches.

2014 Superdrug celebrates its 50th birthday and launches two new concept stores, Beauty Studio in Cardiff and the first wellbeing store opens in Banbury.

2015 The online opticians launches.

2017 Superdrug.com offers international delivery to Denmark, Finland and Sweden.

programmes to allow individuals to reach their potential, and has recently revealed plans to recruit for 500 new apprenticeship roles in 2018. The move will see an apprentice placed in every other store across the country. The target of 500 apprentices represented a significant increase to the number of young people joining the scheme in 2017.

Recent Developments

Superdrug continues to grow and opened 25 new stores in 2017, with a further 25 new stores planning over the next three years.

In February 2017, Superdrug's head office moved to a new location in central Croydon.

The 55,000 sq ft building, spread over six floors, was designed to create a collaborative environment, encourage healthy lifestyles and to support the future growth of the business.

In its Leicester Fosse Park store, Superdrug has recently opened a Beauty Studio floor. This offers beauty service areas providing manicures, nail painting, brow threading and tinting, lash treatments, waxing and ear piercing. A hair salon and barber has also been introduced.

Health services also continue to grow with Superdrug offering travel vaccinations, flu jabs as well as sexual and occupational health clinics in store.

Promotion

In 2017, Superdrug unveiled a new TV ad campaign that communicates the beauty retailer's new direction, reaching a wider demographic through inclusive messaging.

Brand Values

Superdrug's vision is to be the best in everyday beauty and health by ensuring that it gives its customers access to affordable and responsible products. Its Social Value is to have a positive impact on the societies in which it operates and its Environmental Value is to have a positive impact on the environment.

TATA
CONSULTANCY
SERVICES

As one of the **top three most valuable IT services brands** in the world,
Tata Consultancy Services (TCS) is also one of the **UK's largest digital employers**.
TCS works in **partnership with over 150 UK customers**, 38 of which are
FTSE 100 companies, spanning a wide range of sectors.

Market

Having been in the UK for over 40 years, TCS has become woven into the country's society and economy – from banking to retail to transport, as well as its engagement with the public sector. The UK now represents TCS' second largest market worldwide. By harnessing the power of digital technologies, TCS continues to work with businesses and organisations to create a fairer, more inclusive society; one which contributes to positive digital empowerment with clients and communities.

Digital technologies such as social, mobile, big data, cloud and artificial intelligence continue to accelerate and transform the modern economy. These disruptive technologies have led to a rapid transition into a new economic era; one where analytics rules over instinct, where customer experience defines your brand, and where the winners will be determined not by size and scale, but by innovation, insight and agility. For companies to maximise

benefits from these technologies, there is a clear necessity for them to adapt their existing processes, services and business models. As the digital economy continues to evolve, TCS is playing a key role in helping the UK respond to these challenges and opportunities.

Product

TCS works with some of Britain's best-known brands, helping them to adapt their business models through digital transformation and create sustainable growth. For example, the world's largest building society, Nationwide, is using TCS' artificial intelligence platform, ignio™, to improve IT responsiveness, resilience and agility, meaning an improvement to efficiency, an increase in accuracy as well as reduced costs.

2017 marked TCS' second year as Official Technology Partner to the Virgin Money London Marathon, as well as the first year that TCS provided the Official Race App, which was downloaded on nearly 300,000 devices. With more than 73,000 concurrent users at peak times during the day, people were able to share in the experience of how digital can empower individuals, teams and communities to achieve their goals.

Achievements

As a result of its industry-leading work, TCS has received a number of major honours including being ranked number one for customer satisfaction by Whitelane Research, for the fourth consecutive year. TCS has also been selected as the UK's Top Employer by the Top Employers Institute for the second consecutive year and certified as the number one Employer in Europe for the fourth year running.

This is in addition to more than 50 major UK and European awards for branding, communications and integrated campaigns. From applying digital technologies to the UK general election, to launching a thought leadership platform at Davos, TCS has been widely recognised for its efforts in engaging with businesses and wider society across Europe.

At the IPRA Golden World Awards, TCS was a winner in two categories: Best B2B campaign and Best Reputation & Brand Management Online, for its #DigitalEmpowers platform. Another campaign highlight was being awarded Gold for Best use of Digital in the Technology, Media and Telecoms sector at the Digital Impact awards.

Recent Developments

In the face of a 40,000 shortfall in STEM graduates across the UK, TCS is working in partnership with schools, universities and not-for-profit organisations to show young people how they can help shape the digital world that they live in. The technology industry in the UK is a great asset to the country and something that needs to be supported in order to keep driving growth and innovation. Through its IT Futures programme, started in 2013, TCS has helped over 200,000 students across 600 schools in the UK.

The Spark Salon series of events was created to showcase the role of technology in helping to create a more sustainable world. Debates have looked at different dimensions of technological change at the intersection of innovation, productivity, growth, disruption and social purpose. In 2017 TCS also started hosting the 'Digital Explorers Experience Work' initiative with MyKindaFuture. With initial events in London and Birmingham, over 800 young people aged 14-18 have completed a ground-breaking, week long programme to experience work in digital industries to increase their chances of succeeding in the sector.

In 2017, TCS also continued to expand its role as a Strategic Partner to the World Economic Forum (WEF) through the launch of its #DigitalEmpowers platform at Davos. With a focus on demonstrating how digital technologies serve as both a vital and dynamic force for good, compelling stories and technology solutions have been shared in the areas of Youth, Wellbeing, Planet, Equality and

DID YOU KNOW?

STEM education programmes by TCS have inspired two million children worldwide towards careers in technology.

Access; from the use of drones to help protect forests in Europe, to the Internet of Things, enabling the improvement of care for the elderly in Asia, digital plays a crucial role in improving lives.

Promotion
TCS is the Official Strategic Partner to the European Business Summit (EBS) and in 2017 launched #DigitalDirections, a platform offering curated content which celebrates the central role technology plays in powering innovation for business, as well as the various paths business and government leaders are forging to navigate the digital era.

TCS, in its role as a digital transformation thought leader, continues to be at the centre of modern businesses digital journeys. For example, in order to explore the important topic of Artificial Intelligence, TCS recently launched its latest Global Trend Study, Getting Smarter by the Day: How AI is Elevating the Performance of Global Companies. The research polled 335 executives across 13 global industry sectors in four regions of the world. Following the initial launch in February 2017, TCS launched part two of the study, delving deeper into the results of each of the 13 industry sectors surveyed, from automotive through to high tech.

In May 2017, TCS hosted the London edition of its annual global Innovation Forum series. Bringing together more than 300 UK C-suite executives and customers, along with over 50 technology innovation speakers, the event explored the topic of, Being Digital. With insight from researchers, technologists and start-ups across a variety of industries, TCS provided a platform for businesses to learn about the latest digital technologies.

Brand Values
As a trusted technology partner to celebrated UK brands, TCS continues to place itself at the heart of major industry developments and promote the wider impact that technology can have on business and society.

Brand History

1968 TCS is founded as India's first software services company. The first UK office opens seven years later.

2004 TCS undertakes the largest private sector initial public offering in the Indian market.

2006 TCS acquires the life and pensions operations of the Pearl Group to set up its BPO unit, Diligenta.

2009 TCS becomes a top 10 player in the global IT software and services industry.

2013 TCS is awarded the Platinum Big Tick – the highest ranking in Business in the Community's Corporate Responsibility Index.

2014 TCS becomes the world's second-most valuable IT services firm.

2016 TCS wins Company of the Year along with the Highly Commended Award in the Social Responsibility Project of the Year category at the Employee Engagement Awards.

2016 TCS becomes the Official Technology Partner of the Virgin Money London Marathon.

TED BAKER

LONDON

Having **launched as a shirt specialist in Glasgow**, Ted Baker quickly became the place to buy **the very best contemporary menswear around**, earning the moniker of 'No Ordinary Designer Label'. Last year marked **three decades since the brand's inception**; the idea first struck during a fishing trip in 1987.

Market

Notoriously competitive and fast-paced, the fashion industry is one of the world's largest and most complex. Within this rapidly-changing context, Ted continues to buck difficult trading conditions and successfully combat quickly-evolving competitors, helped by its model of having significantly more concessions over standalone stores, which has seen it beat a slump in retail footfall. Ted's unconventional approach of direct-to-consumer marketing contributes to this advantage, giving the brand particular strength both online and internationally. Ted's distinctive and quirky British take on fashion continues to make it a leading player in an increasingly challenging market, and it expects to see this impressive record continue for years to come.

Product

From the beginning Ted has had a very clear, unswerving focus on quality, attention to detail as well as a quirky sense of humour, so much

DID YOU KNOW?

Every standalone Ted Baker store across the world **is completely different,** with a theme **inspired by the city it's situated in**, and a bespoke marketing strategy.

so in fact that the first stores used to provide a laundry service for every shirt purchased – something that gained the quickly growing brand the title of 'No Ordinary Designer Label'. Everything produced under the Ted Baker name has his personality woven into its very heart.

As you'd expect from Ted, the approach to marketing the brand remains the same

as it was from day one; primarily by word of mouth and out of the ordinary activity. What other brand would give away Paxo stuffing at Christmas, a can of chocolate bunny hotpot for Easter, or even special World Cup football cards, Roy of the Rovers style? Ted remains one of the only brands to be built into an international designer label without an advertising campaign.

This unconventional approach is and has always been led by Closest Man to Ted, CEO and Founder Ray Kelvin CBE, whose unique vision continues to drive progress and success today. As Ted chooses not to advertise, the brand must do everything it can to support the collections in a more consistent, different and fun manner.

Today Ted's collections cover more than menswear, womenswear and fashion accessories. From bedlinen, tiles, tableware and rugs, to stationery, grooming, cosmetics, audio technology and even bicycles, Ted Baker is truly a global lifestyle brand.

Achievements

As one of the UK's leading designer brands, Ted has consistently increased its turnover and profit year on year, and has taken over £530m in retail sales globally in the past financial year.

In 2017, as well as the blockbuster Spring/Summer and Autumn/Winter collections across all product lines (and activity in 55 countries worldwide), Ted launched brand new collections including; luxury loungewear from Ted Says Relax; a beautiful Tie the Knot bridal collection; Colour by Numbers, a contemporary take on modern minimalism; Cottoned On, an architecture-inspired womenswear capsule; Precious Wonders, a fine jewellery range for ladies; Well Heeled, Italian-made handcrafted footwear for gents; and a collection tailored for the fairway in Ted Baker Golf.

Additionally, Ted's Grooming Room launched in Canary Wharf, as well as a fresh look and formula for the product range. Ted also opened in St. Pancras with a railway-inspired store

Brand History

1987 The idea for a global brand came to Ray Kelvin CBE while fly-fishing.

1988 Ted opens its first store in Glasgow.

1990 Covent Garden becomes the site for Ted's first London store.

1993 Ted launches the first womenswear collection.

1996 Ted begins wholesale operations in the USA.

1997 Ted Baker floats on the London Stock Exchange.

2000 Ted's first footwear collection launches and The Ugly Brown Building opens.

2001 Eyewear beccmes the next major launch for Ted, and is now distributed globally.

2004 Global expansion continues with Ted's first shops in Australia and New Zealand.

2010 The first Ted's Grooming Room opens in Cheapside.

2011 'The Closest Man to Ted', Ray Kelvin, is awarded a CBE for services to the fashion industry.

2016 Ted works with Hollywood Director Guy Ritchie on the 'Mission Impeccable' AW16 campaign.

2017 Ted launches an unprecedented number of new collections, continuing its success in 55 countries worldwide during a difficult year for retail.

---

as well as in Oxford Westgate along with a second village-within-a-village at one of Britain's top tourist attractions, Bicester Outlet Village. Meanwhile, overseas Ted gained ground in Miami, Tokyo, Sydney, Paris, Shanghai, LA, and Kuala Lumpur.

Recent Developments

As well as continued success on the high street, online and internationally, there have been several significant developments behind the scenes at Ted that are important company milestones as well as investments in its future. The company recently purchased its headquarters in King's Cross, London (humorously yet aptly referred to as 'The Ugly Brown Building'), with extensive plans to redevelop it as a hotel, retail complex and fashion school, and to double the size of the brand's offices.

Additionally, Ted has consolidated its existing warehouses and distribution network into one enormous complex in Derby, helping to streamline fulfilment for its rapidly expanding and successful e-commerce business. Further supporting this, Ted also implemented a completely new IT system across its global business to futureproof its infrastructure capabilities for predicted expansion.

Promotion

Social media presences across various global territories are supported with wider strategic developments of new platforms to support emerging markets. Using Ted's unique tone of voice and eye for detail to articulate the brand in a memorable fashion, Ted's in-house Brand Communications team works to deliver bespoke strategic and creative output across all channels. Fun, engaging and unforgettable ideas are

developed with one simple objective in mind: to connect and engage customers with Ted Baker, resulting in increased loyalty and high levels of return on investment.

Brand Values

Ted's mission is to build a successful company through the creation of a leading designer brand. It aims to achieve this by encouraging team members to conduct themselves in an efficient and courteous manner and by maintaining Ted's high standards and integrity. Ted prides itself in always being in a position to satisfy the needs of its customers. In order to protect the ethos and persona for which Ted has gained an enviable reputation, the team is always asking themselves the question 'Would Ted do it that way?'

tommee tippee® is **the number one baby feeding accessories brand** in the UK (Source: IRI November 2017) and one of the top brands of infant products and accessories in the global market **providing innovative, intuitive and stylish products** loved by babies and recommended by generations of parents.

Market

The UK baby accessories marketing is estimated to be worth approximately £170m (Source: IRI 2017 & Company Data) and encompasses everything from bibs and bottles, to monitors and harnesses. It does not include nappies, wipes, toiletries, formula milk, baby food or nursery furniture. tommee tippee® is number one in five of the top 10 categories in the baby accessories market (Source: IRI November 2017).

tommee tippee® has more than one-third of the total market share by value (Source: IRI November & Company Data 2017). Internationally, it is sold in over 70 countries.

Product

Every tommee tippee® product has been designed around one key principle – to make the life of parents easier. Since the introduction of the original spill-proof cup, tommee tippee® has earned a reputation for its clever ideas and the quality of its intuitive products that support children on their journey from their first feed to independent feeding.

In recent years, significant additions to the product portfolio have included Closer to Nature®, Perfect Prep™ and Sangenic® Tec. Closer to Nature® feeding bottles are the corner stone of the tommee tippee® portfolio. Designed to mimic the natural flex, feel and movement of a nipple, the original breast-like teat can be found on all Closer to Nature® Bottles, for a natural latch and smooth transition from breast to bottle.

Described as a '3am lifesaver' the Perfect Prep™ machine is designed to make preparing formula bottles quicker and more accurate, giving parents the extra peace of mind that comes from knowing their baby's bottle will be perfect every time. Meanwhile, the Sangenic® range helps ensure hygienic nappy disposal in the home by wrapping dirty nappies in antibacterial film. The Sangenic® Tec is the only nappy disposal system to twist and wrap each nappy for unbeatable odour block.

DID YOU KNOW?

Four Closer to Nature® bottles are **sold every minute in the UK***.

*Source: IRI & Company Data, Nov 2017

Achievements

Now in its fifth decade, tommee tippee® continues to impress industry professionals and parents alike with its products winning an array of awards. Once again, tommee tippee® swept the boards at the Loved By Parents awards with 11 awards in total, including seven Platinum across Perfect Prep™, Steamer Blender and Electric Steam Steriliser products as well as an additional Gold award for its Closer to Nature® Feeding Bottles.

Perfect Prep™ is highly regarded amongst parents and experts alike, winning a total of five awards in 2017 including Platinum, Best Innovative Feeding Product from Loved By Parents and Silver in, 'Can't Live Without' Parenting Product, from Made for Mums. Sangenic® Tec was also highly awarded, winning the Consumer Choice Award at Best Baby & Toddler Gear Awards.

Recent Developments

In 2017, following the acquisition by Shanghai Jahwa, tommee tippee® launched into China, the single largest baby goods market in the world which, in 2015 was estimated to be 13.2bn RMB and is expected to continue to grow at circa 15% per annum, 2015 - 2020. Shanghai Jahwa's existing distribution partners created a good strategic collaboration, which prioritised the launch of the brand into 180 Kidswant stores and across key online platforms (TMall and JD.com). China's large-scale market and rapid growth potential will help to continue to drive the global growth of tommee tippee®.

Since launch, tommee tippee® has exhibited at the CBME trade show in Shanghai attracting new distributors as well as significant media interest and collected the coveted Innovation in Feeding Award for the Closer to Nature® Glass bottle. Digital and social activity has also been ramping up, with tommee tippee® reaching an incredible 1.5m consumers via various platforms, including Wei Bo and We Chat, within the first 12 months from launch. This strategic move will consolidate its market leadership position and realise the tommee tippee® vision of becoming the world's most loved baby brand.

Brand History

tommee tippee® continues to drive its product portfolio forward with further launches planned for 2018, including Perfect Prep™ Day & Night, the latest edition to the Perfect Prep™ portfolio.

Promotion

Tommee tippee® is committed to a digital first approach across all aspects of its business and has invested heavily in a dynamic digital programme including social media marketing, SEO, PPC and online retailer activity. In addition to this, it also receives a substantial amount of PR and editorial endorsement from the parenting press and online as well as having a strong relationship with the parenting blog community.

In 2017, tommee tippee® launched Changing Times, a digital campaign designed to help parents embrace the changes in their lives and promote the Sangenic® range. tommee tippee® knows that changing nappies won't be top of any new parent's priority list – but it's certainly one of the biggest things to get to grips with. Using social media, the Changing Times campaign aims to embrace these changes and asks parents to share their stories online.

tommee tippee® is also one of the key exhibitors at the UK Baby shows, which attract more than 75,000 parents and pregnant women every year. The one-on-one interaction ensures that the brand is closer to parents, engaging them with product demonstrations and answering feeding questions.

Brand Values

For over 50 years, tommee tippee® has been designing and producing innovative, intuitive and stylish products to help parents on the rollercoaster ride of bringing up baby.

Now tommee tippee® has created a new global platform that unites, encourages and empowers parents to trust their instincts and #ParentOn.

TONI&GUY™ | OFFICIAL SPONSOR LONDON FASHION WEEK

TONI&GUY has long been renowned as an **innovator within the hairdressing industry**, **bridging the gap between high fashion and hairdressing.** Toni Mascolo OBE's franchise model has maintained the company's **high education and creative standards, protected the brand and made successes of thousands of TONI&GUY hairdressing entrepreneurs** worldwide.

Market

In the years since the birth of TONI&GUY, hairdressing has become a sophisticated industry worth billions, spawning some of the most influential and creative artists in the beauty and fashion sector. From individual salons to global chains, competition is fierce with consumers demanding the highest quality and service.

Having helped to change the face of the industry, the multi-awarded Superbrand has more than 600 salons internationally, covering 48 countries, whilst sister brand essensuals has more than 135 salons worldwide, with three essensuals London branches operating in America.

Product

TONI&GUY salons aim to offer a consistent level of service, guaranteed quality, exceptional cutting and innovative colour – in simple but well-designed salons at an affordable price. All techniques practiced by the stylists are taught by highly trained and experienced educators in 20 academies around the world.

The multi award-winning label.m Professional Haircare range was created by Toni and his daughter, Sacha Mascolo-Tarbuck in 2005. The brand now boasts more than 80 products and is the Official Haircare Product of London Fashion Week. In 2016, label.m launched its most premium range yet – Diamond Dust, utilising real diamonds alongside other luxurious ingredients.

Achievements

TONI&GUY has a worldwide brand presence and is recognised for its strong education network. "Education, education, education", was often quoted by Toni Mascolo as it is considered the cornerstone of the hairdressing powerhouse. An average of 100,000 hairdressers are trained each year, with more than 5,500 employees in the UK and a further 3,500 worldwide. This philosophy of motivation, inspiration and education are key to the brand's success.

DID YOU KNOW?

Co-Founder and **CEO Toni Mascolo OBE** still cut hair one day a week, **alternating between London's Sloane Square and Marylebone** stores, until shortly before he passed away in 2017.

Co-founder and CEO, Toni Mascolo OBE, sadly passed away in 2017. In his illustrious career he guided the direction of TONI&GUY and received much recognition for his work. Toni won London Entrepreneur of the Year and received an OBE for his services to the British hairdressing industry in 2008. He was also honoured with an International Achievement Award from the Fellowship for British Hairdressers and an International Legend Award from the Association Internationale Presse Professionelle Coiffure Awards. Toni was also an Honorary

Professor of Durham University and recognised as one of the 10 most successful Italians in the UK. As one of the most celebrated entrepreneurs in hairdressing, Toni also received the Primi Dieci Award at BAFTA.

Toni's daughter, Global Creative Director Sacha Mascolo-Tarbuck, was the youngest ever winner of Newcomer of the Year at 19 years old. Additional awards include London Hairdresser of the Year, Hair Magazine's Hairdresser of the Year, Creative Head's Most Wanted Look of the Year, and its Most Wanted Hair Icon in 2009, and Fashion Focused Image of the Year from the Fellowship for British Hairdressing as well as Hairdresser of the Year.

Recent Developments

The legendary Artistic Team, under the direction of Sacha Mascolo-Tarbuck, has received numerous awards over the years. Most recently this has included British Hairdressing Awards in 2017, which brings its impressive tally to 67.

Although established more than 50 years ago, the globally recognised brand prides itself on 'moving with the times' and investing in the careers of young hairdressers. In 2017, Katie Prescott from TONI&GUY Canary Wharf was one of four to earn a place on the highly coveted Fellowship Hair F.A.M.E Team 2018, a prestigious accolade and one that counts industry heavyweights such as Errol Douglas MBE, as well as British Hairdresser of the Year, Umberto Gianni and Jamie Stevens as past recipients.

Promotion

TONI&GUY juggles the need for consistency, the desire to be fashionable and the reassurance of solid service values, with the excitement of avant-garde styling, supported by its philosophy of continual education.

TONI&GUY.TV launched in 2003 to enhance in-salon experience. Containing up-to-the-minute content, it still receives more than 90,000 views per week in the UK.

Brand History

1963 TONI&GUY is launched from a single unit in Clapham, south London by Toni Mascolo and his brother Guy.

1982 The TONI&GUY Academy launches.

1985 TONI&GUY's first international salon opens in Tokyo, Japan.

1987 TONI&GUY's first franchise salon opens in Brighton.

2001 The TONI&GUY signature haircare range is launched. The following year, Toni and Pauline Mascolo launch the TONI&GUY Charitable Foundation.

2003 TONI&GUY Magazine and TONI&GUY.TV are launched in the UK. The brand also expands into different markets, opening an optician and a deli-café.

2004 TONI&GUY becomes the Official Sponsor of London Fashion Week.

2005 label.m Professional Haircare by TONI&GUY launches, growing to include nearly 60 products distributed in over 50 countries.

2008 Toni Mascolo receives an OBE for his services to the British Hairdressing industry.

2010 Sacha Mascolo-Tarbuck and James Tarbuck join the British Fashion Council/Vogue Designer Fashion Fund.

2011 TONI&GUY becomes Official Sponsor of the British Fashion Awards.

2013 TONI&GUY celebrates 50 years of hairdressing success with a festival for over 5,000 staff.

2014 TONI&GUY celebrates 10 years as Official Sponsor of London Fashion Week.

2015 TONI&GUY launch its first dedicated barber shop in Shoreditch London and label.m celebrates 10 years of success.

2016 TONI&GUY announce its partnership with Samsung who provide 150 salons with the latest window screen technology, revolutionising the way salons communicate brand messaging.

2018 Katie Prescott from TONI&GUY Canary Wharf is one of four to earn a place on the highly coveted Fellowship Hair F.A.M.E Team.

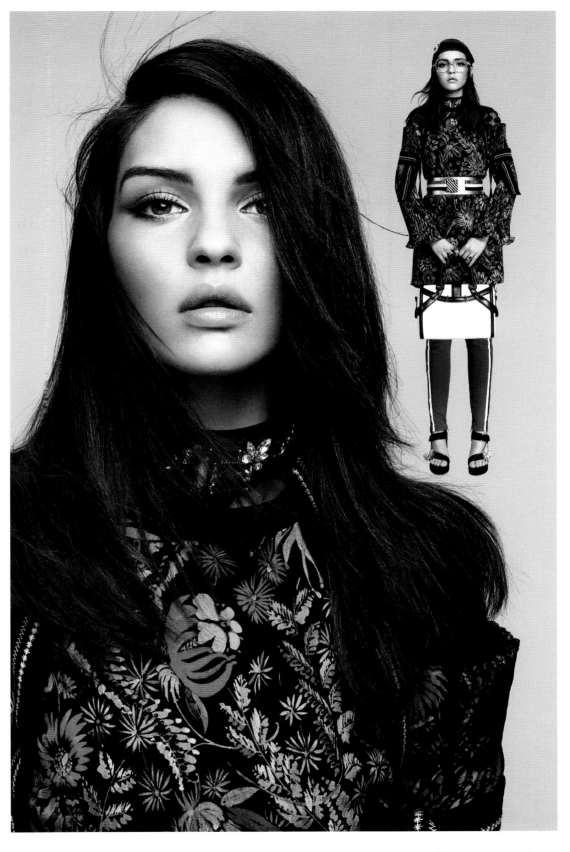

TONI&GUY Magazine was also launched in 2003 to communicate the brand's heritage and philosophy, focusing on key trends in fashion, arts, beauty and travel. Distributed in salons across the global, the magazine promotes the inspirational, accessible face of the company. Furthermore, it won Best Consumer Publication in 2011 at the APA Awards.

Fashion has always been a major pillar of the brand. In 2004, the link grew even stronger when it first began sponsoring London Fashion Week.

More than 25 seasons later, the partnership continues to grow through the endorsement of its professional haircare range, label.m, which is the first product line London Fashion Week lent its name to. In addition, for the 11th season, TONI&GUY and label.m offered support backstage to key designers showing at the 2017 London Fashion Week Men's as well as providing an onsite salon.

The TONI&GUY Session Team works on more than 80 shows per year in London, New York, Paris, Milan Tokyo and Shanghai, offering support to key designers including Mary Katranzou, Pam Hogg, Paul Costello and House of Holland, among many. TONI&GUY has also been awarded as a Consumer Superbrand for 11 years and is proud to support the industry as a leading sponsor of the British Fashion Awards.

Brand Values

TONI&GUY's reputation has been built on an impeccable pedigree and foundation of education, fashion focus and friendly, professional service. TONI&GUY aims to encompass the importance of local and individually tailored, customer-led service, promoting an authoritative, cohesive and – most importantly – inspiring voice.

In 1810 the Reverend Henry Duncan did something revolutionary. He built the Trustees Savings Bank, whose sole purpose was to **help hard working local people thrive.** Four years ago, TSB, Britain's challenger bank was re-born based on his values, to make **banking better for all UK consumers.**

Market

In 2013 the big five banks controlled over 85% of all UK bank accounts. Following the banking crisis, TSB was created to bring more competition to UK banking and ultimately make banking better for all consumers.

TSB delivers a different kind of retail banking that it calls 'Local Banking'. The bank only serves local people and local businesses, to help them and the communities they live in to thrive. It refuses to engage in any risky practises like overseas speculation and investment banking. In short it's High Street, not Wall Street.

Product

Fundamentally, TSB believes in working in partnership with its customers; at its heart is the principle that when people help people we all thrive together.

That's why TSB designs its products the way it does. Its Classic Plus account, with no monthly fee, has a 3% interest rate which doesn't disappear after a year. TSB offers this because it believes the more a customer puts into a partnership the more they should get back. Likewise, its Fix and Flex personal loans and mortgages enable people to borrow well by allowing them to take repayment holidays should life change.

DID YOU KNOW?

On average, 1,000 people a day are voting with their feet and joining TSB.

It's also why TSB calls all its staff Partners, and rewards them when they do as much as they can to actively help people not when they just sell them things. There are no sales targets for TSB Partners and the TSB Award is paid annually to everyone (from the CEO to front-line branch staff) as the same percentage of salary.

Achievements

At launch, TSB's market share was just over 4%, whilst its infrastructure (branches and digital capability) was around 6%. Therefore, TSB decided to grow this by attracting a 6% 'share of the flow' (SoF) in the current account market, equating to an ambitious 50% growth in new customers.

TSB's different approach to banking has paid off and has enabled the bank to deliver on these goals. In fact, TSB has achieved its 6% SoF ambition every year since launch with an average of 7.1%. Indeed, it has achieved the strongest net switcher growth of any bank in Britain (Source: Current account switching data, BACS, 2017), with over 1,000 people joining TSB every day.

TSB's Partners and customers appear to notice how TSB is different too. TSB is one of only four UK companies to be recognised in both the Great Places to Work and Best Big Companies lists. And TSB has been voted Britain's most recommended high street bank (Source: BDRC Continental, 2016/17) and Best Current Account Provider (Source: yourmoney.com, 2017).

The value of TSB has grown as a result. In July 2012 the unbranded TSB was valued at £665m. At the time of the sale to Sabadell in March 2015 the overall business was valued at £1.7bn. In 2014, TSB's first full year as a challenger bank, the TSB

Brand History

1810 The Trustee Savings Bank is established by Reverend Henry Duncan of Ruthwell.

1986 TSB Group PLC is founded.

1995 TSB is bought by Lloyds Bank. TSB disappears as a separate brand, living only as part of the name LloydsTSB.

2013 TSB separates from Lloyds Banking Group, and becomes an independent entity, tasked by the EU with increasing competition in the British banking sector after the banking crisis.

2014 TSB Bank PLC goes public with successful IPO.

2015 TSB is bought by Sabadell, Spain's fifth largest banking group, becoming independent from Lloyds Banking Group.

2016 TSB is recognised as Britain's most recommended high street bank.

brand itself was valued at an impressive £507m (Source: Brand Finance, 2017) and a year later this had risen by a further 20% or £100m.

Recent Developments

TSB recognises and celebrates local people and their communities through its #TSBLocalPride programme. At its heart is a long-term partnership with Pride of Britain and Pride of Sport. Pride of Britain is the nation's biggest annual awards ceremony of its kind, celebrating the ordinary people across the UK who've gone to extraordinary lengths to help others.

The bank also has a Local Charity Partnership programme, supporting over 450 local charities, and a partnership with Sported, who enable people to help others through sport in over 3,500 local sports clubs across the UK.

At the same time, TSB prides itself on creating a culture which encourages and builds diversity and inclusion. For example, TSB was one of the first companies to proactively publish and explain its gender pay gap.

DID YOU KNOW?

TSB is Britain's most recommended high street bank.

And whilst many people believe that banks will use digital technology to reduce services, TSB continues to invest in providing the best of both worlds: human interaction when people want it, combined with the opportunity to bank wherever, whenever and however they like through digital technology.

Join the bank that's not like other banks.

We're the only major bank that uses every penny our customers deposit to help our other customers.

tap | click | call | visit

Local banking for Britain

TSB is currently addressing the barriers some customers have around digital banking, including pioneering iris scanning and facial recognition to provide the highest levels of security in its mobile app.

Promotion

At TSB the brand is not just a wrapper. It's the entire customer experience. Whenever, wherever and however people come into contact with the bank, TSB seeks to deliver a differentiated and consistent brand experience driven by its purpose, values and a set of behaviours that it describes as 'neighbourly with know-how'. Every touchpoint delivers the experience, be it the advertising, branches, Partners, online or the mobile app.

Brand Values

The bank is driven by a set of values (pioneering, straightforward, transparent, collaborative and responsible), which are very different from those which banking has come to be associated with. They continue to inform everything TSB does, just as they have done from the very start.

But, even though the brand has achieved a great deal, TSB's work is far from done. Whilst the business is growing, the dominance of the big banks remains. That is why TSB is going to continue to challenge the market, leading by example and being a different kind of bank, to fulfil its mission of making banking better for everybody.

Founded in 1934, William Hill is the most **recognised and trusted brand in an increasingly competitive betting and gaming market.** With a diverse range of sports betting, gaming products and services, William Hill is now a **truly global brand, attracting millions** of customers from the UK, Spain, Italy, Australia, Nevada and more.

Market

In 2017, the UK gambling industry was worth £13.7bn and employed over 100,000 people. Remote betting, which is predominantly online, is now the largest sector at 34%. The UK is also the world's largest regulated online gambling market, four times bigger than Italy or Australia. Employing over 16,000 people in nine countries, William Hill continues to invest in its people and technology to maintain its market-leader status.

Product

William Hill is a leading provider of licensed betting offices (LBOs) in the UK, with 2,372 shops nationwide.

In its shops, customers will find a wide array of betting opportunities, from football to horse racing, virtual racing and numbers betting. Today, every major event comes with betting odds attached, from royal weddings to Royal Ascot, general elections and reality TV. Customers can bet over-the-counter with a betting slip or coupon, or electronically through self-service betting terminals. For gaming, it offers electronic roulette, blackjack, slots and an array of other casino-style games on its gaming machines.

Since 1998, William Hill has also been providing online betting services, and is now one of the leading online betting and gaming providers in the UK. With more than a million betting opportunities on offer every week, William Hill provides in-play and pre-match sports betting as well as a wide range of gaming products.

In-play (betting during the course of a live event) has become increasingly popular in recent years and amounted to nearly half of William Hill's sports turnover in 2017. The bookmaker is also the leading provider of online casino games to the UK, with its exclusive Vegas platform proving very popular, particularly with sports betting customers.

In all of its retail and online channels, William Hill encourages responsible gambling, with a range

of tools to help customers gamble safely, from setting time and spend limits on gaming machines to information on support services and self-exclusion systems.

Achievements

The increasing use of mobile technology has been a key trend in the gambling industry in recent years, and mobile betting and gaming continues to be a major focus for William Hill. Its Sports iOS App is the most downloaded Sportsbook app in the Apple App Store, with over 2.8m downloads.

The bookmaker has also taken its mobile and online offering into a number of other countries, focusing on markets with a strong gambling culture and a competitive, regulated industry which gives it the ability to offer a broad sports betting product range and casino gaming. William Hill is now a top three online sports betting operator in Italy and Spain, and one of the largest online betting companies in Australia with nearly 250,000 active customers.

Recent Developments

Project Trafalgar – the biggest technology project ever undertaken by William Hill – has been a major step forward on its technology journey. Trafalgar was a comprehensive overhaul of the entire web architecture; with a new front-end experience

Brand History

1934 William Hill begins business as a post and telephone betting service.

1961 On 1st May betting shops become legal in the UK.

1966 William Hill buys into betting shops and starts to acquire existing betting businesses.

1971 William Hill dies, having retired the previous year.

1994 It becomes legal to accept football pools coupons in betting shops.

1997 Nomura purchases William Hill for £700m from Brent Walker.

1998 William Hill launches its online Sportsbook.

2000 William Hill is the first major bookmaker to offer a deduction-free betting service through the internet.

2000 William Hill launches an online casino.

2002 William Hill is floated on the London stock exchange at 225p per share.

2011 American Wagering Inc, Neva Sportsbook Operations and Brandywine Bookmaking in the US are aquired.

2012 William Hill becomes the first European gaming operator to be awarded a full gaming license in Nevada.

2014 William Hill's Sportsbook app passes two million downloads.

2017 Project Trafalagar, its biggest technology project ever undertaken, goes live.

for desktop, mobile web and native app users, which gave William Hill complete control over the interfaces that customers experience.

Technical updates can now be released much faster, moving from around 10 a year to multiple releases in a single day, which enables William Hill to further enhance its position as a market leader. The company has also unlocked the ability to deliver a single experience across multiple digital platforms, from mobile to desktop to retail, supporting its omni-channel strategy that aims to bring a more consistent 'one William Hill' experience to customers.

Project Trafalgar also helped William Hill learn more about its customers' use of its web and mobile products, constantly mapping their journeys to improve and evolve the products customers currently enjoy, as well as launching new output that anticipates what they will want in the future. This has allowed William Hill to further differentiate its betting and gaming experiences, which is increasingly important in the competitive landscape.

DID YOU KNOW?

At it's peak, **William Hill processed 10, 346 bets per minute** during the 2017 Grand National.

Promotion

With a network of 2,372 shops, there is a good chance that one of William Hill's shop posters or digital screens will catch the eye of those frequenting the high street. Throughout the year, the company also runs ads in the most popular UK national newspapers and impactful TV ads around live sporting events on Sky, ITV and BT Sport.

William Hill's marketing strategy has evolved to reflect the growth of online and mobile betting. It invests heavily in social media, SEO and paid search, the latter of which now commands the largest share of the bookmaker's online spend.

William Hill also sponsors a wide range of sports and events, such as the William Hill World Darts Championship, tennis, boxing and football, including the William Hill Scottish Cup.

The bookmaker is also an official partner of three of the most iconic teams in English Premier League, Chelsea, Everton and Tottenham Hotspur. All these key partnerships enable William Hill to engage with the supporters of these sports and clubs on a regular basis.

Brand Values

William Hill firmly believes in aiming to 'go one better' than its competition, with the mantra 'It'll do will never do' used as a guiding principal for everything it does. The company is also committed to providing betting and gaming experiences that its customers can enjoy responsibly.

Anytime, Anywhere

Redefining the rules of customer engagement

NICK MORRIS
Founding Partner, Canvas8

Back in the early 90s, Stu Allan was instrumental in my discovery of new music. He was a DJ at Key 103 in Manchester, and before that, at Piccadilly Radio. On Friday nights, I'd stay in to listen to him, furiously scribbling down his setlists as I held my cassette player on record in my other hand.

Last year, when Canvas8 explored shifts in people's music habits for Red Bull Music Academy, we pieced together a picture that looked very different from my teenage self in the 90s.

While a handful of hardcore fans carved out dedicated time for finding new music, the majority of passionate fans – people committed enough to go on holiday to see bands that they loved – rarely made a point of searching out new music. Instead, music discovery was a part of their music listening. They were always receptive to something new; discovery didn't have to be allotted a separate time and space.

Today, this same attitude applies to just about everything people consume. Just as music and sound are woven into the fabric of everyday life, new technology – and mobile, specifically – have broken all types of discovery out of their neatly contained boxes. Whether it's design buffs on the lookout for a new furniture piece, or cinema lovers

in the market for new media, people expect to encounter inspiration naturally in daily life, rather than having to actively seek it out.

Once upon a time, there was a time and place for everything. To get a handle on current affairs, we turned to The News at 10. For updates on football, we scanned Ceefax page 302. And for shopping, it was Saturday afternoon. But now, the phrase "let's go shopping" has become increasingly rare. It seems unnecessary – and a little backwards – to assign boundaries to something that can happen anytime, anywhere. And that's no exaggeration – among Britons, 20% shop on their daily commute, and a quarter even admit to shopping while they're on the loo.

> "People expect to **encounter inspiration naturally** in daily life, rather than having to actively seek it out."

But now that the rules of customer engagement – once so neatly outlined – have dissolved into thin air, how do we navigate this space? How can we find smart ways to reach people in a discovery free-for-all?

The traditional purchase cycle was comfortingly linear. People would experience a need, research options, and shop to satisfy that need. And while that's still true in some cases, the bulk of customer engagement is being swallowed up by ambient discovery. As futurist Chuck Martin observes: "We're in the midst of a revolution in the way people shop, in how they decide to buy, and in all behaviours associated with the entire purchase process." Thanks to mobile, which is now involved in 45% of all retail journeys, ambient discovery is here to stay – particularly as carving out time for active discovery becomes laughable with the pace of contemporary life.

While this shift might be a hurdle for some, many of today's challenger brands are turning it into an asset. From the coral colour of Monzo's bank card that's designed to provoke conversation, to Airbnb's website pushing people to stumble upon new travel destinations, the normalising of discovery is helping brands to get on the map.

So, if ambient discovery is here to stay, how can brands follow in Monzo and Airbnb's footsteps by enabling it?

It comes down to four things – ambient discoveries need to be found, validated, remembered, and actionable.

For discoveries to be effectively found, they need to feel natural, rather than forced – whether through the suggestions of friends, algorithms, or niche communities. Communities lend themselves especially well

to discovery, by marrying an environment of trust with exposure to new things. It's a model that's worked well for platforms like HYPEBEAST, which has racked up 46m pageviews a month by catering to the niche sneakerhead community.

Beyond this, ambient discoveries need to be validated. As discovery errs towards the accidental, rather than the intentional, it carries a shadow of self-doubt. Given that 96% of American women seek the advice of others before they buy or try products, peer-to-peer communities help people to be confident in their discoveries. It's something that beauty brand Milk has gotten right with their community of 84 micro bloggers, known as Generation Milk.

Thirdly, discoveries need to be remembered – otherwise, there's no point in being found. Discovery is less focused than the mission-based shopping of yesterday, meaning that whatever's found can just as easily be lost again. Services like Whilo are addressing this by letting people create

wishlists for any occasion, while Instagram has launched Bookmarks, allowing people to save and organise the content discovered on its platform.

> "Discoveries need
> to be remembered –
> otherwise, there's
> no point in being found."

Lastly, ambient discoveries need to be actionable – and new technology is being built to make this happen as seamlessly as possible. It's already being put into practice by brands like ASOS with their 'visual search' that lets people take photos of whatever inspires them, and search for similar items in ASOS's online catalogue. With upcoming AI-powered technology, pointing a smartphone at a restaurant will be able to connect people to reviews or let them book a table – effectively bridging the gap between discovery and action.

So what does this mean for marketers? It means don't stalk people with targeted banner ads, don't push your wares forcefully on them, and don't get lost in the noise once you're found. Take a cue from HYPEBEAST, Milk, Whilo, and ASOS – and support people in discovery.

About Canvas8

Canvas8 helps businesses understand people to make better strategic decisions. With a deeper understanding of what people really want they inspire innovation in some of the world's leading brands, agencies and organisations.

CANVAS8

The Path to Organic Growth

Adding tangible value through branding in the B2B market

MARK LETHBRIDGE

CEO of Gravity Global and
Founding Partner of Branding
Business (EMEA)

Driving profitable organic revenue growth is becoming increasingly difficult for many of today's B2B enterprises. In recent years, this burden has increasingly fallen on the shoulders of the CMO. Whereas the discipline of marketing encompasses many functions, CEOs are increasingly preoccupied with just one priority: lead generation to support sales. CMOs have been under pressure to automate lead generation through complex marketing technology stacks, overhaul their team skill sets, and prove their line-of-sight contribution to revenue.

While some CMOs are making progress, many struggle to meet the rising expectations of impatient CEOs and sales leaders. Lofty lead pipeline goals increase the pressure on CMOs and their marketing teams as CEOs turn to mergers and acquisitions to 'buy growth'.

Is this approach sustainable? Is it the best path forward for delivering sustainable organic revenue growth? Or is there a better way?

Examining the underlying reasons for the CEO/CMO schism, we believe there are three factors at play:

(1) CEO investment priorities: CEOs are comfortable making investments in technology, processes and capital equipment – but often feel lost when it comes to investing in, and building, a sustainable brand.

(2) CEO attitudes toward branding: CEOs see branding as an arcane concept borrowed from the consumer-packaged goods (CPG) industry that has little relevance in the world of B2B. It's also true that marketing agencies have sold 'branding' and delivered little more than campaigns that spike awareness but don't deliver sales.

(3) CEO understanding of buyer behaviour: CEOs are out-of-touch with modern B2B buyer behaviour. Today, buyers trust peers more than brands and want to be educated, not sold. As a result, CEOs often promote an outdated model of aggressive marketing and sales tactics for short-term gain at the expense of long-term customer lifetime value.

What can B2B CMOs do to build CEO Trust and increase revenue?

Sustainable, long-term financial gains are not found in quick-fix tactics such as MarTech automation or clever advertising slogans – they are found in creating and sustaining a brand that offers the three things buyers want: trusted advice; experiences (instead of products); and an emotional connection (feeling good about the vendors they buy from). This requires B2B companies and their CMOs to rethink their antiquated view of brand strategy and customer engagement.

We recommend that CMOs consider three ways they can transform their brand to drive sustainable revenue and become a growth partner with the CEO.

CMO Imperative – Number One:
Establish a connection between the brand and business value

No amount of argument or cajoling is going to change a CEOs entrenched prejudice about branding. If the word can't even be used in the c-suite it's a real problem. What the CEO will listen to is data. He needs to know where growth is going to come from.

The brand must first be framed in terms of what the market values (not what the vendor thinks is valuable). This requires discovery via primary buyer research to understand what they define as value.

> "Technology now allows rigorous analysis and reporting on a broad range of deliverables."

It's true, there is a complexity of data and analytics available to CEOs, but the old maxim 'data rich, information poor' still holds true. Mobility, social media and emerging technologies are transforming entire industries, commoditising products and reshaping customer interaction with brands. To bridge the divide between brand strategy and business value, there are quantitative market insight tools available to B2B brands.

Within a landscape of key competitor activity, such tools analyse in detail brand performance against specific buyer segments consisting of attribute clusters and, critically, identify the segment with the strongest buyer affinity with your brand and the greatest potential for growth. The output is highly accessible to management teams and gives both the CMO and the CEO confidence to make major brand investment decisions based on the data.

Finally, this insight allows the CMO to build comprehensive data analysis capabilities and create a dashboard of metrics that covers all channels, integrating data into a single portal to give the business and your CEO 24/7 access to one dashboard, evidencing the tangible value marketing delivers.

Technology now allows rigorous analysis and reporting on a broad range of deliverables. It can monitor brand and product sentiment down to city level, define where the opportunity and threats within customer sets exist and provide a thorough analysis of the customer journey from initial contact, re-targeting, and a direct link between marketing and sales. This is hard data you can defend and use.

CMO Imperative – Number Two:
Shift your message focus to become relevant to buyers

For decades, marketing and sales professionals have been taught to talk about their company, products, awards, and customer case studies. Websites are packed with product information while sales presentations often begin with an overview of the business and its solutions. As mentioned earlier, buyer dynamics have changed, but the sales and marketing tactics employed by many B2B companies have failed to adapt. For example, Forrester Research found that 59% of B2B buyers now prefer online research because sales reps push an agenda instead of helping them solve a problem.

You can't grow revenue when buyers tune-out your messages and avoid your sales people.

According to CEB research, business value perceptions hardly vary at all between brands, either within an industry or even across industries. In fact, a whopping 86% of B2B buyers stated they could not see any meaningful difference between suppliers. This is costly. McKinsey found that companies unable to articulate business value experienced 20% deeper discounting to win the sale.

B2B CMOs need to shift the focus of their message strategy and content from products to the business outcomes that buyers seek. This requires brands to flip their approach, starting with the end-goal in mind and working backwards.

A best practice five-step approach:

(1) Define the ideal customer profiles (ICPs) that represent the most attractive revenue growth within a brand's business strategy.
(2) Conduct buyer persona and journey research to document the buying process, information needs by stage, decision stakeholders, conflict that stalls deals, decision criteria, and more.
(3) Develop Message Maps for each market that quantifies value propositions (business value, personal value) and insight-led sales talking points at a segment level, buyer persona level, and account level (for AMB).

(4) Audit existing content libraries for alignment of message narratives to buyer journey stages, buyer personas, preferred mediums.
(5) Capture unscripted voice-of-customer stories and develop personalised content to support lead generation campaigns and modular sales enablement assets.

Real content personalisation happens when messages are tailored to individual buyers. Effective message personalisation includes appealing to both business value and personal value. Business value refers to how a solution helps the buyer deliver on business priorities, or solve a problem. Personal value appeals to the professional benefits, social benefits, emotional benefits and self-image of the buyer.

CMO Imperative Number Three:
Go beyond products, sell experiences

In the B2B world buyers are looking for experiences, not transactions. The sales experience, the on-boarding experience, customer support, the functionality and user experience of the website – it all matters. Those that get it wrong are left competing for the scraps in a race to the bottom in terms of profitability. Customer experience is critical, not just in determining the long-term value of a customer, but of their willingness to recommend your company (essential when you consider up to 92% of purchasing decisions are influenced by word-of-mouth recommendations).

This reality has left many B2B brands ill prepared and struggling to remain relevant to buyers.

This gap between selling products and delivering experiences is being accelerated by the expectations of Millennials, who seek meaningful connections with the brands they buy.

A 2017 Forrester Research report entitled, Millennial B2B Buyers Come of Age, states: "While recent research indicates that 73% of Millennials are involved in B2B purchasing decisions, their rise to power is largely going unnoticed. Companies that purposefully adapt their marketing and sales strategies to better mesh with the Millennial mindset will outperform the competition.

In Summary

When done correctly, this triple-pronged approach to aligning marketing and sales communications along the buyer journey can drive superior financial performance and revenue growth:

- Brands that articulate business value can shorter sales cycles by up to 24%, according to Sirius Decisions, and avoid price discounting of up to 20% (McKinsey & Company).
- Brands that map content to customer journeys experience 73% lead (MQL) conversion rates (Source: Aberdeen Research).
- Brands that personalise communications to buyers realise up to 50% lower customer acquisition costs and up to 20% improvement in marketing ROI (McKinsey & Company).

Inside some organisations, there is an opportunity for the CMO to enlighten c-suite counter-parts as to the value of brand strategy, activation, and experience delivering on both short-term lead generation and long-term financial health. In other organisations, don't try to change the CEO's mind about the value of branding – deliver results with a growth-based brand strategy.

Thanks to contributions from Branding Business: Alan Brew/ Steve Patti

About Gravity Global

This award-winning dedicated global B2B agency network serves clients around the world that face challenging business issues and environments. The results Gravity's clients achieve are testament to its marketing models, process and industry leading creativity.

GenZ and the UK Retail Market

Understanding the new breed of digitally savvy consumer

JAMES McCOY
Research Director, Research Now SSI

Millennials, of whom Generation Z (GenZ) are the youngest cohort, represent a quarter of the world's population. As this generation moves to become the primary consumer base, retailers need to think out of the box when looking to attract the digitally savvy subscriber. To understand these emerging consumers better, Research Now SSI conducted extensive research across seven countries – the UK, France, Germany, Italy, Australia, Canada and the USA. The survey of over 1,000 members of GenZ in each country provides a unique insight into the mindset of these consumers, including how they want to be marketed to, where to reach them and what tone to strike in any messaging.

How GenZ see themselves
An important step in targeting GenZ is understanding how they view themselves. In the UK, this generation describe themselves as "honest", "funny", "realistic" and "reliable", a similar pattern seen in other countries surveyed. However, GenZers in the UK are more likely than their counterparts in any other EMEA country surveyed to describe themselves as "independent" and "individual". This directly correlates to how retailers should approach GenZ through their advertising: when asked to rank digital ad features in order of importance, "fun" (31%) ranked highest, followed by "originality" (25%).

For UK retailers wanting to target this generation, marketing messages with authenticity, originality and humour will strike the right chord and help them stand out from the crowd. Additionally, because this generation wants to believe that they are understood as individuals, personalisation has never been more important. Retailers need to demonstrate that they 'know' and understand the individual GenZer and customise the end-to-end shopping experience, across all channels and touchpoints.

Which platforms
GenZ is the first truly digital generation, having grown up with social media, mobile and online channels, this is where retailers need to focus their marketing outreach.

GenZers are currently using some form of social media daily, providing opportunities to target this true digital native. Snapchat is by far the most popular platform in the UK, with the highest daily usage of any country surveyed and an average of 11 visits or more a day. Brands utilising the Snapchat platform will gain more exposure and reach a larger portion of this audience.

> "In the UK, this generation describe themselves as "honest", "funny", "realistic" and "reliable.""

YouTube is popular across all countries surveyed, with nearly 100% penetration in each, and is rated as one of the most acceptable ways of contacting the GenZ consumer. Aside from the blanket term 'social media', GenZers across all countries surveyed feel that 'video adverts (e.g. on YouTube)' are the best way for brands to reach them to advertise their products and services.

GenZers have been raised on mobile, with smartphones integral to how they interact with the world. 39% of GenZers in the UK spend between 11 and 30 hours per week on their phone, with a further quarter devoting a whopping 30 hours or more. Clearly retailers need to be mobile aware – when both targeting and selling to this generation – via apps or mobile optimised websites. This is not optional.

Buying Behaviours
UK GenZers are more likely than their counterparts in the other EMEA countries surveyed to prefer shopping online because it's convenient with their lifestyle, matched only by the US. Retailers must put considerable effort into making the online shopping experience as easy as possible for this generation. Next day delivery, try before you buy and one click purchasing are all extremely attractive

> "Snapchat is by far the most popular platform in the UK, with the highest daily usage of any country surveyed and an average of 11 visits or more a day."

to the fast-paced GenZer; recommendations, pairings and abandoned basket features are essential for this 'individual' and 'authentic' generation. When asked about buying behaviour influences, price came out on top, which is somewhat unsurprising given the limited expendable income this generation has. Next came "social media" and "talking to friends and family", indicating that word of mouth is extremely important to this generation. What should retailers do to tap into this? Campaigns encouraging consumers to engage on social media such as River Island's #IMWEARINGRI or Calvin Klein's #MyCalvins represent an imaginative way to engage this audience, using peer influence.

Marketing strategies need careful planning Research Now SSI's survey findings reveal a wide variety of metrics that set UK GenZers apart from the crowd – not only from older generations, but from their counterparts in other countries surveyed. Retailers aiming to target the world's first truly digital native consumer will need to plan their marketing strategies carefully.

This article is taken from a wider report, which demonstrates how research commissioned from Research Now SSI can be utilised to formulate actionable insights for companies and clients, helping to make better business decisions to achieve better results.

About Research Now SSI

Research Now SSI is the global leader in digital research data for better insights and business decisions. The company provides world-class research data solutions that enable better results for more than 3,500 market research, consulting, media, healthcare, and corporate clients. Research Now SSI operates globally with locations in the Americas, Europe, and Asia-Pacific, and is recognised as the quality, scale, and customer satisfaction leader in the market research industry.

Appendix

Superbrands Selection Process

Introducing the Experts

Council Profiles

Highlights of the 2018 Results

Qualifying Brands

Superbrands
Selection Process

Superbrands UK Annual Volume 19, 2018

The annual Consumer Superbrands and Business Superbrands surveys identify the UK's strongest business-to-consumer and business-to-business brands through an extensive and robust research process.

Brands do not apply or pay to be considered for Superbrands status. Over 3,000 brands – representing the major names across 145 categories – are instead evaluated. This process identifies the best brands in the country, not just the best among those submitted.

For the past 12 years, both surveys have been independently managed by The Centre for Brand Analysis (TCBA), which undertakes a wide range of brand research, brand evaluation and brand strategy projects. The Centre's audit and consultancy services help shape brand, marketing and business strategies, enhancing brand reputation and underlying business growth. In mid-2017, TCBA took over the UK license for Superbrands and continues to run the research process as follows:

Consumer Superbrands
Chosen by 2,500 British adults voting on a list of just fewer than 1,600 brands across 78 different sectors. The list is also ratified by the independent and voluntary Consumer Superbrands Council, comprised of leading marketing experts.

Business Superbrands
Jointly chosen by 2,500 British business professionals, with purchasing or managerial responsibility within their business, and the independent and voluntary Business Superbrands Council, made up of leading leading business-to-business marketing experts. Both audiences vote on a list of just over 1,500 brands, across 62 categories.

Definition of a Superbrand

All those involved in the voting process bear in mind the following definition:

'A Superbrand has established the finest reputation in its field. It offers customers significant emotional and/or tangible advantages over its competitors, which customers want and recognise.'

In addition, the voters are asked to judge brands against the following three factors:

- **Quality -** Does the brand provide quality products and services?

- **Reliability -** Can the brand be trusted to deliver consistently?

- **Distinction -** Is it well known in its sector and suitably different from its rivals?

Please visit Superbrands.uk.com for full details of the research methodology or for more information about TCBA please visit www.tcba.co.uk

To access the consumer and business professionals, that vote in our surveys, TCBA has partnered with the global leader in digital research data, Research Now SSI.

About Research Now SSI

Research Now SSI is the global leader in digital research data for better insights and business decisions. The company provides world-class research data solutions that enable better results for more than 3,500 market research, consulting, media, healthcare, and corporate clients. Research Now SSI operates globally with locations in the Americas, Europe, and Asia-Pacific, and is recognised as the quality, scale, and customer satisfaction leader in the market research industry.

researchnow.com

Introducing the Experts

The Business Superbrands (B) and Consumer Superbrands (C) Expert Councils are chaired by Stephen Cheliotis, Chief Executive at The Centre for Brand Analysis (TCBA).

Business Superbrands Council

Darren Bolton
Executive Creative Director,
OgilvyOne Business

Kirsty Dawe
Managing Director, Really B2B

Gail Dudleston
Global CEO, twentysix

Steve Dyer
Managing Director, Oil the Wheels

James Farmer
Publisher & Founder,
B2B Marketing

Jennifer Janson
Chairman, Six Degrees

Nick Jefferson
Partner, Monticello

Steve Kemish
Managing Partner, Junction

Mark Lethbridge
CEO, Gravity Global

Claire Mason
Founder & CEO, Man Bites Dog

Clive McNamara
Founder & Chairman,
The Marketing Practice

Stephen Meade
Chief Executive, McCann Enterprise

Vikki Mitchell
Director, Corporate Practice,
KANTAR

Rob Morrice
CEO, Stein IAS

Michael Murphy
Senior Partner,
Michael Murphy & Ltd

Rebecca Price
Partner, Frank Bright & Abel

Louise Proddow
Founder, Tweak Marketing
& Rejuvage

Sandy Purewal
Founder, The Octopus Group

Shane Redding
Managing Director, Think Direct

Dave Roberts
Executive Brand Director,
The Partners

Susanna Simpson
Founder & CEO, Limelight

Paul Stallard
International MD, Berkeley

Terry Tyrell
Worldwide Chairman,
Brand Union

Alan VanderMolen
President, International,
WE Communications

David Willan
Co-Founder & Adviser,
Circle Research

Professor Alan Wilson PhD
Professor of Marketing,
University of Strathclyde

Consumer Superbrands Council

Jenny Biggam
Founder, the7stars

Ed Bolton
Creative Director, BrandCap

Catherine Borowski
Managing Director, PRODUCE UK

Emma Brock
Founding Partner, Brock & Wilson

Colin Byrne
CEO, UK & EMEA, Weber Shandwick

Hugh Cameron
Chairman, PHD UK

Brian Cooper
Chief Creative Officer,
OLIVER Group UK

Claire Cootes
Managing Director, LIDA

Luke D'Arcy
President, Momentum Worldwide

Christian Dubreuil
Managing Director UK,
Research Now SSI

Emily Hare
Managing Editor,
Contagious Communications

Lucy Hart
Head of Influence, Mischief

Andy Hayes
Managing Director,
Northern Europe and Middle East,
Lambie-Nairn

Vanella Jackson
Global CEO, Hall & Partners

Owen Lee
Chief Creative Officer, FCB Inferno

Nick Liddell
Director of Consulting, The Clearing

Avra Lorrimer
Managing Director,
Hill + Knowlton Strategies

Fiona Lovatt
Director, Mash Strategy

Mick Mahoney
Chief Creative Officer,
Ogilvy & Mather London

Amy McCulloch
Co-Founder & Managing Director,
eight&four

Nick Morris
Founding Partner, Canvas8

Richard Moss
Chief Executive, Good Relations

James Murphy
Founder & CEO, adam&eveDDB

Thom Newton
CEO & Managing Partner
Conran Design Group

Tim Perkins
Deputy Group Chairman,
Design Bridge

Julian Pullan
Vice Chairman &
President International,
Jack Morton Worldwide

Crispin Reed
Founder, Skyscraper Consulting
& Director, The Taunton
Cider Company

Tom Roberts
CEO, Tribal Worldwide London

Hugh Robertson
Founding Partner & CEO, RPM

Gary Robinson
Creative Partner,
Studio of Art and Commerce

Jonathan Simmons
Chief Strategy Officer, Zone

Chris Walmsley
Co-Founder, Cubo Group

Dylan Williams
Chief Strategic Officer & Partner,
Droga5 London

Matt Willifer
Chief Strategy Officer,
WCRS and DF & Partner, Engine

JENNY BIGGAM (C)

Founder
the7stars

After a career at Zenith Media and Carat (where she was a Board Director), Jenny set up the7stars in 2005 which has since won numerous awards (including Campaign's Agency of the Year in 2015) and grown to be the UK's largest independent media agency with clients including Suzuki, Nintendo and Iceland Foods. Jenny chaired the Media Week Awards in 2016 and has spoken at a number of conferences and events including FT Women at The Top and Mediatel's The Year Ahead.

DARREN BOLTON (B)

Executive Creative Director
OgilvyOne Business

With over 20 years' experience in B2B and consumer marketing, Darren has helped generate successful integrated campaigns for many global brands. He is responsible for all creative work that comes out of the agency. His team are an in-house creative department of more than 30 talented experts with skills across all areas of the marketing mix, from copy, design and multimedia to UX and digital design and build.

ED BOLTON (C)

Creative Director
BrandCap
@TalkBrandCap

Ed heads up all things creative at BrandCap. A relatively new player, BrandCap holds a unique position in the market – a business consultancy that combines commercial acumen with creative, entrepreneurial brand thinking to transform the performance of organisations everywhere. See their work and culture on Instagram at we_are_brandcap.

CATHERINE BOROWSKI (C)

Managing Director
PRODUCE UK
@catinsky

Catherine is a practising artist and placemaking specialist with more than 16 years' event industry experience. She created PRODUCE UK as an artistic event-making and placemaking agency and has built a network of cultural programmers, conceptual artists, producers, digital strategists, designers and creatives that specialise in media and creative brand experiences. Catherine has a diverse work portfolio including Argent LLP and the London Design Festival, as well as Hyundai, adidas, 38 Degrees and Discovery Channel.

EMMA BROCK (C)

Founding Partner
Brock & Wilson
@emmabrock

Emma's background is in both leading global advertising agencies and brand design consultancies. As a result she really understands how to build strong iconic (and award winning) brands that connect with consumers. She talks around the world about how to create brand desire. Her client experience includes Diageo, Coca-Cola, Nestlé, Unilever and McDonald's. She founded her own brand design agency last year, who specialise in premium, fashion, sport and drinks brands.

COLIN BYRNE (C)

CEO, UK & EMEA
Weber Shandwick

Colin is one of the UK's leading PR practitioners with 40 years' experience spanning domestic and international public relations programmes, communications and campaign strategy, politics and public affairs, CSR and issues management. For eight years in a row, Colin appeared in GQ's annual '100 Most Influential Men in Britain' ranking and is a regular commentator and speaker on communications issues as well as sitting on the judging panels for many key industry award programmes.

HUGH CAMERON (C)

Chairman
PHD UK

Hugh is part of PHD's UK leadership team who, over the last seven years, have received a sweep of marketing and media industry awards including Media Week Agency of the Year 2016 and, for four consecutive years, being one of The Sunday Times Best Companies To Work For. Hugh is an instinctive challenger and believes that if you are not challenging something you don't have a strategy or perhaps a future. This challenger behaviour has been central to PHD's success.

BRIAN COOPER (C)

Chief Creative Officer
OLIVER Group UK
@_briancooper

With a career that has taken in BBH, McCann-Erickson, Mother, Wieden + Kennedy and Dare, Brian is a multi-award-winning creative with experience working on brands including Sony, Vodafone, MasterCard, Barclays, Lynx and Audi. He has also worked at Apple as Head of Creative and Strategy EMEA.

CLAIRE COOTES (C)

Managing Director
LIDA

Having previously worked at both OgilvyOne and Iris, Claire joined LIDA, part of the M&C Saatchi Group, in 2013. The agency aims to create the most valued brands in the world and as a managing partner Claire held responsibility for the agency's O2 account. Having worked at LIDA for four years, she took on the position of Managing Director in April 2017.

LUKE D'ARCY (C)

President
Momentum Worldwide

Named one of their Global Agency Innovators of the year by Internationalist Magazine, Luke has worked across numerous global networks and independents including IPG, Havas and Iris. He has also worked client side at Virgin as Partnership Director of their Formula 1 team before returning to agency life as global CMO of Momentum and now UK President. Outside work his fitness regime is focused on four kids who frankly run rings around him.

KIRSTY DAWE (B)

Managing Director
Really B2B
@kirstydawe

Co-founder and director of award-winning B2B marketing agency Really B2B – whose work includes campaigns for clients including the BBC, Orange Business Services, Compass Group, Santander and HSBC – Kirsty is also Marketing Director for the MarketMakers group. With a particular interest in emerging B2B channels in the digital space, Kirsty is also a member of the IDM B2B Council.

CHRISTIAN DUBREUIL (C)

Managing Director UK
Research Now SSI

Chris has been in the data insights industry for over 20 years and is the Managing Director UK of Research Now SSI – the leading global digital data collection business. In addition, Chris serves as a board member for the Market Research Society's Company Partner think tank, helping to drive thought leadership in the industry. A frequent speaker and data industry commentator, Chris is fascinated by how people interact with brands in the digital space.

GAIL DUDLESTON (B)

Global CEO
twentysix

Previously Director at Rapp, Gail founded twentysix in 2005 and has grown the agency from six to an international team of 150, with a turnover of more than £15m in 2017. Gail is passionate about the digital world, serious about strategic thinking and dedicated to delivering technical innovation. Employing the very best people to deliver true digital creativity and innovation for clients, in over 101 markets, is paramount for Gail.

STEVE DYER (B)

Managing Director
Oil the Wheels

Steve has a unique blend of client-side industry knowledge with over 25 years' B2B agency know-how. He understands industrial/manufacturing decision makers and how to motivate them, because he used to be one! His industrial strength approach to brand marketing has fuelled a recent agency rebrand: Oil the Wheels. A strategic communications marketer, he's a Fellow of the CIM and IDM and has held senior positions on various B2B committees within the DMA.

JAMES FARMER (B)

Publisher & Founder
B2B Marketing
@MarketingB2B

James Farmer is founder of the information provider, B2B Marketing. Launched over 10 years ago, James has led the business from a small start-up, UK magazine to a global media, with a portfolio of products from business data, news and reports to events, awards and training. James is also one of the founding members of the marketing association, the Business Marketing Collective.

EMILY HARE (C)

Managing Editor
Contagious Communications

Emily covers leading advertising, consumer culture trends and new technologies for Contagious magazine and Contagious I/O. She helped build consultancy division Contagious Insider, speaks at industry events including Most Contagious, Ad:Tech and Advertising Week and has judged at London Innovator Awards and D&AD New Blood. She was also selected as a 2015/16 Marketing Academy scholar.

LUCY HART (C)

Head of Influence
Mischief

Lucy's current role is at one of the country's top consumer PR agencies, Mischief. She spends her time connecting brands to their consumers via the world of influence marketing, which covers everything from dark social communities to big names on the social platforms. She's worked in the PR industry for 14 years for a range of brands from baby brands to beer companies, energy companies to energy drinks, and much more in between.

ANDY HAYES (C)

Managing Director, Northern Europe and Middle East
Lambie-Nairn
@andyjhayes

Andy oversees offices in the UK and Germany as well as the business in the Middle East. He plays a key role in developing new and existing client relationships and ensures Lambie-Nairn's work always meets the highest standards. With 20 years' international branding experience, he has worked for clients across many sectors, including the BBC, Sainsbury's, Saudi Telecom, flydubai, Electronic Arts, Vodafone, JLL and Airbus.

VANELLA JACKSON (C)

Global CEO
Hall & Partners

Vanella has always been passionate about brands and communications. Prior to her current position, Vanella spent 20 years working in some of the UK's best advertising agencies, including BBH, AMV/BBDO and JWT. As a strategic brand consultancy, Hall & Partners has a reputation for pioneering new thinking to inspire the industry, with its award winning initiative, The Hub, creating a new vision for insight in this new, digital, business world.

JENNIFER JANSON (B)

Chairman
Six Degrees

As a specialist in reputation management, Jennifer has overseen successful campaigns for large multinational companies over the last 20 years. Jennifer wrote The Reputation Playbook: a winning formula to help CEOs protect corporate reputation in the digital economy (Harriman House, 2014) and is a regular contributor to the Wall Street Journal's Risk Report. She is also a member of the CIPR and recently founded start-up, My Business Bookclub.

NICK JEFFERSON (B)

Partner
Monticello

A partner with the advisory firm, Monticello, Nick is a strategy consultant with particular expertise in the space where brand meets culture. A former CEC of two creative agencies, he is an Englishman who speaks Spanish and French and works all over the world. Nick writes for both the Marketing Society and the Huffington Post as well as sitting on the Governing Body of The BRIT School.

STEVE KEMISH (B)

Managing Partner
Junction

Steve is a multi-award-winning marketer and public speaker who has worked in digital marketing since 1997. He has had experience client-side, helped grow a leading email service provider, consulted to numerous clients on digital strategy, and helped build one of the most respected and awarded B2B marketing agencies in the UK. He is also an IDM tutor, a member of the IDM Digital Council, and a guest lecturer at various British universities.

OWEN LEE (C)

Chief Creative Officer
FCB Inferno

Owen has spent his career creating advertising for brands such as Mercedes-Benz, BMW, the UK Government and Oreo. Since becoming joint Chief Creative Officer at FCB Inferno, the agency has won the Grand Prix at Cannes two years running. Previously, he ran his own adverting agency, Farm Communications.

MARK LETHBRIDGE (B)

CEO
Gravity Global

Specialising in brand development, Mark is the Founder and CEO of Gravity Global, a specialist B2B marketing and communications agency, which represents global brands. Mark is also President of MAGNET that acts for more than 800 brands worldwide setting best practice in global marketing and communications across 42 agency locations. Prior to this, Mark founded and was CEO of the AGA Group – a communications group focused on B2B and brand development.

NICK LIDDELL (C)

Director of Consulting
The Clearing

Nick leads the strategy team at The Clearing, an award-winning independent brand consultancy in London. With over 16 years' experience, Nick has worked with global business and consumer brands from Amex, Guinness and Prada to McLaren, Sky and The United Nations. A regular conference speaker, Nick is a Visiting Fellow at Cranfield University, author of the popular book, Business is Beautiful and a contributor to the Huffington Post.

AVRA LORRIMER (C)

Managing Director
Hill + Knowlton Strategies
@AvrainLondon

Throughout her career, Avra has worked on many of the world's best known and most beloved brands. She has experience across a diverse array of sectors including FMCG, travel and automotive. An American expat residing in North London, Avra lives with her husband and daughter. In her free time she reads, occasionally blogs and is an aspiring voice over artist.

FIONA LOVATT (C)

Director
Mash Strategy
@fionalovatt29

Fiona is a director at Mash, a brand strategy consultancy, and has 20 years' marketing experience, 18 spent client-side solving brand challenges at companies like Diageo, Magners and Twinings. She loves uncovering consumer insight to create meaningful brand propositions and strategies that really drive growth.

MICK MAHONEY (C)

Chief Creative Officer
Ogilvy & Mather London

Mick has been rewarded by every major advertising festival, with over 150 industry awards including: a Cannes Grand Prix, three Gold Lions, six Silver Lions, a One Show Best in Show, five D&AD Silvers, five BTAA Golds and a TED Ideas Worth Spreading Award. He has created campaigns for some of the world's top brands including Stella Artois, Nike, BA, Vodafone and Durex and has enjoyed a career spanning some of London's best creative agencies.

CLAIRE MASON (B)

Founder & CEO
Man Bites Dog
@manbitesdogb2b

Specialist B2B marketing and communications consultancy, Man Bites Dog is an award-winning consultancy which unleashes big ideas to fuel PR, marketing and BD campaigns with remarkable commercial impact. Claire is proud to work with some of the world's smartest organisations, from the Big Four and magic circle law firms, to innovators including BP and Google. Claire was recently named Female Marketing Leader of the Year by the Chartered Institute of Marketing.

AMY McCULLOCH (C)

**Co-Founder &
Managing Director**
eight&four

Amy is the Managing Director of eight&four – a Modern Comms Agency with creative and social expertise at the heart of the business. The agency focuses on creating relevant moments to transform relationships between brands and audiences. eight&four holds specialist experience in the Travel & Hospitality, Food & Beverage and Not for Profit sectors.

CLIVE MCNAMARA (B)

Founder & Chairman
The Marketing Practice

Clive founded The Marketing Practice (TMP) in 2002, bringing his extensive marketing experience to enterprise clients in the technology and professional services sectors. He is driven by an unwavering focus on results, bringing marketing and sales together to deliver commercial value – a focus that runs through everything TMP does. Fifteen years later, The Marketing Practice works with global organisations including Microsoft, Salesforce, Xerox, Capgemini and Sage, and has offices in Oxford, London, Munich and Seattle.

STEPHEN MEADE (B)

Chief Executive
McCann Enterprise

Stephen is CEO and founder of McCann Enterprise, a corporate and B2B specialist agency within McCann Worldgroup, and recently voted 'Best B2B Marketing Agency' by the RAR. Prior to setting up McCann Enterprise, Stephen was European and UK Head of Planning for McCann. He joined McCann from Springpoint, where he was Managing Director, having previously spent some 15 years at both Publicis and HHCL, Campaign's Agency of the Decade in 2000.

VIKKI MITCHELL (B)

Director, Corporate Practice
KANTAR

Vikki is a specialist in branding and positioning, corporate reputation and creative development research. She regularly partners with FTSE brands to align insight with corporate and communications strategies, delivering optimal impact for her clients. Vikki sits on the BIG Group board – representing B2B research and market intelligence services – is a frequent speaker at B2B events and writes articles for various business and research magazines.

ROB MORRICE (B)

CEO
Stein IAS

Under Rob's guidance, Stein IAS has become a truly global B2B agency force. Named Business Marketing Association's B2B Agency of the Year five times, it has collected numerous global B2B awards since its inception in 2013. With locations across North America, EMEA and APAC, Stein IAS works with brands including Samsung, Juniper Networks, Western Union, NCR, Ricoh, Merck, Ingredion and Trelleborg.

NICK MORRIS (C)

Founding Partner
Canvas8

In 2008 Nick founded Canvas8 to challenge the formica world of market research. Canvas8 is a behavioural insight practice that helps businesses, brands and organisations understand people so they can do what they do best. Canvas8 has helped the Bill and Melinda Gates Foundation understand the science of influence, Weber Shandwick become Global PR agency of the year, Nike plan for the World Cup and the Euros, Google pivot and the British Government prepare for life post Brexit.

RICHARD MOSS (C)

Chief Executive
Good Relations
@wordofmoss

Richard currently runs one of the UK's leading PR and Content agencies. Starting his career in FMCG marketing, managing the Andrex, Carlsberg and Mr Kipling brands, he moved into public relations to pursue his passion for 'Contagious Truthtelling'. Today his agency's clients include Subway, Airbus and Trustford.

JAMES MURPHY (C)

Founder & CEO
adam&eveDDB

James co-founded adam&eve in 2008. Merging with DDB in 2012 to become adam&eveDDB, it has gone on to become one of the UK's most successful agencies. Most notably for its multi award-winning John Lewis and Foster's campaigns, high profile work also includes Google, Volkswagen, YouTube, Waitrose, Financial Times, Harvey Nichols as well as charities including Save the Children and Great Ormond Street Hospital.

MICHAEL MURPHY (B)

Senior Partner
Michael Murphy & Ltd

Michael has had a long career in public relations. Four years ago he established his own advisory firm, Michael Murphy & Ltd, which provides non-executive and advisory services around the world to a range of marketing and communications consultancies and agencies as well as firms in other sectors. He also mentors and advises a number of senior business leaders and is Chairman of Waypoint which provides financial advisory services to the marketing and communications sector.

THOM NEWTON (C)

CEO & Managing Partner
Conran Design Group

A progressive leader, with over 20 years' experience in the design industry, Thom took over as Conran Design Group CEO in 2012. He has led the agency through the most dynamic period of growth in its 60-year history – 129% from 2013 to 2017 – through the development of the in-house studio offer, the naming and packaging offering as well as expansion into the US. Conran is part of the Havas network, where Thom is a member of the Havas UK Board.

TIM PERKINS (C)

Deputy Group Chairman
Design Bridge

Tim joined as Design Director for Asia Pacific 25 years ago and has since worked with brands across markets from China to the US, from Columbia to Laos, gradually moving over to building long term client relationships with global brand owners such a Diageo, Unilever and JTI. In his current role, Tim has responsibility for the company's core client relationships, he still likes to keep things simple and visual, fuelled by plenty of tea!

REBECCA PRICE (B)

Partner
Frank Bright & Abel

Rebecca is a brand strategist and communications specialist. She has a knack for finding what matters and expressing it well, and knows that the right creative expression is about so much more than design alone. She is Co-Founder and partner of creative consultancy Frank, Bright & Abel.

LOUISE PRODDOW (B)

Founder
Tweak Marketing & Rejuvage

Louise is a global business leader, entrepreneur and pro-age advocate. She is a passionate pioneer of branding and marketing and has launched successful technology start-ups. With a career that has embraced branding innovation and commercialism for over 25 years, Louise is also the author of two books.

JULIAN PULLAN (C)

Vice Chairman
& President International
Jack Morton Worldwide

Julian is Vice Chairman and President International of brand experience agency, Jack Morton Worldwide. Rated among the top global brand experience agencies, Jack Morton Worldwide integrates live and online experiences, digital and social media, and branded environments that engage consumers, business partners and employees for leading brands everywhere.

SANDY PUREWAL (B)

Founder
The Octopus Group

Sandy has over 20 years' of sales, marketing and PR experience, advising B2B brands from global blue chips to disruptive startups. He co-founded Octopus Group and has spearheaded its award winning Brand to Sales proposition combing comms, creative and technology to accelerate demand. Sandy's experience includes working with Vodafone, Cisco, Accenture, PwC and Adecco on both local and international programmes. Sandy has been a PRCA Council Member and is in the PR Week Powerbook.

SHANE REDDING (B)

Managing Director
Think Direct
@ShaneRddng

Shane is an independent consultant with over 30 years' international B2B direct and digital marketing experience. Shane uses her skills and knowledge to help businesses transform their marketing by implementing and using automation tools; combining data, best practice marketing skills and software to get results. Shane's clients include Lexis Nexis plc, British Dental Association, Dennis Publishing and she has worked with ITV plc, Telefonica, as well as the Institute of Directors.

CRISPIN REED (C)

Founder
Skyscraper Consulting
Director
The Taunton Cider Company

Crispin has worked in leading global advertising and design agencies, brand consultancy as well as client side in the fragrance and beauty sectors. In addition to starting his own management, marketing and brand consultancy in 2016, he also became part of the team reviving the once iconic Taunton Cider Company. He is also the co-author of The 7 Myths of Middle Age – Implications for Marketing and Brands.

DAVE ROBERTS (B)

Executive Brand Director
The Partners

Dave is the multi-award winning Executive Brand Director at The Partners, with a passion to bridge the gap between creativity and strategy. With his wealth of experience, he has developed some of the world's most revered brands including Argos, Investec, Nokia, Nespresso, Samsung, HSBC, Molton Brown and Kew Gardens. At the heart, Dave is committed to helping clients accomplish authentic business strategies and finding ways to turn them into meaningful and highly crafted creative solutions.

TOM ROBERTS (C)

CEO
Tribal Worldwide London

Tom leads Tribal Worldwide London, part of the Tribal DDB Worldwide network, held by marketing services giant Omnicom, as CEO. Tom has responsibility for the agency's strategic direction, expanding client relationships, and managing the executive team. Tom heads up both large-scale national and international projects, most recently leading the team that designed the multi award-winning digital connected customer journey for Volkswagen UK. He is also a member of the DDB UK Executive Board.

HUGH ROBERTSON (C)

Founding Partner & CEO
RPM

Hugh founded the award-winning, independent, creative agency RPM 24 years ago. He sits on the Advertising Association Council, is a member of the Marketing Society and a board member of the Marketing Agencies Association. Hugh is passionate about improving the diversity of talent in the industry and supports a number of initiatives to address this. In 2015 Hugh walked to the North Pole with a team that raised over £500,000 for The Prince's Trust.

GARY ROBINSON (C)

Creative Partner
Studio of Art and Commerce

Gary recently joined Studio of Art and Commerce and has helped them produce a series of mini documentaries for Walgreens Boots Alliance as well as the first advertising campaign for BrewDog, the successful crowd funded brewery. He was previously Executive Creative Director at FCB Inferno – the agency responsible for the multi award winning This Girl Can campaign.

JONATHAN SIMMONS (C)

Chief Strategy Officer
Zone

Jonathan, one of Zone's founders, leads projects for clients including Barratt Homes, BMW, Unilever, and The Glenlivit. Jonathan is an industry expert on charity and social purpose, and has worked with 50 of the UK's leading charities including Girl Effect, CRUK, The Scouts and RNIB and helped brands like Tesco, Nike, and Aviva deliver large scale social purpose projects.

SUSANNA SIMPSON (B)

Founder & CEO
Limelight
@SusannaSimpson

Susanna is Founder of Limelight, which exists to give talented and ambitious businesses the recognition they deserve. Limelight's major skill lies in building business thought leaders for corporately and privately owned companies. Working exclusively in the B2B sector, Limelight delivers reputation-driven growth for businesses including VW, Saatchi & Saatchi, Gallup, Equimedia, Personal Group, Pinsent Masons, Diamond Logistics and Bybox.

PAUL STALLARD (B)

International MD
Berkeley
@Paul_Stallard

Paul is responsible for building the international footprint of the comms agency through acquisition and partnerships. Berkeley helps digital, technology and consumer brands on a global scale to gain the recognition they deserve. Storytelling is used to create emotional connections that help shape how people perceive the brand and compel them to interact with it.

TERRY TYRRELL (B)

Worldwide Chairman
Brand Union

Terry co-founded Brand Union in 1976 and today it employs more than 500 people in 23 offices across the world. Responsible for major branding programmes, Terry leads teams across the Brand Union network. Recently these have included Schroders, Shell, HSBC, Canon, SABMiller, Qatar National Bank and Durham University. Terry is also Chair of the Design Council.

ALAN VANDERMOLEN (B)

President, International
WE Communications
@AlanVanderMolen

Alan runs WE Communications businesses outside of the US. He designed the agency's Brands in Motion and Stories in Motion studies, which now form the backbone of the agency's point-of-view and approach to client assignments. Alan also spearheaded the launch of PLUS, a WE-led, anti-network group of global, independent specialist agencies helping brands shake the shackles of mundane, holding company 'solutions'.

CHRIS WALMSLEY (C)

Co-Founder
Cubo Group

Chris co-founded creative agency Cubo in the same year Superbrands was born – 1995. In the ensuing 23 years, the original Cubo has evolved into a communications group containing five specialist agencies. Each company in the group is full of natural collaborators who work closely together to create campaigns that make clients' brands stick in their consumers' minds.

DAVID WILLAN (B)

Co-Founder & Adviser
Circle Research

David has spent a lifetime in B2B research. Having co-founded BPRI and sold this business to WPP, he was one of the prime movers behind Circle Research. Circle is the UK's foremost B2B research agency and is now part of Next 15. David is a Governor of the University of Portsmouth and also a Director of a league one football club.

DYLAN WILLIAMS (C)

Chief Strategic Officer & Partner
Droga5 London

Dylan came to prominence in 1998 upon appointment as BBH's youngest company director. A move to Mother in 2004 culminated in Campaign voting him the industry's 'Number One Strategist' and Mother its 'Agency of The Decade'. After two years as Global CSO at Publics Worldwide he joined Droga5 London as CSO and Partner in 2016. He also sits on Facebook's Client Council and Tech City Advisory Board at Downing Street.

MATT WILLIFER (C)

Chief Strategy Officer
WCRS and DF
Partner
Engine

Matt joined BMP DBB from Oxford University in 1995. He has been Head of Strategy and part of the management team at M&C Saatchi, where he won APG Global Strategy Agency of the Year. He has also been Chairman of the APG, and CEO of a games developer. At WCRS

PROF. ALAN WILSON PHD (B)

Professor of Marketing
University of Strathclyde
@ProfAlanWilson

Alan is a Professor of Marketing at the University of Strathclyde Business School. Before joining the University, he was a senior consultant at a London-based marketing consultancy. He has written numerous articles on corporate reputation, customer experience management and branding, and is also a Fellow of both the Chartered Institute of Marketing and the Market Research Society.

Highlights of the 2018 Results

Revealing the finding of the Superbrands research

STEPHEN CHELIOTIS

Chief Executive,
The Centre for Brand Analysis (TCBA)
& Chairman, Superbrands and
CoolBrands UK

The Superbrands research has been running since 1995, adopting its current methodology in 2006. This years vote involved over 2,500 British consumers, 2,500 UK business professionals – with purchasing or managerial responsibility within their business – 26 senior business-to-business industry leaders – on the independent and voluntary Business Superbrands Council – and 34 leading consumer marketing experts – on the Consumer Superbrands Council. They have all voted on the UK's major brands to identify the nation's Superbrands.

Over 3,200 brands were judged and voted on; just fewer than 1,600 business-to-business brands, across 78 different sectors, and just over 1,500 consumer brands, across 62 categories, were reviewed by the audiences. As ever, brands were judged both against the Superbrands definition and against the three core factors making up a Superbrand; namely quality, reliability and distinction. With all the voting data now in and analysed, we can reveal a new leader atop both the Consumer and Business Superbrands rankings.

In the Consumer Superbrands league table, LEGO has built its way to the top of the leader board, the culmination of a solid upward swing started in 2014. At that time, it was placed 25th in our rankings, but over the subsequent four years climbed steadily; 11th in 2015, before jumping to third in 2016, second last year and now number one. Whether it's LEGO films, consumer-made movie trailers using LEGO, art shows made from LEGO, new products and spin offs such as Star Wars LEGO, or simply producing great toys that still inspire and develop children to think creatively, LEGO has felt to have real positive momentum over recent times. It feels appropriate that the brand has hit number one this year, being the 60th anniversary of the LEGO brick. Although no new kid on the block,

interest just continues to grow, for instance eBay reported in January that in the last week of that month alone, there were 20,000 searches for LEGO, or one search every 30 seconds! All this positivity, interest and brand momentum however is not entirely transferring to the bottom-line, as lower sales and redundancies were announced by the group in September 2017.

> "This year has seen a change in leader atop both the Consumer Superbrands and Business Superbrands rankings."

Gillette, despite challenges from new competitors, such as Unilever's DSC (Dollar Shave Club) or UK rival Cornerstone, claimed runner-up spot, climbing up from fifth last year. It has been omnipresent in the top 10 since 2014. Taking third is Apple, which recovered from last year's fall of two places to jump back up six positions, from ninth last year, despite increasingly difficult markets, comparisons and focused rivals.

Other notable movers in the top 20 include Disney, whose last appearance in the leading pack was back in 2013. Also coming back into the top 20 for the first time since 2013 is Heathrow. The UK's busiest airport jumped back into 16th, following the Governments initial decision to grant permission for its planned third runway. A brand, based at Heathrow however had a not so positive year, with British Airways descending from first to land in 27th position. Still elevated compared to rivals, this drop was not unexpected, after a challenging period, but it's essential the brand arrests its slide and recovers at pace, before it falls into a tailspin that is hard to recover from.

Aside from Disney and Heathrow, other new entries into the Consumer Superbrands top 20 included oil majors, BP and Shell. The latter made its first entry into the top group since 2014, and the former its most recent feature since 2013. Positive performances from BMW, Kleenex and Visa, enabled all three to join the elite 20, while Häagen-Dazs made last year's absence from the top 20 a one-year wonder by re-entering. Among the fallers from the top 20 on the other hand were Kelloggs, it first non-appearance since 2012, Dyson, which had featured for the last three years, and Fairy. Notably Google and Amazon fell out of the top 20, while Facebook continues to be nowhere near challenging for a top 20 berth. Falling out of the top 20 last year, there was also no return for tech giant Microsoft.

> "In the vast majority of cases, the **category leaders are hard to dislodge**. Of the 78 categories reviewed, only 13 witnessed a change in leadership."

Outside of the top 20, it is always interesting to see if, at a direct competitor level, many changes in sector leader have occurred. What is clear, as seen in previous years, is that in the vast majority of cases, the category leaders are hard to dislodge. Of the 78 categories reviewed, only 13 witnessed a change in leadership. The most significant of these include Colgate, losing its long-term advantage in the Oral Care category to Oral-B, Marks & Spencer overtaking John Lewis to re-establish its lead, RAC taking over pole position from the AA, and perhaps most surprisingly Sky taking the top of the media TV category from the BBC, the first time ever in our research that the BBC has not topped it category in the poll.

Looking at the overall Consumer Superbrands list, the biggest risers among the 1,555 brands reviewed included many fairly young disruptive brands, such as Deliveroo, Purple Bricks, Snapchat and AO.com. Other risers however were more established, including impressive rises from KFC and Starbucks. The biggest riser overall however was GAME, the UK's leading games retailer, albeit probably helped by a slight rebrand from GAME Digital. Conversely, some of the biggest fallers included Dorset Cereals, Hartley's and Gale's, while tech brands Pioneer and Olympus were both among the top 10 largest fallers.

As would be expected, and following the long-term trend, volatility at the top of the business-to-business rankings is not dramatic, with just four constituent changes in the top 20. That said, as seen with the Consumer Superbrands, the number one brand has changed. Once again, British Airways falls from the top position, albeit dropping less dramatically to place fourth. Replacing it is Apple, which had been second for the previous three years and third the year before that. Prior to that, in 2014 it held top position, so has been consistently solid and continues to perform more strongly in our business survey than in our consumer survey. GlaxoSmithKline and Bosch both returned after a one-year absence outside of the top 20. Barclaycard also re-entered the top group, after a slightly longer absence, dating back from 2014. Just to exasperate the pain for British Airways, the other new entry in the top 20 was gulf-based airline, Emirates.

Replicating the trend seen within the Consumer Superbrands survey, the vast bulk of category leaders retained their sector leadership year on year. Of the 62 categories reviewed, only 13 saw a change in leader. Among these changes, Boeing lost its headship of the Aerospace & Defence category to a recovering Rolls-Royce Group, while Slaughter and May took over number one in the Legal Services category from Clifford Chance, BP moved ahead of Shell, and British Land took over from the Canary Wharf Group in the Real Estate – General sector.

Among the biggest risers overall were chemicals company Sika, distributor Fagan & Whalley, FTSE 250 engineer Meggitt and FTSE 100 assurance, testing, inspection and certification services giant, Intertek.

This year has seen a change in leader atop both the Consumer Superbrands and Business Superbrands rankings. There have been numerous changes in both top 20s, while equally most of the constituents have retained their placing; whilst the vast majority of brand leaders within their sector have again outperformed their rivals. Looking more widely, a range of disruptive brands are fast moving up the rankings and it will be interesting to see how far they can progress and how quickly. We look forward to seeing how these trends develop next year.

More detailed analysis of the results will be posted online and also feature within the Superbrands Guardian Supplement.

Rank	Consumer Superbrands 2018	Business Superbrands 2018
1	LEGO (+1)	Apple (+1)
2	Gillette (+3)	BP (+12)
3	Apple (+6)	Microsoft (-)
4	Andrex (-)	British Airways (-3)
5	Coca-Cola (+5)	Emirates (NE)
6	Disney (+30 NE)	Google (-1)
7	Marks & Spencer (+7)	PayPal (-3)
8	Boots (+4)	Shell (-2)
9	Heinz (+8)	Visa (+3)
10	BMW (+23 NE)	Mastercard (-1)
11	Cadbury (+2)	American Express (-3)
12	Rolex (-10)	London Stock Exchange Group (+7)
13	BP (+30 NE)	Virgin Atlantic (-6)
14	Shell (+29 NE)	IBM (-3)
15	John Lewis (-9)	JCB (-2)
16	Heathrow (+28 NE)	Samsung (-1)
17	Jaguar (-1)	GlaxoSmithKline (+5 NE)
18	Kleenex (+13 NE)	Bosch (+8) NE
19	Visa (+4 NE)	Barclaycard (+4 NE)
20	Häagen-Dazs (+10) NE	Intel (-4)

NE - New Entry

QUALIFYING BRANDS

Brand	Code
3M	B
7-Up	C
A-Plant	B
AA	C
ABB	B
Abbott	B
ABSOLUT VODKA	C
ABTA	B C
Acas (Advisory, Conciliation & Arbitration Service)	B
ACCA (The Association of Chartered Certified Accountants)	
Accenture	B
Access Self Storage	B
Acer	B
Actimel	C
Activia	C
adam&eveDDB	B
Adecco	B
adidas	B
Adobe	B
ADP	B
ADT	B
Aegis	B
Aegon	C
Age UK	C
AIG	B
AIM	B
Air France	C
Airbus	B
AKQA	B
AkzoNobel	B
Aldi	C
Alfa Romeo	C
Alka-Seltzer	C
Allen & Overy	B
Allianz	C
Alpen	C
Alpro	C
Alstom	B
Alton Towers	C
Always	C
Amadeus	B
Amazon	C
Ambre Solaire	C
AMD	B
Amec Foster Wheeler	B
American Airlines	B
American Express	B C
American Express Travel	B
Amey	B
AMV BBDO	B
Anadin	C
Anchor	C
Andrex	C
Anglo American	B
Ann Summers	C
Antofagasta	B
AOL Advertising	B
Aon	B
Apple	B C
Aquafresh	C
Arcadis	B
ArcelorMittal	B
Arco	B
Argos	C
Ariel	C
ARM	B
Arriva	B
Arsenal FC	C
Arup	B
ASDA	B
Ashridge Executive Education	B
AstraZeneca	B
Atkins	B
Atlas Copco	B
Audi	C
Aunt Bessie's	C
Auto Trader	C
Autodesk	B
Autoglass	B C
Avast	B
Avery	B
Avis	C
Aviva	B C
AXA	B C
Axis Security	B
B&Q	C
Babcock	B
Bacardi	C
Badenoch & Clark	B
BAE Systems	B
Baileys	B
Bain & Company	B
Baker McKenzie	B
Balfour Beatty	B
Bank of America Merrill Lynch	B
Bank of Scotland	B
Barclaycard	B C
Barclays	B C
Barnados	C
Barratt Homes	C
BASF	B
Basildon Bond	C
Bassett's	C
Baxi	B
Baxter	B
Baxters	C
Bayer	B
BBC	C
BBC Children in Need	C
BBH	B
BCG (Boston Consulting Group)	B
BDA (British Dental Association)	B
BDO	B
Bechtel	B
Beck's	C
Beechams	C
Ben & Jerry's	C
Benchmark	B
Benylin	C
Best Western	B
Bet365	C
BHP Billiton	B
BIC	B
Biffa	B
Big Yellow	B
Biogen	B
Bird & Bird	B
Birds Eye	C
Birmingham Conference and Events Centre (the BCEC)	B
Bisto	C
Black n' Red	B
BLACK+DECKER	B C
BlackBerry	B
Bloomberg	B
Bloomsbury Professional	B
BMA (British Medical Association)	B
BMW	B
BNP Paribas	B
BNP Paribas Real Estate	B
BOC	B
Bodyform	C
Boeing	B
Bold	C
Bombardier	B
Bombay Sapphire	C
Bonjela	C
Booker	B
Booking.com	C
Boots	C
Bosch	B C
Bose	C
Bovril	C
Box	B
BP	B C
Braemar	B
Brakes Group	B
Branston	C
Braun	B
BRC (British Retail Consortium)	B
Breville	C
Brewers	B
Bridgestone	C
Bristol-Myers Squibb	B
Britax	C
British Airways	B C
British Chambers of Commerce (BCC)	B
British Council	B
British Gas	C
British Gas Business Energy	B
British Gypsum	B
British Heart Foundation	C
British Land	B
British Red Cross	C
Britvic	C
Brother	B
Brunswick	B
BSI	B
BT	B C
BT Sport	C
Budweiser	C
Buildbase	B
Bulmers	C
Bunzl	B
Bupa	B C
Bureau Veritas	B
Burger King	C
BuroHappold Engineering	B
Butlins	C
Buxton	C
CA Technologies	B
Cadbury	C
Caffè Nero	C
Calor	B
CALPOL	C
Cambridge Judge Business School	B
Campbell's	C
Canary Wharf Group	B
Cancer Research UK	C
Cannon Hygiene	B
Canon	B C
Capco	B
Capgemini	B
Capita	B
Capital & Regional	B
Capital FM	C
Captain Morgan	C
Cargill	B
Carillion	B
Carlsberg	C
Carphone Warehouse	C
Carr's Group	B
Carte D'Or	C
Carte Noire	C
Carter Jonas	B
Casio	B
Cass Business School	B
Castrol	B C
Caterpillar	B
Cath Kidston	C
Cathedral City	C
Cathy Pacific	B
CBI	B
CBRE	B
CEMEX	B
Centaur Live	B
Center Parcs	C
Central Hall Westminster	B
Centrum	C
Cesar	C
Channel 4	B
Chelsea FC	C
Chevron	B
Chubb	B
Chubb Fire & Security	B
Churchill	C
Cillit Bang	C
CIMA (Chartered Institute of Management Accountants)	B
CIPD (Chartered Institute of Personnel and Development)	B
Cisco	B
Citi	B
City & Guilds	B
Clancy Docwra	B
Clarks	B
Classic FM	C
Clear Channel	B
Clearasil	C
Clifford Chance	B
Clyde & Co	B
CMI (Chartered Management Institute)	B
CMS	B
Co-op Food	C
Co-operatives UK	B
Coca-Cola	C
Coca-Cola London Eye	C
Colgate	C
Colliers International	B
Colman's	C
Comfort	C
Comic Relief	C
comparethemarket.com	C
Compass Group	B
Concord	B
Continental	B
Convatec	B
Converse	C
Cornetto	C
Corona	C
Corsodyl	C
Costa	C
Costain	B
Cosworth	B
Courvoisier	C
Cow & Gate	C
Cranfield School of Management	B
Cravendale	C
Crayola	C
Credit Suisse	B
Croda	B
Crowdcube	C
Crown Paints	C
Crown Trade	B
Crowne Plaza	B
Cummins	B
Cunard	C
Cuprinol	C
Currys	C
Cushelle	C
Daily Mail	C
Dairylea	C
DB Schenker	B
De La Rue	B
De Vere	B
De'Longhi	C
Debenhams	C
Deep Heat	C
Del Monte	C
Dell	B C
Dell EMC	B
Deloitte	B
Deloitte Real Estate	B
Delta	B
Derwent London	B
Dettol	C
Deutsche Bank	B
DeWALT	C
DFS	C
DHL	B C
Digital Cinema Media (DCM)	B
Direct Line	B C
Disney	C
DLA Piper	C
dmg events	B
Dolmio	C
Domestos	C
Domino's Pizza	C
Doritos	C
Douwe Egberts	C
Dove	C
DowDuPont	B
DPD	B
Dr Pepper	C
Dreams	B
Dropbox	C
DS Smith	B
Dulux	C
Dulux Trade	B
Dun & Bradstreet	B
Dunlop	C
dunnhumby	B
Duracell	C
Durex	C
Durham University Business School	B
Dyson	C
E.ON	B C
E45	C
Early Learning Centre	C
easyJet	B C
eBay	C
Echo Falls	C
EchoStar Satellite Services	B
Ecolab	B
Eddie Stobart	B
Edelman	B
Eden Project	C
EDF Energy	B C
Edwardian Hotels London	B
EE	C
Egon Zehnder	B
Elastoplast	C
Electrolux	B
Elsevier	B
Embraer	B
Emerson	B
Emirates	B C
EnServe Group	B
Epson	B
Equifax	B
Equiniti	C
Equinix	B
Ericsson	B
Esso	B
Etihad	B C
Euronext	B
Eurostar	B C
Eurotunnel	B C
Eutelsat	B
Eversheds Sutherland	B
evian	C
ExCeL London	B
Exhibition Centre Liverpool	B
Expedia	B
Experian	B
ExxonMobil	B
EY	B
F-Secure	B
Facebook	C
Fagan & Whalley	B
Fairtrade Foundation	B
Fairy	C
Fanta	C
Farley's	C
Febreze	C
Federation of Small Businesses (FSB)	B
FedEx	B
Felix	C
Ferrero Rocher	C
Ferrovial Agroman	B
Filofax	B
Financial Times	C
Finish	C
Finsbury	B
Finsbury Foods Group	B
First	B
First:Utility	B
Fisher-Price	C
Fitch Group	B
Flash	C
FleishmanHillard Fishburn	B
Flora	C
Flymo	C
Foot Locker	C
Ford	C
Forrester	B
Forth Ports	B
Foster's	C
Fox's Biscuits	C
Fred Perry	C
Freeview	C
Freightliner Group	B
French Connection	C
Freshfields Bruckhaus Deringer	B
Frost & Sullivan	B
Fruit Shoot	C
FSC (Forest Stewardship Council)	B
FTI Consulting	B
FTSE Russell	B
Fujitsu	B
Funding Circle	B
G4S	B
Galaxy	C
Galliford Try	B
Gallup	C
GAME	C
Gap	C
Garmin	C
Garnier	C
Gartner	B
Gatwick Airport	C
Gatwick Express	B
Gaviscon	C
GE	B
GfK	C
Gillette	C
GKN	B
GlaxoSmithKline	B
Glencore	B
Glenfiddich	C
Goldman Sachs	B
Goodyear	C
Google	B C
Gordon's	C
Gorkana	B
Graham	B
Grant Thornton	B
Grant's	C
Great Ormond Street Hospital Charity	C
Great Portland Estates	B
Green & Black's	C
Green Energy UK	B
Green Flag	C
Greggs	C
Guinness	B
Gulf Keystone Petroleum	B
Gumtree	C
GW Pharmaceuticals	B
H&M	C
Häagen-Dazs	C
Habitat	C
Halfords	C
Halfords Autocentre	C
Halifax	C
Hallmark	C
Hamleys	C
Hammerson	B
Hanson	B
Hapag-Lloyd	B
Hardys	C
Haribo	C
Harris	B
Havas	B
Hawker Siddeley Switchgear	B
Hay Group	B
Haymarket	B
Hays	B
Head & Shoulders	C
Heart	C
Heathrow	B
Heathrow Express	B
Heidrick & Struggles	B
Heineken	C
Heinz	C
Hellmann's	C
Help for Heroes	C
Henkel	B
Henley Business School	B
Henry Boot Developments	B
Herbal Essences	C
Herbert Smith Freehills	B
Hermes	C
Heron International	B
Hertz	C
Hexagon Group	B
Highland Spring	C
Hill+Knowlton Strategies	B
Hilti	B
Hilton Food Group	B
Hilton Hotels & Resorts	B C
Hire Station	B
Hiscox	B
Hitachi	B C
Holiday Inn	B C
Holland & Barrett	C
Homepride	C
Honda	C
Honeywell	B
Hoover	C
Hornby	C
Hotels.com	C
Hotpoint	C
House of Fraser	C
Hovis	C
Howden	B
Howdens Joinery	B
Hozelock	C
HP	B C
HP Sauce	B C
HSBC	C
HSS Hire	B
Huawei	B
Huggies® Wipes	C
Iams	C
ibis	B
IBM	B
Ibstock	B
Iceland	C
ICM Unlimited	B
iEnergizer	B
IKEA	C
Imagination	B
IMODIUM	C
Imperial College Business School	B
Imperial Leather	C
Informa	B
Infosys	B
Initial	C
Inmarsat	B
innocent	C
Instagram	C
Intel	B
Intelsat	B
Interserve	B
Intertek	B
Intuit	B
Investec	B
Investors in People	B
IoD (Institute of Directors)	B
Ipsos MORI	B
iris	B
IRN-BRU	C
Iron Mountain	B
Irwin Mitchell	B
ISS	B
ITV	C
ITV Media	B
iZettle	B
J.P. Morgan	B
J2O	C
Jack Daniel's	C
Jacob's	C
Jacob's Creek	C
Jaguar	C
Jameson	C
JCB	B
JCDecaux	B
JD Sports	C
Jewson	B
Jiffy	C
Jim Beam	C
JLL	B
JobServe	B
Jobsite	B
John Deere	B
John Frieda	C
John Lewis	C
John West	C
Johnnie Walker	C
Johnson & Johnson	C
Johnson Controls	C
Johnson Matthey	B
Johnson Service Group	B
JOHNSON's Baby	C
Jordans	C
Juniper Networks	B
JUST EAT	C
Just for Men	C
Kantar Media	B
Kaspersky Lab	C
Keller	C
Kellogg's	C
Keltbray	C
Kenco	C
Kenwood	B
Kenwood (Kitchen Appliances)	C
KETTLE Chips	C
Kew Gardens	C
Keyline	B
KFC	C
Kickstarter	B
Kier Group	B
KIMBERLY-CLARK PROFESSIONAL	B
Kinder	C
Kindle	C
Kingsmill	C
Kingspan Group	B
Kingston Smith	B
KitKat	C
Kleenex	C
KLM	B C
Knight Frank	C
Knorr	C
Komatsu	B
KONE	B
KP	C
KPMG	B
Kronenbourg 1664	C
Kuehne + Nagel	B
Kwik Fit	C
L'Oreal Elvive	C
Lacoste	C
Ladbrokes	C
Ladybird	C
LafargeHolcim	B
Laing O'Rourke	B
Lakeland	C
Lambert Smith Hampton	B
Lancaster University Management School	B
Land Rover	C
Land Securities	B
lastminute.com	C

Please note that this list reflects the brands as presented in the Superbrands research voting process; brands may subsequently have been altered or entirely rebranded, while others may no longer be sold or operational.